The Interplay of Opposites

The Interplay of Opposites

Opposites

A DIALECTICAL ONTOLOGY

by

Gustav E. Mueller

Professor of Philosophy
University of Oklahoma, Norman, Oklahoma

Bookman Associates : New York

Copyright, 1956, by Gustav E. Mueller

Dedicated

to

Paul Häberlin

my first guide to Philosophy

at the University of Bern forty years ago.

Contents

Questions and Answers

AN INTRODUCTION

Q. What are you trying to do?

A. I am not merely trying—I'm doing it—and I have done it.

Q. Are you then, presenting the finished product, the final result of your philosophy?

A. In philosophy, there are no such things as finished products or final results—they are as nothing apart from the activity of thinking, which is forever beginning anew; and unless they are re-born in other minds, they are dead stuff, gathering dust on library shelves.

Q. Are you not contradicting yourself?

A. Yes, I am this living contradiction—and so are you.

Q. Why?

A. Because you ask real questions, and expect true answers. Questions make no sense without answers, and answers make no sense if they do not answer questions, and what was supposed to be an answer, may become a starting point of a new question. Thus, we grow and mature in a living process of overcoming our former self in a wider or expanding self. We are this dialectical movement of a never-ending beginning.

Q. So this is what you mean by Interplay of Opposites? Why do you call it an Interplay?

A. I like aesthetic terms—philosophy, like art, thinks the concreteness of life—a cosmic dance in which sometimes one, sometimes another partner comes closer—or a play in which director, actor, and audience together enact the whole show. The chapter on Language and Imagination deals with this analogy of philosophy and art, but if you prefer, I could also speak of "reciprocity" or "mutuality" of opposites.

Q. Explain.

A. I am what I am by not being you, and you are what you are by not being me—and so, together, we are engaged in the same situation; think of husband and wife as another example: man makes woman, and woman makes man. They are mutual partners in a dialectical whole—the family.

Q. Have you other examples?

A. If you will look at the table of contents, you will find quite a list.

Q. I am looking—and it looks rather bewildering to me. Is there any order in this?

A. If you mean by "order," a gradual progression from a more simple to a more complex knowledge—as in mathematics, empirical object sciences, or in language studies—then there is no order. Since reality is equally present in all points, you may start reading anywhere.

Q. If there is no order, then how shall I find my way around?

A. I did not say that there is no order. There is an order of complementary *contraries* where one value is known by what it is not, as for example, art is not science—and you have to keep all those related differences in mind—and there is also the order of *contradictories,* where one value maintains itself by overcoming its negation—as for example, in the struggle of truth against error, evil against good.

Q. Where and how did you find your opposites?

A. I found them in myself as well as in the history of metaphysics.

Q. What is metaphysics?

A. As I use the term, metaphysics means whatever man has found to be ultimately real and important to his existence . . .

Q. . . . And if I find money to be ultimately real and important to myself . . .

A. . . . Then acquiring money is the practice of your metaphysics— the chapter on the Essence of History deals with many such obsessions—but in the history of metaphysics, the problems of nature, of history, and of the whole of reality, encompassing both, have been the perennial and major metaphysical concerns of man; they are also called "world," "soul," and "the Absolute," or "God." The book is arranged in this order—but every one of these themes is also contained in the two others.

Q. Is this the meaning of your sub-title: A Dialectical Ontology?

A. Yes—Being is the unity of all opposites, the Coincidencia Oppositorum as Nicolaus Cusanos called it. The word "ontology" is derived from the Greek word for "Being." Philosophy thinks that which is. My metaphysics, you see, is an ontological affirmation of many equally important aspects of the One Being, a multi-universe.

Q. Why do you philosophers always use Greek and Latin words?

A. What would you think of a Christian theologican who would avoid the Bible? They are our sources—well-springs of wisdom.

Q. Is there anything that is *not* dialectical?

A. Certainly. Dialectic itself eternally *Is*—it has no opposite outside of itself.

Q. Are you joking?

A. An absolutely certain uncertainty. But seriously speaking—as you would understand the term "seriousness"—everything can be thought undialectically—simply isolate it and keep it in a neat little box—in a cute "ism"—as you see, the table of contents teams with such undialectical "isms." All special-isms melt in the loving embrace of dialectic. They all meet their doom as well as their resurrection. They all are cancelled as well as preserved. It is the necessary function of abstraction to fix and isolate; it is a necessary function because without it, dialectical wholes would not become articulate.

Take for example, a mathematical law as if it were real, apart from the infinite irrationality of qualitative events which it is supposed to measure: If you forget this radical inequality of the measured contents, then you can be quite safe with your exact equations; or, if you abstractly think a moral law apart from the evil to which it is opposed—and by being opposed to it defines it as evil—then you have a perfectly lovely undialectical goodness in your heart.

Q. Are you sarcastic?

A. I'm merely "trying"—to be true to life is always "trial."

Q. Can one learn to think dialectically—as one can learn a science?

A. You can not avoid dialectic if you will pay respectful attention to what the "schools" of philosophy say with reference to one another—or if you simply are honest with yourself. Dialectic is a developed self-knowledge.

Q. How long does it take to read your book?

A. Just a few hours.

Q. Are you serious?

A. As serious as a physicist who measures time by split-seconds; or as serious as a busy executive who is so bored with what he has to read, that he has acquired the art of reading diagonally.

Q. Are you hinting that there is an other than scientific time?

A. Why don't you look into the first chapter on This Temporal World —and you will find out—but take an easy chair and a bottle of old wine—to sip . . .

Q. Are there pre-requisites for understanding your book? You consider it advanced, don't you?

A. The more advanced, the more heart-felt—think of artists. There are no "pre-requisites" in philosophy—except having a mind for it. I have seen unwarped minds without training understand perfectly and I've also seen warped minds with a lot of training understand nothing at all. Everywhere and in everything, there are levels of understanding which must be understood in turn.

Q. You are not writing for experts then?

A. I'm writing for you. If I were writing for experts, in their very own privileged jargon, then no pundit would ask me: "For whom do you write?" Philosophy is for Everyman—according to his level.

Q. What good would I get out of it?

A. No less than you put into it. But that is merely starting . . .

Q. Starting toward what?

A. Starting towards finding balance in movement, harmony in conflict, truth in errors, peace in troubles . . . God in creation.

Q. This sounds mysterious—almost religious—but I do not believe much in what is not factual and useful, or scientific—philosophy can not make atom bombs.

A. No, philosophy is not that glamorous. But this belief of yours is of course a belief in a metaphysical dogma—you see, you have a metaphysics whether you know it or not—but there is no dogma that is not questionable—and if you will find the answer to this question: What is the value of the "factual," "scientific"? then you will have become contemporary.

Q. Do you expect many followers? Is dialectic American?

A. Ask a pragmatist that. Since we are involved in dialectic anyway, the question is not one of "following," but of self-knowledge— without which we would have no philosophical voice to proclaim our dynamic multiplicity and its unity to the world.

This Temporal World

That from which things take their origin, into that again they pass away, as destiny orders; for they are punished and give satisfaction to one another for their injustice in the ordering of time . . .

—ANAXIMANDER 600 B.C.

Time is that being which in so far as it is, is not and in so far as it is not, is—the looked-at-becoming . . . not in time all things appear and disappear but time itself is this becoming, appearing, and disappearing . . . Chronos giving birth to and destroying his offspring . . . because things are finite, therefore they are temporal: not because they are in a time do they disappear but the things themselves are this temporality; to be thus is their objective nature. The process of real things itself makes the time . . . their duration is only relative . . . eternity must be distinguished from all durations. Time itself is eternal in its self-comprehension and is therefore absolute presence. Eternity is not that which will be or was, but it is. Time is not a part of a process but contains both eternity and process as its two sides and is in itself unproceeding. . . .

—HEGEL
System der Philosophie,
Werke IX, 257, 258.

FINITE OR INFINITE?

Has the world a beginning and end in time, or is it infinite and eternal? has been asked at all times. The conviction of the finitude of the world stems historically from a religious metaphysics for which the world is a mortal creature of the eternal God; the conviction of the infinite and eternal world expresses a secular metaphysics rooted in an endless experience where everything depends on precedents.

Metaphysics always says what man believes to be important and real. In his metaphysics of time man reflects on the ultimate meaning of his own temporal existence in this temporal world.

Let us distinguish: If I take myself as an object of my own observation—either as external physical body, or as organism, or again as psychical process which I record—I perceive myself as a temporal object which moves in time relative to other temporal objects; when they surround me I find myself in space, when they precede or succeed me I find myself in time, "in line."

On the other hand, in order to "time" perceived objects (myself included) I have to exist. This I-existence is temporal in itself. There was a time (for the perception of others) when I was not, and there will be a time when I shall not be.

There would be no "measured" times without that "measuring" existence with reference to which phenomena appear as "earlier" and "later," as "before" and "after." Measured times presuppose always, at all times, temporal existence—"that from which things take their origin, into that they pass away . . . in the order of time." This "destiny" is eternal "justice." Temporality and mortality characterize existence-perceived, "measured," scientific times belong to the external, appearing aspects of existence.

In this temporal world, *for* any existing world part, time is *both* the condition of its own existential appearance and disappearance, and also the condition of perceiving other world parts come and go. Time is both in and for itself.

The successive coming and going of one part after another characterizes it as "part," as partial and as participating, there are no enduring "eternal objects" in experience.

Temporal existence is one with its non-existence. It exists between cradle and grave as a word exists and makes sense only in between other words. Existence is "dead-sure" of its finitude. And it projects its existential dialectic (this unity of existence and non-existence) out into its perceptual time. It perceives appearance to appear and disappear in times. In this perceived time-succession, what will be is not now, its non-being future is the condition for its "coming to pass." The present cannot last, time itself would disappear if it would last and would not "pass away." All perceived phenomena thus appear in the "bad infinity" of an endless regression and progression. We cannot arbitrarily break it off. There is no empty timeless time outside, "before" or "after" this process. Any "before" or "after" makes sense only within the infinite relativity of observed time processes dating one another. The world of all "possible experiences" has no beginning or end in time.

Eternity does not mean a timeless time outside existential temporality and/or experiential times. It is an ontological term. It refers to Being itself. Being or World-itself as a whole is found in no time, since all times are within it. That all Becoming is temporal is an eternal ontological truth. This truth points to the absolute ground and unity of all temporal worlds; or, also, the ontological truth and ground of time is present at all times NOW.

The absolute unity of all opposites is always both temporal and eternal, partial and whole, temporally relative and eternally restoring its unbroken presence in all temporal changes. It is not either endlessly transitory or exempt from time. There is neither a non-temporal Being, which would leave time outside of itself, nor is there an existence which would be nothing but temporal—because such an absolutely finite existence could not know temporality as eternal destiny of its own existence.

The Absolute is always beginning and ending as well as unbeginning and unending. This dialectic is explicit in our reflective human existence. Our temporality is our eternal destiny.

EXPERIENTIAL TIME

We began with a result—now we describe the way by which we reached it. The way belongs to the result, as a garden-path belongs to the owner of the house to which it leads.

Experiential, scientific or clock-time is useful for telling what time it is, to keep appointments and to guide missiles—but not what time itself is. The factual-empirical question: What time is it? has little, if anything to do with the ontological-essential question: What is the nature of time? "What then, is time? If no one ask of me, I know; if I wish to explain to him who asks I know not. Yet I say with confidence, that I know that if nothing passed away, there would not be past time; and if nothing were coming, there would not be future time; and if nothing were, there would not be present time." [1]

---

[1] Augustine. *Confessions*, Book XIV, chapter 14.

Kant analyzed the essential nature of experiential time in the Transcendental Aesthetics of his *Critique of Pure Reason.* It is shown to be a "pure and apriori form" of perceptions. Every individual "I" must experience sense-objects with their sense-qualities in the order of temporal sequences and spatial arrangements. If the individual disregards the particular objects and abstracts from their particular qualities it can still imagine any objects in temporal and spatial orders—this is space and time as ideal and imaginary form of possible sense-experience, the apriori and subjective "pure intuition" as basis for geometrical and serial quantification, and the mathematical sciences. This necessary and universal (apriori) time-sense of perceiving individuals, articulates and illuminates—not reality—but reality in the form of appearance to individuals, as "empirically real and given." If this experiential and scientific time is confused with reality, the illumination turns into illusion. (*Erscheinung* becomes *Schein.*)

From the history of the problem three thinkers can be selected whose results jointly converge on the Kantian solution of experiential time. Aristotle worked out the antinomies, the relativity and self-contradictoriness of experiential time; Augustine discovered and added its subjectivity; *Newton's* "absolute time continuum" illustrates what Kant means by his "transcendental illusion"; Newton, according to Kant's *Critique,* confused the necessary and universal but subjective, imaginary, relative time of physical object-science, with a form of reality.

The time of physics, Aristotle says,[2] "would make one suspect that it either does not exist at all or barely, and in an obscure way. One part of it has been and is not, while the other is going to be and is not yet. Yet time—both infinite time or any time you like to take— is made up of these. One would naturally suppose that what is made up of things which do not exist could have no share in reality."

Following this passage is a detailed discussion of the relativity of physical time. I paraphrase and illustrate this discussion with two clocks. On the first clock the hand moves forward and the dial is at rest. The hand eventually returns to its starting point. On the second clock the dial moves backward and the mark of a future hour reaches the fixed hand. The first clock pictures time as a forward moving; if I identify myself with the moving hand I march forward in time in order to reach the meeting with you, which then becomes our presence; if I identify myself with the second clock, I am awaiting your

---

[2] *Physics,* Book IV, 10.

arrival, "flowing" from the future into my present and past me into the remembered past. In the first clock the present moment moves and time stands still; with reference to this present moment other moments become past and future. In the second clock time moves and the present moment stands still; the marks moving backwards on the dial become present and past as they pass by the fixed onlooker. The relation of the two clocks illustrates the relativity of experiential times. It makes no difference whether you, looking out of the window of a moving train, see the landscape rushing by, or whether you rush by the landscape. Real in either case seems only the present moment—but as soon as we try to hold it, it also vanishes. It is shrinking to an imaginary and unextended "infinitesimal" limit "between" two moments, of which the one is not yet and the other is no more.

The cosmic model for our mechanical clocktime is the year of the sun's seeming revolution around the earth. Aristotle criticizes those who think that time can be identified with such constant and repetitious motions. True—the sunbeam would strike at the same point at the same hour and at the same angle as the year before—but all this begs the question of what experiential time is. "The change of movement of each thing is only *in* the thing which changes or where the thing itself which moves or changes may chance to be. But time is present equally everywhere and with all things. Again, change is always faster and slower, whereas time is not: for "fast" and "slow" are defined by time—"fast" is what moves much in a short time, "slow" what moves little in a long time; but time is not defined by time, by being either a certain amount or a certain kind of it. Clearly then it is not movement . . . nor independent of movement." [3]

Aristotle's question: How can an experiential time be real, if it consists of non-existing moments and ideal limits, is taken up by Augustine. His answer is: Time is real because it is a necessary, unavoidable form of experiencing subjectivity:

"There are three times; a present of things past, a present of things present, and a present of things future. For these three do somehow exist in the soul, and otherwise I see them not: present of things past, memory; present of things present, sight; present of things future, expectation." [4]

---

[3] *Physics,* Book IV, 10, 218b.

[4] *Confessions,* Book XI, chapter 20.

"Let no man tell me that the motions of the heavenly bodies are time, because, when at the prayer of one the sun stood still, but time went on." [5]

Still, the model of the sun-clock remained practically useful in "measuring" factual times. Time as mathematically quantified in so many "exact" units of measuring was identified with the physical time of moving bodies.

But as time passed, irregularities were noticed. The calendar had to be revised and the original identity of mathematical and physical time had to be abandoned. Newton states this break between mathematical or "absolute" and physical or "relative" time, as follows:

> I must observe that the *common people* conceive those quantities under no other notion but from the relation they bear to sensible objects. And thence arise certain *prejudices,* for the removing of which it will be convenient to distinguish them into absolute and relative, true and apparent, mathematical and common. Absolute, true, and mathematical time, of itself, and from its own nature, *flows* equably without relation to anything external, and by another name is called duration: relative, apparent, and common time, is some sensible and external (whether accurate or unequable) measure of duration by the means of motion, which is commonly used instead of true time; such as an hour, a day, a month, a year.

The sensuous image of a "flow" retained in Newton's definition hides the ambiguity that in such an "absolute" time nothing earthly could move. Equal moments or intervals do not "flow" mathematically, they are discrete divisions of a continuum ("duration"), formulated as a "compact or dense series, which contains a term between any two terms" (Bertrand Russell). Newton's hostility against the "prejudice" of "the common people" is based on his own prejudice that mathematical time can be both "absolute" and nevertheless physical-experiential. The only thing that moves in thinking such a continuum is the mathematician's mind, who must take an earthly time to draw out his line of "equal moments," as Kant remarks.

MATHEMATICAL, PHYSICAL, PSYCHOLOGICAL TIMES

Although Newton's definition excluded mathematical time from the "relation to anything external," it nevertheless served as a standard

---

[5] *Ibid.*, chapter 23.

of measurement in the physics of mechanisms in the image or "schema" of the clock.

But when post-Newtonian physics turned to the actual empirical flow of events, the distinction between mathematical and physical time became necessary for physics itself. It rediscovered the Platonic world of Becoming, in which all times are relative: "Out of motion and change and admixture all things are becoming, relatively to one another" (*Theaetetus*, 151E). The arrival and departure, the coming and going of observed events date one another. The coming and going of events is indifferent to a pure series of equally repeated quantities, as their relative times are determined by the fastness and slowness of their appearing and disappearing movements, which are fast and slow with reference to each other. The clock-time is a symbol for the regular movement of the celestial mechanism, but "if sun and moon and stars would stop moving, time would not. The potter would still turn his wheel in its own appropriate time." [6] And "since motion appears different from different stars, there must, if it is to be taken as the measure of time, be as many times as there are stars in the universe" (Aristotle, id. 218b). There are as many experiential times as there are faster and slower movements with reference to one another.

Such relative times permit of no exact measurement. The time interval which occurs in one becoming event is not the same in another. The "same" time required for a dog to grow old and die brings a child to his adolescence. But the chief reason for not being able to measure measure is, that any flowing interval cannot be preserved in time, to serve as a measuring unit. The supposed measuring of experiential and relative time goes on in time, and that time is a new and different time; the measuring itself moves.

This difficulty is reinforced if we add the further difficulties of perception. When the Danish astronomer Roemer discovered in 1675 that the moons of Jupiter did not keep their time table, according to whether they were observed when the planet was farther or nearer to the earthly observer, he discovered an instance of the general truth, that experiential times are linked to the relativity of observing them. It takes time to measure time. This time it takes may be calculated into the result, but that does not alter the fundamental principle of relativity. Standards of time are arbitrary. The "same" clock tells different times according to whether the observer moves with it, away from it or towards

---

it, not only for the mechanical reason of relative systems of motions, but because observation, taking place in such movements, itself is a temporal process.

Not being able to return to an absolute time, and yet still needing a definite time-order to meet his appointments in a man-sized world, pragmatism and positivism assert time as an operational or practical method of predicting events. This is true as far as it goes, and it is philosophically valuable, if it is remembered to have grown on a skeptical evaluation concerning the necessary inadequacy of accurate knowledge of experience: Given in scientific or nonscientific observation are perceived events. An anticipated event involves anticipation of its being perceived in the future. This anticipated perception is present as my anticipation "now," the actual perception of the event takes place in a different "now." The temporal actuality of the first "now" is not the same actuality as the second "now"; there is no anticipation of experiential time—I may die in the meantime—and even if I do not, the second "now" is a new and different qualitative event. The sequence of the anticipated and the actual perception moves in a time order different from the sequence of the perceived events themselves. The event is indifferent to the role of verifying your anticipation. In the same way, a remembered event "before" is never identical with the unique time-quality which it had when it occurred with reference to all other events. It was not experienced as a "before." Plato, for example, had no inkling that he was living "before" Christ.

Result: "absolute" or mathematical time is to the relativity of physical times what physical times are to the subjectivity of psychological times. All three forms of experiential times are inseparably linked, one overlapping and blurring the others.

Operational time is plausible because it is useful, physical time is convincing although it is tied to a deceptive spatial image. The hands of the clock move on a quiet spatial plane with fixed numbers. But time does not move in a fixed spatial frame at all; it moves in its own dimensions of earlier and later. Its going-on goes on in wider and other goings-on, all relative to one another. Space itself is going on, because space is precisely this cross section or simultaneity of all events now. Space is frozen time, all times seen as halted. All temporal configurations of events become spatial constellations when stopped. The stars thus create empirical spaces and times in their passage. Time thus dominates space; the technical term for this truth is "the four-dimensional space-time continuum." Since there are many times going on at once, thus plurality of times, looked at, appears as space. Space is the simultaneity of many times externalized ("looked at").[7] Every spatial point may be considered to be outside of and indifferent to any other point; it can be traversed "up" or "down," "right" or "left," depending on the point of reference chosen. But this is considering space as if it could be separated from time, which is an abstract illusion. What seems external in space is in the making, it is temporal. Space is the perceived becoming in a time that is irreversible, while space abstracted from this temporal becoming of all events, seems to be free from such irreversible direction. But time as a spatial line is an abstract isolation which misses the most essential feature of the going-on of time: its irreversibility. This can be understood better after considering time as form of all existential becoming.

ONTOLOGICAL TIME

I, as temporal individual, experience you as my temporal object in the sequence of earlier/later, before/after, "measured" in long/short, slow/fast, durations.

All such experiential times of perceptions and perceivings appear uncertain, overlapping, and producing wavering borders. And this uncertainty of all appearing experiential times is its ontological status and truth. We are such that we can experience nothing except through time and as temporal, which is equivalent to saying that we can experience nothing as certainly fixed or placed. Experience fixed in an "absolute" quantity, pretending to be time, is an abstraction from all content. But time is "absolute" in the sense of a necessary, universal, *a priori* condition; this *a priori* means that we cannot exist without locating experiences, and that we cannot locate experience with reference to us now, without existing as temporal beings. In this sense time belongs inextricably to us, being the condition both of our experiencing something, and of something being experienceable. This is the ontological truth of time as a non-perceptual limit of all empirical perceptions, Kant's "pure form of intuition," which is only one aspect of world-itself:

All beginning is in time and all limit of extended things is in space. Space and time, however, are only in the sense-world.

---

[7] Kant: Space is the form of external perceptions, time the form of all perceptions. *Kritik der Reinen Vernunft*, Transcendentale Aesthetik, §8.

Hence only appearances *in* the world exist conditionally, but *world-itself* is limited neither conditionally nor unconditionally.[8]

This ontological "eternal time" is that by virtue of which we are enabled to distinguish and to criticize the various experiential modifications of time. It is the dialectical unity of all such distinctions. In the discovery of a star, for example, we distinguish the star's time, the time of its light appearing on earth, the time of the observer or observers in historical times. All such distinctions occur within the one time, which is the condition both of appearances to appear and of experiences to be experienced. As totality of all experiential differentiations, time itself is not found among them, as one item or one kind among others. As unity and totality of all its own possible time sequences and durations, time is unlimited or infinite, indivisible and all-pervasive.

It is not a logical class because it does not subsume subordinate or coordinate classes; it contains sequences and durations in each of which the problematic character of experiential times is present. We grasp time itself through its own various inadequate forms. We see both its ontological inevitability and its limited but never finished experiential processes together.

Ontological time contains the whole field of all possible temporal experiences, and pervades the whole field of all possible empirical consciousnesses. As pure form of intuition it is the precondition of both. It is the going-on at every instant—I-perceiving-thinking myself, one and not one with myself, in past, present, and future. We cannot think its going on not to go on, because we would have to produce such a thought without time, to prove the possible absence of time. As not identical with mathematical, physical, or psychological time, and as not outside or apart from them, ontological time is at once their limiting concept and their unity.

All antinomies of time, stated by the Alexandrian skeptics and restated by Kant, arise from a confusion of ontological time with given experiential sorts of time. By not recognizing the dialectical nature of time as being both finite or limited in its experiential modifications and infinite or unlimited as their universal and necessary presupposition, by trying to avoid the absolutely certain relativity or uncertainty of all temporal

---

8 "Aller Anfang ist in der Zeit und alle Grenze des Ausgedehnten im Raume. Raum und Zeit aber sind nur in der Sinnenwelt. Mithin sind nur Erscheinungen *in* der Welt bedingterweise, *die Welt selbst* aber weder bedingt, noch auf unbedingte Weise begrenzt." *Der Antinomie der reinen Vernunft*, Neunter Abschnitt, I.

experience, antinomies or necessary self-contradictions are seen in the objectified mirror of a time which is neither ontological nor experiential. A "given temporal whole" is self-contradictory, because on the one hand it thinks the finite going on of time not to go on, and on the other hand it denies the infinity of time by confusing the totality of all temporal series with a given or accomplished experience.

EXISTENTIAL TIME

Plato's *Politicus* myth presents the created world as growing older and younger at the same time. This is the dialectical time of existence.

Aristotle, after pointing to the relativity and self-contradictions of experiential time, turns to the real and existential time in his famous definition: "When we perceive a before and after, then we say that there is time. For time is just this—number of movement in respect of "before" and "after." This sounds like another statement of clock-time and it has frequently been interpreted in this sense. But Aristotle's context and comments make it sufficiently clear that what he has in mind is a real-existential time.[9] The real and existential whole of a living movement "is like the unit of number" only; "number," then, is an analogy to something else. This something else is a present temporal whole of life, which steps into actuality in meeting other like "units." It is "like" number, if number is understood as a totality of moments counted, which annihilates the previous "number." Time is a discontinuous stepping out in totalities of actual presents, in which the new totality is always at the "same time" the disappearance of the "old." The real and actual presence is "always" perishing in order to give place to a new formation. Every I-existence is comprised in the temporality of its actual world, in which it appears and disappears now. "In so far then as the 'now' is a boundary, it is not time but an attribute of it: in so far as it numbers, it is number; for boundaries belong only to that which they bound, but number (e.g., ten) is the number of these horses, and belongs also elsewhere" (ib220a20). The "number" here is the real presence of "these ten horses," an actual totality of living forms, and such actualities are also "elsewhere" in the present and temporal world. If such totality is diminished or increased it is always by qualitative leaps. Whereas the abstract "boundary" of the imagined scientific clocktime is merely an "attribute" of real and existing temporality of all things in this temporal world.

---

[9] Hedwig Conrad-Martins. *Die Zeit, München.* Kösel Verlag, 1954, p. 47f.

The real-existential time "quanta" are always perishing and are always reformed: they are that which "numbers," which "counts," which "matters." This activity of actively forming totalities is that which is the real time always present.

Existential time is living time, *Lebenszeit*. The scientific objectified series of before/after chooses some body and its movement as point of reference; before/after with reference to a living center of activity is past/future, older/younger. Existential time is the time which we *are,* in enacting it. Hippocrates observed the healing/harming process of time in sickness and health. This dialectic of existential living-time is not to be taken in the Bergsonian sense as psychological time, as opposed to the objective or physical time. Psychology, as object-science, measures psychical processes by the same clock as any other object-thinking, and describes the subjective time sense of its patients as deviations from the objective clocktime. Existential time is subjective ontologically, not merely psychologically; the subject's living-time and living through his time or being temporal, is the ontological non-temporal essence of living and temporal reality. Existential time is the necessary pre-condition of any kind of experiential time.

We and the world grow at once older and younger. The beginning of a new time at every moment is identical with getting older. With reference to this aging the past is young, it is our youth, but with reference to this past as long ago in comparison with our time-consuming present now, the past is what is old or ancient. We refer to the "cradle" of nations and cultures, while we are old and experienced; existentially this being old is not a sum of years, but living memories stored up in our embodiments, our institutions, and traditions. The older the individual (biological or cultural) grows, the shorter seem psychologically its later years, because they are cast on the perspective of vast times lived through. On the contrary, the latest arrival in time is the youngest member of the temporal family, in comparison with which the world is ancient; it was hoary with old age, when it was youngest. Our ship moves upstream and the water flows past, but both the ship and the waters are the same existential time, they both exist as temporal.

"Ship" and "water" are inadequate means of communicating a dialectical relation. The ship is the image for the renewing, rejuvenating time; we reach into the future for the new things to come; their non-being today is the condition of their being-there tomorrow; we hope for the future to carry old things away. The future is the well of possibility, the time dimension favored by activists, whence time flows through our actualizations and thus becomes our past. If the ship moves downstream, then the flowing water stands for the accumulation of past conditions in my present time, enabling me to exist and to act, the time dimension favored by contemplative minds. The regard for the past, for origins and traditions, renews their actuality in the present. If actualities did not sink into the "what was being," treasured as background and condition for all present action, and if the not-yet-being of future possibilities did not constantly widen the hope and anticipation of "better times to come," there would be no present and no existential time. The present exists dialectically as, and in, the annihilation as well as the preservation of the past as having been mine, and in the annihilation and preservation of the future as my potential being.

The present is the concrete "at-once," the dynamic polarity of those temporal opposites, separated from which concrete temporal existence they are abstractions. "This wonderful being, the at-once, lies between rest and motion, existing outside of all time, and in it the movement passes into rest, and the resting into movement . . . but as it passes, it does so in the moment, wherein it can be in no time, and neither rests nor moves." [10]

There is only a past for us when we remember, or regret, as there is only a future for us when we plan, hope or fear. Existence without remembrance and anticipation would not be a human existence. The present time with reference to "I exist" is duration, the past with reference to "I exist" is memory, the future with reference to "I exist" is anticipation. Each existence lives its own time. It carries its own temporal dialectic within itself. It is its own standard.

If many existential time-structures are correlated, we have a historical time or age, a structure of existential times analogous to the simultaneity of observed events in space. The scholastics called this historical age the *aevum*. The *aevum* is the collective or social duration of correlated existential times. "Spiritual creatures as regards their affections and intellections, in which there exists succession, are measured by time; as regards their natural being, they are measured by the *aevum;* and as regards their vision of glory, they participate in eternity." [11] The *aevum* thus is the middle ground between individual

---

[10] Plato, *Parmenides,* 156.

[11] St. Thomas, *Summa Theol.,* I, QX, art. 5. The term "natural" refers to human nature as social-political.

existential time and the paradox of an eternal time, implied in the standard of the eternal *nunc stans*.

Why are we so partial to our *aevum?* This is an evaluation unwarranted by a logical analysis of time. "What was being" is no less real than my time now; why, then, should I prefer it to an existential past or future time? And why should I select one *aevum* and give it a privileged status over others?

The secret of this preference lies in what Augustine calls *cura;* the present time is the time of moral decisions and responsibilities. I make myself responsible for the right or wrong use of my time. This in itself creates the "historical moment." This *cura* embraces the past and the future. In repentance, the past is remade, in contradiction to the chronological record which reports the fact as a dead and gone derelict of time. Repentance turns a shame over a past action into a renewing source of good. The past, in *cura,* reaches the present as an authoritative and warning voice. And on our moral decision hinges the course of the future. And the future changes the meaning of the past. Caesar's conquest of Gaul, for example, received a new cumulative meaning and reality through the birth of the French nation centuries later.

The value of existential time is not a function of an experiential chronology or clock-time. It depends on the *cura* to live time, to span time, to create durations, cohesive through impulses and responsibilities, through the will to renew and encompass traditions and claims on the future. A decisive time, whether constructive or destructive, is great, regardless of whether it is long or short in external counting, while an idle and empty time is small, although interminable in length. Boring times are long to live through and short in memory. Mere duration, long-living mediocrity, is no value in itself, because it shuns the dialectic of time as a responsible process of renewing memory and renewing hope. It closes its eye to death as the real limit of time-embodiment in existence. Existential time is discontinuous.

Art is alive to the value of time; it shapes the dialectical time process in enduring imaginative symbols. It crowds the full process of life into the lasting images of its work. Such a work presents and beholds the rhythms of existence in epochal concentration.

The relativity which we found to invalidate any ultimate claim of exactness and certainty in experiential times is the projection of our existential uncertainty. All experiential time-measurement finally has to refer back to observation and perception. But those are functions of an individuated life wrapped up in its own living time.

The second, for example, is derived from the heartbeat. It is composed of moments, and the moment, the *momentum* or *punctum temporis*, is the time which it takes to become conscious of a sense-impression. *Momentum* comes from *movere* and designates the jerk following the prick of a pin. Hence, a second may be "long" when filled with such vivid "moments." The German *Augenblick*, the glance of the eye, means the number of visual impressions which we are capable of having at one glance. Both moment and *Augenblick* are units of existential time. Various psychological experiments with moving pictures establish a rate of 8 to 16 impressions per second. We live faster or slower, that is, we may have more or fewer impressions at the "same" time. If our existential moments are slow we can look at one thing many times before we notice any change; the seeming stability of things depends on the time-rhythm which we live.

If we shorten our life-span but accelerate its movements, we then would have in one month as many experiences as we have now in eighty years; we could follow a bullet comfortably with our eyes, as if seen through an extremely slow time-lens. If we again reduce our life-span but retain the same number of moments of experience, then we would live only a few minutes but with as many experiences as now. In this condition we could not notice any change in the world at all, and we probably would not see but hear the light. We would know nothing of a change of night and day.

If, on the contrary, we think our lifetime extended but our moments slowed down, then our years would make the impression of hours, the seasons would race by, and we would see tall trees grow like mushrooms. Days and nights would be like alternating minutes of light and darkness. The sun would appear like a swishing rocket.

Such fictions serve to make us aware of the relativity of existential times, and the uncertainty of our time-sense. We have analogies to these extreme illustrations in the different time-sense of different ages and periods of culture. The rhythm of our living existence is the basis of experiencing things in terms of time. Their relativity and uncertainty is the mirror in which is reflected the uncertainty of our human mode of existing.

ETERNAL TIME

The paradox of eternal time unites the ontological and existential time in one dialectical synthesis.

Temporality is equivalent to mortality. Both are the eternal signature on all things finite. We are not mortal because we are in time, our finitude is our mortality and our temporality. We reach out for our own end, we live our own death. But we are also trying to overcome our finitude of existing in the here and now, we are fighting this limitation by retaining our own past, as we "live it down," and we are hopefully anticipating a future as a consoling possibility. And still more fundamentally, we realize our mortality, which means that we compare it with a being which would be free of our temporal limitations. "Eternal time is the total and perfect possession of interminable life in its simultaneity," says Boethius. And Augustine: "Their hearts flutter in the past and future movement of things and is full of vanity. Who will steady it and move it to stand, that it may grasp something of the splendor of eternity and compare it with the never resting time." [12] In attempting this comparison, Augustine agrees with Plato that God creates the world not in time, but that he creates the world as temporal creature, a moved image of his eternal being.

We cannot will not to be born, we cannot avoid experiencing all things in time, we cannot escape making decisions now. All such dialectical negations affirm time in all kinds and in all its uncertainties and relativities as an absolute order of the world, as absolute presupposition of all experiential knowledge and existential self-changes. Eternal time is thus known as timeless truth and essence of existence. As Hegel puts it, "It is not past or future but it *is*." [13]

That things begin and end is the unbeginning and unending truth and being of time. Eternal time expresses the inevitability of the Now in all its passages. Ontology thus eternalizes the absolute fugitivity, mortality, temporality of all durations, regardless of their relative positivity or durability in experience and existence.

What leaps into existence now, and what is struck from the book of time now, are like words which in themselves make no sense; but only because words end, do sentences become possible. Being is the sentence which the temporal words spell. Being is articulate in and through the periodicity and rhythm of its temporal content. These changes carry their own times with them. The non-temporal being of time is nothing outside and apart from the discontinuous sequences

---

[12] *Confessions*, IX, 11.

[13] *Encyclopedia*, §258.

and durations of which it consists and in which its ever present nature becomes clear.

Ontology thus knows time as a timeless truth, as the paradox of eternal temporality. Eternal time is the ineluctable modality of all existence and of all experience, the inescapable omnipresence of temporality in all existential becoming as well as in the experiential presentation of all events.

Plotinus may further illustrate this paradox: "A life instantaneously entire, complete, which belongs to the authentic existent by its very existence—this is eternity . . . contemplated by what is eternal in the self. . . . Being cannot be treated in terms of intervals, unfoldings, progression, extension . . . does not depend on any quantity. . . . Putting forth its energy in act after act, in a constant progress of novelty, the soul produces succession. Time, then, is contained in differentiation of life; the ceaseless forward moving of life brings with it unending time; and life, as it achieves its stages, constitutes past time . . . the unity of succession must be the image of oneness, the moved image of eternity. . . . Time is not to be conceived outside of soul; eternity not outside of the authentic existent . . . soul begot at once the universe and time; in that activity of soul this temporal world sprang into existence. . . . The movement of the All will be measured according to time, but time will not, of its own nature be a measure of movement. The reiterated perception of movement—the same extent traversed in such and such a period—will lead to a definite conception of a time past. . . . Time is that in which all the rest happens, in which all movement and rest exist smoothly and in eternal order." (*Enneades*, III.)

TEMPORAL DIALECTIC

This ontological dignity of time means, then, that every man, regardless of his natural conditions (sex, young or old, white or black, etc.) or of his cultural values (practical, theoretical, aesthetic, religious) lives his own time and dies his own death. His temporality is his reality and his temporal reality is identical with his mortality. He not merely has time, but enacts his temporal being. He has time, he takes time out to direct his attention to intellectual verities or to practical values. In the meantime he is living forward towards his end, no matter whether he employs his time usefully or whether he wastes it.

His past sinks irrevocably away from him. At the "same time" this, his own past time, builds up a body of habits, reputations and personal conditions, which partly determine what steps he can or cannot do into the future. Most of his past time is forgotten, or disfigured by an imagination which is colored by present interests. And the time will come when all his time will be forgotten and will have sunk into the Hades of oblivion. So it is with this historical time of mankind: Only a few islands of remembered names or documents survive more or less, like some high peaks above the general sea of fog in the Alps. The past cannot be held and preserved. It slips through our fingers like sand. Man does not like this. He makes heroic efforts to preserve and to remember. The whole of all historical sciences, archives, museums, witness this search for a lost time. On the other hand man wants to forget. He feels encumbered by the "dead hand of the past." Perhaps he also likes to forget, because many deeds and steps of his past life are shameful, painful, guilty moments. Both his greedy search for the past and his anxious flight from the past, are all-too-human. Opposite attitudes, equally unsuccessful: the clinging to the past does not bring it back, the flight from the past does not eliminate it. Psychoanalysis has demonstrated, on the contrary, that a guilty past, when covered up and inhibited, may exert an indirect and devastating effect on the present.

Equally dialectical is man's relation to the future. A ruthless optimism, as Schopenhauer called it, anticipates the future as if it were man's right and property. Man lives as if he and his time were unlimited, as if his way of living his time were perfectly desirable, as if the future were as certain as a fool-proof bank-investment. The pessimist, on the contrary, regards the future with a not entirely unfounded suspicion. He is hesitant, he would prefer to retard time, because the eventual outcome, the death of all plans and purposes, is clear to him. Opposite attitudes towards the future, equally uncertain: the optimist may find his disappointment, the pessimist may live to a happy old age.

The present seems to be the most certain time to cling to; it is the time of decision. Any minute, if taken seriously, is a minute to prove your worth. But precisely this minute of a full responsibility may turn this precious present into a nightmare. Man shirks his responsibility, he loses the present in dead routines, fritters his opportunity away. And then inevitably, the present is the fugitive and futile emptiness, which is already gone and is not here yet.

And thus, in the dialectic of our three existential time-dimensions, we live all our days, tumbling from past to future and from future to past, both receding potentials, our present being a gamble of hit and miss. We are thrown into temporal existence and hurled away. The next, please!

Nevertheless: <u>Time is an eternal ontological reality, omnipresent and all-pervasive.</u> We find ourselves in a temporal community with all men. We share and understand our temporal situation. And from this eternal being of time in and at all moments, our philosophical attitude towards the three-dimensional temporality receives a value, which time does not have, if the ontological being or reality of time is denied. The past is in truth and in reality not less real, because it is past for us and has slipped away from us. The cultivation of the past, history and memory, are therefore ontologically grounded and justified. The future likewise will be what it will be, irrespective of our optimistic rashness or our pessimistic misgivings. The caring for the future, therefore, has the same ontological dignity as the caring for the past. And the present with all its waste, friction, and part-fulfillment, is also an eternal mode of all times. Temporal dialectic as a whole both discloses, and is the reality of, all temporal changes and movements.

This whole, however, is not the whole of each individual existential time. Existentially man is incomplete, imperfect and perfectible. What perfection he has depends on the others, by whom he is nurtured, educated, influenced, and to whose life he can contribute his mite. His own time is like an incomplete phrase, like a time-measure or beat in a symphony.

<u>Existential time is limited in birth and death.</u> It is beginning and ending. Man does not know where he came from. He may stretch his historical neck to find out how other souls lived before he did. But this does not expand his own existential time one minute. As far as he is concerned, he emerges out of non-being into being. Naturalistic speculations tell him that he is merely a reshuffling of already given chemicals, cells, genes, etc. He knows that such talk is thoughtless. He as this individual—"I exist"—is not identical with arrangement of stuff-particles. They are psycho-physical materials his organism is endowed with and with which he has to make a living arrangement. Theological speculation, on the other hand, stimulated by Plato's myth of pre-existing souls, pretends to know exactly that this pre-existing soul is joined to organism at the moment of conception. But, Plato says, that people who take myths literally are "painful men" (*"deinos aner,"* *Phaidros*, 229). The plain truth is that we do not know. The only thing we know is that each human individual is a new and unique modification of a race of temporal creatures, called human. The limit of existential

time is also the limit of existential knowledge. But as such a limit it is known and is important. It prevents any sort of absolutization of existential time. It limits man within the ontological fullness of all existential times, which he represents in living his own limited dialectic.

The other limit is death. Thoughtless naturalism consoles man over death in telling him that his elements and atoms will be used in a new combination. Plato also wrote myths of the post-existence of souls, showing what they have done with their times to an infallible and impartial judge. Just as the logical meaning of his pre-existence is that the soul has access to truth which is logically prior to its earthly temporal acts of apprehension, so the meaning of his post-existence is that, indeed, what each soul has worked out in merits and demerits in this life, is now on record and can never again be undone or wiped out from the book of being. But again the "painful men" of literal-minded and conscience-tortured phantasy have transcended the limit of knowledge in death and have frightened people into hysterics about "the life to come." All we know is that, as we have emerged from non-being, so we also descend into non-being. It is within our own time that we have to work out some *analogia entis,* carving out a time-shape, "a moved image of eternity," as Plato puts it. If we succeed in doing this, we have done well. We would not wish to have an endless continuation, which would be a cursed existence, as the one told in the legend of the wandering Jew who can never die. Neither our environment would like us to go on forever spinning our own yarn, which is not long enough for an endless time; nor would we like to go on making endless new adjustments to ever changing conditions. Only the measureless, the limitless people, indulge in the formless, shapeless toils of an endless, measureless, and limitless life.

IMPORTANCE OF TIME

Existential times are non-physical processes, whereby we participate in our common human history. This "we" expresses a solidarity, we help one another to shape a common world of historical and existential times, which we remember in piety, which we anticipate in hope and fear, and which we embrace as present time in love and responsibility. Man is the creature who is enabled to speak of "our" common temporal world, in which he enters as shaper and participant, and through which he is lifted out of the accidental and contingent time of his location and province. Our common time frees him from his private-psychological time, which runs like sand in the hour-glass.

As participating in the same time-world of piety, hope and love, all historical men are contemporaries, they are weaving the same loom. But as future and past with reference to one another, they are un-contemporaries, they are each other's futures and pasts. As heirs of our fathers we are under obligation not to disappoint their hopes. As fathers of our descendants we are under obligation to transmit to them what we have learned. Briefly, the historical process is the time of education. This is the importance or value of historical-existential time. This distinguishes it from a biological time of naturally growing older. This is one of the many fallacies of Spengler's *Decline of the West*, that he cannot distinguish between existential-historical and biological times. Historical time is the form of a spiritual succession, of a common struggle to share and to come into the enjoyment of a universal human time. The pupil may be a biologically old man, the teacher may be a biologically very young genius. What makes the biologically young individual old, and the biologically old man young, is the spiritual "fact," that the one has to impart values, which the other has to learn, if he wants to participate in the same human world of historically significant time. The teacher is older in as far as he knows and has to impart something which the biologically older pupil has yet to learn. If both enter this educational relation they both believe that their time is well applied to this common undertaking. They show by their action that they believe in a meaningful time-sequence in which our common humanity is being worked out.

Death is the most decisive "argument" for the spiritual meaning of existential time. We advance into time-positions vacated by death. The legal order assumes that the old order is worthy to be preserved, that the new order is worthy to preserve it. Biologically, in the animal world, the descendants know nothing of their ancestors, and the parents know nothing of their offspring. They do not care. We care, and we show this caring and caring-for in the legal order, by which the future and the past are intellectually and spiritually regulated. We exist consciously in the solidarity of this common legal time-order. Biological death is here the condition of temporal continuity and succession. This continuity does not mean the unchanged prolongation of a past, it means on the contrary a re-newation, a new shape of life made nevertheless possible through a believed continuation of historical time. Existential-historical time is the continuous order of appearances and disappearances, which differentiates it from the steady flow of equal moments in the experiential-scientific clock-time.

The latter goes together with an abstract intellect. Its abstract general objects are supposed to be timeless. A scientific law is not located in time, but is a relation of general terms, holding together an indefinite number of phenomena, applicable to them at any time; from this is derived the fiction, as if thought itself would need no time. If this abstract and quantitative attitude dominates education, education as a concrete historical process is fatally weakened.

Let us take a class-period in philosophy as a small logical model of the historical-existential time-process. The first and basic requirement for successful teaching is that teacher and pupils are willing to give their time to each other. The importance of this mutual sacrifice must become evident. If it is absent, time is only considered as a clock-unity of fifty minutes to be rushed through.

The pupils begin where the teacher ends: at the last thought of his life's work. They are not contemporaries, but are trying to struggle through towards a common and shared time. Time is an existential task, and the situation is dialectical, a unity of temporal opposites. This is the reason why we can take the class-room period as an historical "syllogism."

The time is decisive: Whilst it lasts, the participants are in a position to ask and answer, to correct misunderstandings, to grow. If the pupil is to grow and if the teacher is to get his point across, there can be no hurry. The process is slow, "takes time." The rush towards a preconceived, abstract content of instruction, the covering of vast quantities, is not existential learning, but bluff.

Both pupil and teacher have to wade through misunderstandings. If there is no opportunity for misunderstanding, if everything is simple and easy, then we may have a transfer of some useful pieces of information, but no dialectical situation. To overcome misunderstanding is the prerequisite for a genuine discipleship which is at the same time a liberation of the pupil to his own deeper self-realization. Any Platonic dialogue will illustrate what is meant. If the pupil merely repeats, copies, and reproduces what the teacher says, then time is not seriously employed. The teacher then is merely the organ or mouth-piece of an abstract science. If, on the contrary, difficulties are enountered and faced in common, then the time of the teacher has become the time of the pupil. The battle with errors takes time, is existential time itself, and is the importance of this time. The dialectical tension between teacher and pupil is the time-process in which it becomes explicit and in which it is bridged. This time is the living source of all sciences and of all arts—in distinction from the "body of knowledge" which is the abstract sediment of that process, stored up in libraries and museums. The time-span of existential study is the span of decisive changes, transformations, corrections of misapprehensions. A teacher who has never been misapprehended has never said anything of importance.

If the teacher merely encloses the pupil in the teacher's own time, then he robs the pupil and makes him small. If the pupil merely exploits the teacher's time by not becoming engaged himself, he does not enter the historical dialectic of time. Through the teacher all times before the pupil's birth are met in a living present. The teacher, on the other hand, sees in the pupil all the times to come, for whose shape this moment is of decisive importance. Thus both teacher and pupil sacrifice their times in order to transcend themselves into the common spiritual community which is one with temporal humanity, and which is always actual in the beloved mutual presence of men thus transcending themselves.

THE MYTH OF TIME

Myth is the aura of truth; it is truth in the alluring shape of a transcendental imagination. As such it is as necessary for the lives of most men and most cultures as is the atmosphere in its moods and colors. Myths of time speak clearly of the various aspects of time, thought out in philosophy and "measured" in the sciences.

Greek culture affirms and feels time as a rhythmic order of natural and eternal recurrence. The mathematical language of nature is not foreign to the worship of the sun god. And as the seasons of the year and the ride of the sun god recur, so the *kosmos* itself is ordered in the rhythmic recurrence of immense cycles, the "great year" of aeons or world-periods. In these periods cultures are born together with their worlds and are destroyed in order to rise again in their next proper time. How could we find new values, Plato asks, if what has been found by cultures long ago had not been destroyed? Such a feeling for time is at once the expression of creative energy and also of the idea of limited possibilities, of finite perfections. In this rhythmic and cyclical destiny of the time order, "justice" resides and reigns. Things are balanced 'in the long run," and Greek art celebrates this balance in the *choros* and *Chronos* of life. And as the eternal being of the world is always present in the aeons, so the beauty and substance of human culture is made manifest in the seasonal celebrations and festivals of the year of the soul.

Over against this absolute affirmation of being in the recurrences of natural time lies the *Hindu* negation of time. The cycle of recurrence here is the wheel of torture, the fate of an endless and therefore meaningless rebirth. The thirst for pleasure is thirst for becoming, and the thirst for becoming is the ground for perishing. Life, death, and suffering are the unholy trinity of time and of temporal existence. But this flickering time of illusion in experience and existence collapses in the white light of knowledge. "The wheel is broken, the dried-up river flows no longer, this is the end of suffering," Buddha teaches. The being of knowledge is the eternal negation of temporality and its illusions of actions and passions.

The *Old Testament* knows time as the natural order of creation, a footstool for the glory of the creator of the universe *ex nihilo*. It is for the pagan to fear the signs of heaven as signals of destiny. The times of nature are trivial external experiences, measured by God's time, which is the time of his revelation and the time of history over which He presides. God is the God of historical time, and His prophets expect the fulfillment of time in His own messianic or apocalyptic future, which will be the end of all times. Also, the similar, because moral-activistic, conception of time in the *Persian* religion, sees the end of all time in the triumph of the good over the evil will and principle. The *Germanic* Orlog, on the contrary, is a term uniting the ideas of a time order of destiny and the idea of war and battle-order. The present time and the present world live between catastrophes, the world will come to an end in cold or in heat. Time is the time of heroic battle against annihilation.

Chinese wisdom cultivates, against this activism and pragmatism in and for itself, the maxim, "Do nothing." All is already done, it roots in the holy origins, and in the eternal being-order of Tao. The meaning of life is to remember, to preserve, and to keep pure these principles of traditions. The worship of the ancestors keeps the great tree of life watered, growing, and connected with its roots and soil. In all changes and transformations, even in the daily constellations of events, the immutable law, the eternal Tao, manifests its motionless fluidity. To become infinitely patient, adaptable, and flexible: the wise man sees the ten thousand appearances and he looks into them as into a mirror where he beholds himself. If you are "creating new things," know that nothing of it remains with your own, it all returns to the great origin.

Compared with these five myths, the *Christian* myth is a synthesis. God the timeless and ever-present, creates the world, not in time, but as the temporal creature. But the Creator and Father of time also becomes flesh and appears in time, as the great existential divide, up to which and from which all other times are oriented. He transcends time and He is immanent in time. And His birth, His passion, and His resurrection, form the supernatural and revealed time order of the Christian year. It affirms temporality as mortality and suffering; they are shown to be His will and posited in His will, but they are also left behind and transcended. The natural order of time is superseded and sanctified by the higher supernatural and existential order of God's Life in it. He reconciles the negativity of time, living the life of suffering by embracing it as His own, and He also breaks through the limitations of mortal times revealing himself as the God who is beyond life and death. And in looking forward towards this full revelation of God beyond the cradle and the grave, the Christian myth also embodies the prophetic aspect of time.

"The eternal reason, in which there is no beginning and no ending, knows that all things must begin and end. But this is Thy Word, which is also the origin, as it also speaks to us." [14]

---

[14] Augustine, *Confessions*, IX, 8.

Nature and History

If we look into world history then we see an immense image of changes of infinitely manifold shapes of life, of peoples, states and individuals in restless succession. Everything that may affect the soul of man is actualized. Everywhere purposes are pursued which we acknowledge, whose execution we wish to see; we hope and fear for them and in all those happenings and accidents human action and passion is uppermost; everywhere do we find our inclination engaged. Sometimes we are attracted by beauty, freedom, power; sometimes by energies through which even vices appear historically important. Here a mass of public interests are moved and are dispelled in an infinite complexion of minuteness; there, immense things emerge out of seemingly unimportant small conditions—everywhere a colorful turmoil and if one is dispelled, another takes its place. The general category which appears in this incessant change of individuals and peoples which maintain themselves for a while and then disappear, is the category of change . . . the thought of the mind which manifests, develops and cultivates its powers in all directions. Which powers man possesses we experience out of the manifold of his cultures . . . evolution which in nature is a quiet organic growth, in the spirit is a hard infinite battle against itself. What spirit wants is to reach its own concept but he himself hides his goal from himself and is proud in this self-alienation . . . if we contemplate this spectacle of passions and violence and unreason and if we see evil, misfortune and destruction as a result, we can only be filled with compassion . . . and with indignation of a good spirit if such a one is in us. . . . In seeing history as this altar upon which the happiness of peoples, wisdom of states and virtues of individuals are sacrificed, then the question necessarily arises, For what ultimate end have these immense sacrifices been made?

—HEGEL*

*Werke (Fromann, Stuttgart, Vol. XI, 111, 91).

THE PRESENT MEANING OF HISTORY

Man is an ideational creature. There is not and never has been a culture which was not based on distinctions of real and apparent, important and unimportant, true and false, right and wrong, and so on. Man lives in his own fashion by affirming and denying such values; he believes or disbelieves. He exists in making such decisions, such commitments. A state prior to ideational commitments would not be a historical state of affairs. It would be a chaos of pure immediate experience, which may be approximated in some "primitive" cultures, or in very small children. They would live in a chaos of relative and subjective experiences; they would perceive things small from a distance and large from near-by; they would say one thing one minute and the opposite the next minute, and would be quite happy in such a blooming confusion; they would not notice that they were confused, and would therefore find nothing wrong or right about their experiences. Historical man begins, and he begins very definitely, in what is called primitive culture, by bringing order into, and demanding a consistent explanation of, experience. This is the beginning of history.

Historical civilizations are determined by their philosophies. What they assume to be real and important shapes their conduct and their institutions. Different world views imply different evaluations of life. Such differences often lead to conflicts in geographical space, or to revolutions in historical time; such revolutions take place within one civilization when its philosophical orientation changes from one set of values to another. The great divide of history is a variety of local histories. Between 800 and 400 B.C., man reaches historical existence and self-knowledge in China in Confucianism and Taoism, in India in the Vedas, Upanishads, *Bhagavad Gita*, and Buddhism; in the Near East in the Persian religion and the Jewish prophets, in Europe in Homer, the Greek philosophers and the Roman state and jurisprudence. Karl Jaspers calls this middle of history the historical axis, the discovery of origins, to which we all can return and always find a common ground of humanity in these four-fold foundations. But of the four, it is the European culture which, in transcending itself, has actually proved itself as the one world-historical power, which has brought about the end of all local histories and the beginning of a global history. Today, what happens in one member of a unified humanity affects all.

Today all types of civilizations are aware of one another. They have become close neighbors through the technical conquest of space and through the technical presence of instantaneous communication. To develop neighborliness, then, a "good neighbor policy" is the supreme task of a global understanding. Between such varying historical and present cultures this task cannot be solved without philosophy. Good will alone is blind without understanding. And philosophical understanding means not only that we should be aware of different assumptions underlying different cultures but also that we should be aware of our own assumptions and their limitations. Self-knowledge implies knowledge of our limitations. Every important value demands concentration of all energy on it to master it and to work it out. This is true for individuals as well as for individual cultures. Their strength lies in their self-imposed limits. To ignore such limits is insanity. Sanity lies in the mutual respect of profoundly differing ideals. This is the philosophical foundation of a democratic world civilization. Differences must be lifted from a smug provincialism to the universal plane of rational dialogues, in which different assumptions are clarified and understood as different possibilities of humanity. Mankind can realize its unity by becoming dialectical, that is, by thinking its unity in its many perspectives, expressions, and experiments.

To live in one world with other cultures is made impossible by any fanatical, intolerant totalitarianism, which is uncritical of its own limitations. This is the problem of the future of history, which belongs to the essence of history no less than the past, although its facts are not yet open to scientific-historical inspection. But all history is made with reference to an anticipated future.

The problem, the issue of a coming global or world-history is whether we shall find an order of right of federated continents, in which democratic freedom can be reconciled with socialism, the integration of collective-social industrial enterprises into a free community—or whether an imperialistic world-state and totalitarian planned economy will transform mankind into a prison without freedom and without escape.

HISTORY AND HISTORIA

History is enacted in practical conflicts and value decisions; *historia* is related in stories and interpreted in memory.

History exists because man does not know what he should will. The will of whole peoples or social groups is not more unified than the will of individuals. All historical situations are ambiguous; one party within a state engaged in a total conflict with another state is out for its own immediate power, prestige, and material gains; another party of the same state appeals on the contrary to moral motives, ideals, and the "good of mankind." And whether the particular realistic aims or the universal ideals are the "real" meaning of the historical action is always a secret to all participants. The objective situation resulting out of the cross-current of tendencies and interaction of subjective wills is never identical with the purpose of any one of the parties involved. In history concrete existential time is constituted in the anguish of actual decisions; decisions move from what is already done, *res gesta,* to what is not done, but might be done in one direction or in another. History-making men have to decide on the basis of "fact" *and* on what they suppose will be the next move of their opponents. Both the historical past and the potential future may be misleading in historical action. One party may point in its propaganda to the innocence and righteousness of its actions up to this point, and it may be "right"; while the other party's propaganda may discard the historical facts and records and point to the potential menace of future actions, covered by the hitherto innocuous preparations up to this point, and it also may be "right." Both select and stress "facts" and both take a risk concerning an uncertain future.

Historia seeks to clarify this opaque and tense history. *Historia* is not pragmatic. If historical knowledge were pragmatic we would have no knowledge worth mentioning because the practical-historical future is an undisclosed book, and the past is not a matter of practical decisions. The only thing, Hegel says, *historia* teaches is that man can learn nothing from history, because his existential historical situations and decisions are always "now"; they are concrete and unforeseen and cannot be covered or solved by situations that are past, remembered, and abstract.

The "fact" of *historia* is the central problem of remembered experience, as the muddled "will" is the center of practical history. Events and rumors; selections of what seems important to actors and observers; unifications dependent on time-distance and reports of those involved; interpretations dependent on interested participants and cool, impartial observations—such views and perspectives cross and cancel one another in both "fact" and "will" of *historia* and history.

History and *historia* are interdependent. Without knowledge of the past—and even the latest news-bulletin is a record of past events—

there is no historical action; and without historical actions there is nothing to remember. Problematic decisions and problematic "facts" condition each other.

Today there is such an accumulation of accurately recorded stories that no historian is in a position to know history.

HISTORY AND NATURE

"History" and "nature" are different logical apprehensions of the same living reality.

Life as history is reality apprehended in its individuated becoming. Change becomes transparent and understandable in human individuals. Man reveals in his actions what he is; he makes explicit what is implicit. He produces himself in external "gestures," which are interpreted by others according to their "lights." What he produces depends on his metaphysics, which always consists of those "things" which to him now are ultimately real and important. He holds himself responsible. This being responsible and holding others responsible leads to and constitutes his historical struggles and crises; history is a realm of freedom for and against values. Hegel's definition: "History is the progression in the consciousness of freedom," is wise and profound.

History is aristocratic. Innumerable peoples and innumerable masses of individuals have lived and died without leaving traces. And among the few peoples who have, only a few individuals have decisively contributed to values which have remained, embodied in lasting institutions. The higher and more universal the values are, which have become historically effective, the smaller is the circle of the individual founders. The founders of world-historical religions, for example, are counted on the fingers of two hands. Only what is outstanding in creation or in destruction of values is historical. Individual historical significance is a mixture of qualitative value and the quantity of lasting effects. This protects that which is historically significant from being confused with that which is merely freakish or absurd. Herostratus, who burned a temple in order that he might figure henceforth in history books, achieved his purpose—as an example of what the true historical individuality is not.

The historian is guided in his selection of that which is important and essential, and in his leaving out the unimportant and unessential data, by those values which were important to the people whom he studies. The historian is not evaluative himself; he has to apprehend evaluations of others in logical form. In writing the story of the history of the Reformation, or in comparing "East" and "West," for example, the reader must not have the impression that the writer belongs to one of the parties whose struggle he investigates. History as object-science is neither philosophy nor fiction. Its scientific dignity rests on the faithfulness with which the historian portrays what is valuable not only to him personally, but also to those whom he studies. Value-understanding makes history not less but more scientific than a neutral, natural science. Whether two elements fuse or explode is of no personal concern to a chemist, whereas the success or defeat of a "cause" may be of highest personal interest to the historian himself.

History records individual life in *collective* concepts; they are always unique. History never repeats itself. If it seems to repeat the same pattern it is not any longer history but nature. It is then apprehended by *generalizing* concepts, such as are used in many sociologies, where history is disregarded as a unique and concrete process, and where generalizing descriptive types or recurrent cycles are sought. "The revolution," for example, may show a similar curve of development in many instances. It is a generalizing sociological concept. "The French Revolution," on the contrary, is a unique collective concept, composed of all individuals participating in it. "History repeats itself," and "History never repeats itself" would be contradictory statements if they were not understood as different logical constructions of historical experience. The first is true from the point of view of a generalizing sociology, the other is true from the point of view of an individualizing history.

This is precisely the exciting "charm" of history, even in remembering retrospect, that nothing is settled beforehand. It is exciting to read who wins out and by what means, or why some seemingly strong and entrenched power was dethroned. History shows a relative freedom from antecedent conditions. It is the realm of the surprising emergence of new values and vital energies, full of breath-taking, spellbinding suspense. *Historia* is scientific if it is true to this existential anxiety of struggling individuals.

This selection of individual personalities in their unique collections, "period," "age," "war," "revolution," is only the first step in the concept of *historia*. The concept is developed into continuous wholes, which take the place of "laws," prevalent in natural sciences. What the historian conceives is initially some deed, which is already conscious to an actor and a known expression of a subjective mind. But the development, of which this deed is "seen" as a link and organic member of a whole "objective mind," is not known and conscious to the conscious actors involved. When Julius Caesar conquered Gaul he could not know that this deed would later contribute to the Latinization of the Franks and so lead to the birth of the French nation. This irony of history annihilates intentions and purposes by seemingly fulfilling them. The historian thus knows what no individual agent of history knows. This is the creative understanding of *historia*. There is no natural or genetic continuity of "blood and soil" which would act as a guide in the understanding of historical continuities. The historian apprehends wholes of existential times. He thinks together which individual events, persons, actions, belong together meaningfully, not only genetically or naturally. The historical collective whole contains more and greater significance than the consciousnesses of which it is composed, whereas in the logic of natural sciences the more general structure contains less content than the particular occurrences from which it is abstracted.

Historia is the science of "causal" inequalities. Small events become the occasions of huge revolutions, as a match may become the "cause" of a conflagration destroying a whole city. "Causes," further, disappear in their effects; the new "cause" devours and replaces the old. In so doing *historia* contributes to history in knowing what is "new" and what is "old," out of date, old-fashioned, antiquated. *Historia* does not exist outside and apart from history, which is its own memory. *Historia* as remembered continuity of an historical whole is a constitutive part of history, taught and preserved in education, transmitted to the future as living faith and as educating will to preserve what has been "inherited."

Historia as known, as well as history as enacted, is, finally, subject to chance, luck, contingency. It is fortunate to possess great men, unfortunate to lose them too early; and it is chance to have someone remembering adequately—Socrates was in luck that he found a Plato to immortalize him.

The same living reality which is logically apprehended as history can also be logically apprehended as nature. The logical categories and methods by which reality is thought determine whether reality is thought as an historical or a natural object of knowledge.

Physical science abstracts from understandable qualities, functions, and values, from life and soul, and keeps to their external shell as given to the senses. This abstraction enables it to unify all appearances, human and nonhuman, and to subject them impartially to a purely quantitative measurement. Natural sciences thus achieve systems of law on various levels of abstraction and generality. Nature, in opposition to history, is always identical, exact, clear, necessary, calculable, wide, and "big."

This logical construction of physical science is abstractly separable from the given events; "laws" as scientific objects are one with this formal intelligibility. Nameless "masses" satisfy the abstract intellect and its demand for control of innumerable instances of the same general behavior-pattern or "law."

The objectivity of physical sciences, and their freedom from particular perspectives (which belong to historical understanding of living contents), is easier to achieve than in *historia*—at a high price! The naturalist has once for all resigned his understanding, he never understands what he describes and explains. He is reduced to mass-behaviorism.

Natural science is "democratic," all particulars are equals before the natural "law"—no exceptions permitted: In order to level all appearances and to make them amenable to this reduction to law, their existential and functional event-character must be disregarded, what is common to innumerable instances must be retained in order to enable science to form statistical averages and to make predictions on the basis of such.

There is no such thing in scientific nature as "conscious," "subconscious," and "more-than-conscious," because naturalism keeps to sense-given appearance. It is interpreted in causal equations, where cause equals effect and where their sum remains constant. For natural sciences there is "nothing new under the sun," every causal relation is simply a cause subsumed under the same old and constant equation of cause and effect. Every stone which runs down a hill exemplifies the same old formula of gravitation which is also present and constantly present in all bodies alike.

The time used by natural science is the clock-time of quantitative measurement, which is indifferent against the contents measured, which are said to be "in" time, but which are not temporal creatures with time of their own.

Whereas the apprehension and representation of history requires a strong and artistic individuality who is capable of doing justice to great individuals and events, the naturalist on the contrary is replaceable. He prides himself on leaving all his subjectivity out of his experiments and his measuring. Anyone in his place and equipped with the same methods will have to arrive at the self-same result.

Creative thinking in science, on the other hand, is itself historical. It does not enter the impersonal generality which it discovers as creative thinking enters a work of art as enlivening part of that work.

So called "social sciences" or "sociology" are logically considered imitations of natural sciences. They apply the logical methods of natural sciences to an obstreperous human historical material. The "objects" object!

NATURALISM

The "victory" of machines over men, climaxed by the atom bomb, looks like a scientific-technical blackout of culture. The advent of a global technical efficiency seems the end of a meaningful history. This pessimistic view, however, is not justified. Man cannot be reduced to nature. Pessimism is the "natural" outcome of naturalism. This is an old story. Lucretius' *De Rerum Natura*, for example, has it complete. Man there has the choice between a meaningless whirl of eternal atoms and pleasant and short-lived illusions of sense-appearances. The world is a chance constellation of atomic whirls, life and meaning are products of bodies pushing and hitting one another, and the end of the world is certain and near. What appears in history and as history is sound and fury signifying nothing; a veil of short-lived unstable illusions of pomp and glory in the opinions of the many; a vast graveyard of values once fervently believed and now laid to eternal rest; a slaughter house in which a cunning beast of prey indulges in its maliciousness. The difference between the "old" naturalism engendering pessimism, and the "new" one, is only this, that now the human beast of prey is equipped with bigger and better scientific weapons.

If it is not the empty, futile, greedy, insane will-to-live and will-to-power which puts up the hysterical show (Schopenhauer), then it may be just the stomach which determines the mass movements of history, which alone are "real," while what is called culture is merely a superstructure; or everything is governed by lust and sexuality, and cultural institutions are defense mechanisms, weak dams to hide and stem the flood of sexual vitality (Freud); or, the so-called history is determined by sun spots and other "pressure groups" in our cosmic environment, producing historical rhythms as the moon causes ebbs and floods and directs the appearance and disappearance of seaweeds in the Atlantic

Ocean (19th century positivism); or history is a branch of biologism (orthogenesis), where races grow up in youth, maturity, and old age, like unconnected mushrooms, in which case there is not even a "survival of the fittest," because even the "fittest" race has only a brief preordained span of life (Spengler).

Naturalistic logic, lacking all principle of selection applicable to history, inevitably tends to worship any fact simply because the fact has succeeded in becoming one; and since one fact is just as good a fact as any other fact, history tends to be dissolved into an inarticulate mass of facts.

Chaos, the absence of all organizing form and selective value, is the most radical expression of naturalistic negation of meaning: History is Nonsense. "History is bunk" (Henry Ford). But such naturalistic negations of historical meaning may make history themselves; they become historical expressions of a sick conscience and of desperation.

Desperate ideology says that there is no absolute truth and then goes on maintaining as true that we are not real and that we have no access to any reality and that we have nothing but empty verbalisms. This is the voice of a desperate philosophy wanting to be desperate. Or, it says that something is ultimately real which can in no sense be ultimate, namely, the contingent and transient experiences and pleasures of momentary individuals. This is a desperate philosophy which does not want to admit being desperate. This was the mood prevalent in the decaying last centuries of the Hellenistic world. Or, it denies that man is a subject of knowledge responsible for his social world, and pictures him as an isolated individual "wax tablet" on which things engrave this impression; to accumulate as many such things as possible is supposed to make the man happy. Or, it says that knowledge is not a pursuit of truth, but is only a practical trick to gain advantages for given individuals or groups. This is a desperate philosophy pretending to be cheerful, athletic, and optimistic; it will prefer football to philosophy. Or, it says that the good is the good of my racial, national, or economic group—which is a desperation that has at least the virtue of brutal frankness. To this group belongs Marxism. Man is declared to be nothing but the product of economics and consequently an object of manipulations. All philosophy is alleged to be ideology that is a hypocritical mask for partial economic class interests. One class has nothing in common with other classes. History is the mechanical friction of such collective mass egotisms. And since there is no truth or justice, any means employed in this struggle is natural. This differs in nothing from racism, except that the latter replaces economic classes by racial-national groups as pseudo-ultimate standards of reference. Since Marxism has become a major historical power in this century, it is necessary to have a clear understanding of its negative character. Marxism is a naturalistic ideology expressed in four negations.

The first and foremost negation is the negation of God and of man's believed relation to him, which is religion. A rabid and fanatical atheism fires the imagination of the young Marx. In the preface to his doctoral dissertation on the materialistic philosophy of nature in Democritus and Epicurus he says: "Philosophy does not conceal it: In simple words, I hate all the gods, this confession of Prometheus is also her own confession, her dictate against all earthly and heavenly deities, which do not acknowledge man's own consciousness as the absolute and supreme being. There shall be no other gods beside it."

And in his so-called Critique of Hegel's *Philosophy of Law* he says: "Criticism of religion is the basis of all further criticism. Man has sought in the phantastic realm of heaven only his own reflected image. What he really sought was the superman. This reflected image of himself is pure illusion, it is a man undoing himself *(Unmensch)*, and now he will not any longer be inclined to be satisfied with it instead of with his own true reality which he now must seek. . . . The fight against religion is at the same time a fight against that world, whose spiritual aura religion is . . . religion is the opium for the people."

Friedrich Engels, the inseparable friend and companion of Marx, carries this on as follows: "The fight against religion, our emancipation from it, and the emancipation of the world from it is the purpose of our whole work from morning to night *(einzig Tagewerk)*. . . . The pretension of man to be anything but natural . . . is the root of all untruth and of all lies. Therefore we have declared war on religion and on all religious conceptions."

Marx made it perfectly clear how this war is to be conducted: Religion is not an object of knowledge, which is merely to be criticised, it is "our enemy, which we do not want to refute but to annihilate . . . in such a struggle the question is not, whether the opponent is an equal, a noble or an interesting opponent, the only thing that matters is to strike the mortal blow."

The second negation is the negation of reason. Reason is the center of philosophy. Philosophy is a free and logical reflection on all meanings of the truth. As Hegel puts it: Philosophy must be open to that which is and it must clearly think and say what it is. Reason in that sense is not a natural thing among other things, let alone a physical process which simply occurs. It is rather an obliging and infinite task, a personal commitment and a spiritual reality. As such it points back to, or implies a world-ground which makes it possible.

Marx denies this classical and idealistic conception of reason and philosophy. With his own venomous arrogance he declares in the preface to *Das Kapital* that he has reformed philosophy, that he has put Hegel upside down *(umgestülpt)*, and that philosophy and reason are nothing but ideology.

The term "ideology" he found as a weapon, wielded by French materialists of the eighteenth century. It means that there is no authentic spiritual reality. The implications of this position are terrific. You can never trust what a man says. There is no truth. There is no obligation in any agreement. All such rational conduct of life is nothing but "bourgeois ideology."

Philosophy degraded into ideology becomes the dogmatism of the party line, dictated by momentary power-interest. It is the Marxistic dogma that "all ideality is nothing but material interests fed back through a human head." Since the "human head" is also physical and material, the sentence says that all ideality is nothing but physical matter "transposed" through other physical matter.

All philosophy is only the "superstructure," or ideology, of material and physical class-interests. And since those so-called "classes" are, in accordance with the whole Marxistic hate-ideology, always and inevitably at war, and since war is conducted on the principles quoted above, all attempts at reasonable discussion are futile. If the principle of logic is denied, there is no possibility of any mutual understanding. The well is poisoned. You may have the most sincere and reasonable intentions to be fair and to do justice to legitimate interests—to the Marxist this is merely a ruse and hypocrisy.

Whoever attacks reason and philosophy is the loser. Marxism, by undermining philosophy as an ideological handmaiden of material power-interests, has branded itself as nothing but an ideology; "truth" depends on the momentary tactical decision of those in power, or what sort of double-talk might be the most opportunistic at the moment. Hence the frightening anxiety of all living under this terror to be orthodox and swing along with the party dictation at the right moment. Hence also the impoverishment of thinking, whose richness depends on the freedom of individuals to bring to public discussion their own views and abilities. Truth must be replaced by uniform and cominform propaganda.

The third negation is the progressive abolition of progress. When an epidemic makes progress or when you have a progressive tuberculosis you are subject to a progression which you would rather not have. Progress in this naturalistic sense is the Marxist conception of it. It is thought of as an irrestible natural power in which man is a helpless victim. He can do nothing to stem this sort of progress.

Marx had inherited the term progress from Hegel. But he claims to have reversed its meaning. Hegel speaks of meaning of history as a "progression in the consciousness of freedom." If Marx is correct in saying that he has put Hegel's philosophy upside down, the sentence then would read "the meaning of history is progression in the unconsciousness of slavery."

In Hegel's philosophy the idea of progress is inseparable from a widening, deepening, improved understanding of truth. It is a more mature formulation of what the Enlightenment had in mind when reason was said to liberate man from narrow provincialisms, prejudices, and superstitions. We are entitled to speak of progress, if a former world-view is seen through in its limitations, when its truth becomes a partial aspect of a wider truth. In such a maturing, dialectical progression we preserve the individual differences and former insights, while at the same time we also cancel them in favor of a revised and more comprehensive knowledge. And Hegel is careful to state that such a progress is tied up with the earnest endeavour in seeking truth, and that it is therefore not a blind or irresponsible change in time. What is later in time is not therefore also more spiritual or true in content. "The logical order in ideas must not be confused with their order in the sequence of time." Marx's reaction against Hegel and his step "forward" in "the order of time" is at the same time many steps "backward" in "the logical order of ideas." Marxism is truly reactionary.

To distinguish between a natural progression or change and a meaningful progress we need values, norms, standards, by which we evaluate a change. A change is a progress in a philosophical sense only if life becomes richer, more meaningful, more valuable to individuals and societies; or, to put it negatively, if suffering, misery, and ignorance are diminished. But since Marx assumes that reality is all physical, natural, material, he has no such spiritual value which could serve as a norm of progress or regress.

And since he further believes that philosophy should be replaced by natural sciences, he is bent on finding progress as a natural or scientific law. This he proclaims to have found; all Marxists parrot after him that progress is proved scientifically. As Lenin puts it: "Science is a copy, a reflex, a photograph of matter." This dogmatic and blind scient-*ism* makes scientific progress impossible.

Scientific progress has always rested on logical questions put to nature. Physical phenomena are criticized, not blindly accepted at their face-value. Physical science itself is not physical. It is a logical method by which spatio-temporal changes are measured and predicted. And philosophy of science has shown that this measuring or quantitative description of appearances can never equate its equations with a knowledge of reality. A philosophical scientist knows the limit of his methods. Only when we know our various limitations have we made true human progress.

Marxism has stifled both the scientific as well as philosophical progress. The practical technical application of sciences becomes a mysterious progressive process of nonsense, as if the value quality of human life were dependent on a more efficient mechanism and technicism. Man himself, a physical object among other objects, can now be mechanically manipulated. Man is a mass, subject to impersonal laws. Scientism in political practice leads to the most revolting dehumanization of life known to history.

The fourth negation is the negation of freedom and democracy. The term "democracy" has assumed an ideal meaning for us, which the Greek expression itself does not contain. Whether a "people's rule" is desirable or not depends on what sort of people is going to rule, and by what sort of rule. The tacit assumption that it will be a good people or that its rule is good, speaks well for our confidence in man, but any unexamined optimism is nevertheless a bit naïve. The emptiness of the term itself is demonstrated by the thoughtless communistic stuttering about "people's democracy."

What we really mean by the term is not what the term means. What we have in mind is rather freedom. And all freedom is based on the freedom to think and to say what you think. Without thinking, without sharing universal ideas through which we can communicate and form a community, all other freedoms would instantly collapse. The absence of logical thinking is insanity. If we "lose our mind," we also lose with it our freedom; indeed, we lose everything.

Thinking is a social process. One does not think in isolation. One thinks in meeting the thoughts of others. If I meet you and you represent a thought differing from my own, we exchange ideas and each of us is enriched by this process. I appropriate something from you, you appropriate something from me. The process of exchange, the give and take of ideas is richer than any of the partners who contribute to it. In order to be successful we have to be open to the other and open to ourselves. Without veracity, and trust in the veracity of others, we cannot arrive at any truth. We have to risk ourselves in laying ourselves open, but we also expect kindness and respect from the other if we do so.

The philosophical name for this process is dialectic, derived from the Greek "dialogue," which means to speak something through together. Democracy is the political realization of dialectic. Hegel first conceived the whole of history as such a dialectical process on a grand scale. Marx took the term and, as usual, perverted it into the absurdity of a "dialectical materialism." Marx is related to Hegel's philosophy as a dog is related to the corner of a cathedral!

Hegel's historical dialectic is the clarification of opposites. By working out a principle, its limitations are discovered and overcome in a wider and more comprehensive knowledge. Dialectic is meaningful only if it refers to thinking human beings who can freely express themselves. "Matter" cannot be dialectical and a "Dialectical Materialism" is a wooden iron!

Marx transformed Hegel's logical opposites into a clash of brute power groups. Their "dialectic" is merely a clash of force against force, without a common ground. And these forces, in turn, were narrowed down to economic classes. The whole intellectual, spiritual, moral, aesthetic, and religious culture, and their dialectical relations, disappeared in the bloody monotony of class-struggle between the bourgeois and the proletarian classes.

Their clash is an absolutely unintelligent process, in which the greater mass and the greater number determines the unavoidable result. In an official pronouncement of the Supreme Soviet of 1931, it is not orthodox to speak of this class-struggle as "mechanical-causal," which is proper for machines, but as "deterministic-causal."

Freedom of thought and of speech, the true dialectic of the human mind is incompatible with "dialectical materialism," just as a true democracy is impossible within a "people's democracy." The living human mind and spirit is the creator of all historical realities, including natural sciences and technical machinery, and it is not a product of a "deterministic causality."

The priority of logic over its embodiments and applications is the refutation of "dialectical materialism." But, unfortunately, a logical refutation is not convincing to an enemy who considers an appeal to truth as treason to the party line.

The Communist Manifesto of Marx makes such a distinction between political practice and philosophical theory ridiculous; his "theory" as practice abolishes all private ownership; which gives to the state the right to send you to work where the state pleases; which foments trouble and fans hatred all over the world to soften this world up for a communistic world-conquest. Totalitarian imperialism is merely the secular arm of the Marxist creed.

STATE, CULTURE, RELIGION

Nonsense presupposes sense. Naturalistic-pessimistic condemnations of history are involuntary testimonies of a truth which is not theirs. History is made by men who believe in univeral and shared values or ideals. In reflecting on the meaning of their motivating or "final causes," they produce one-sided or partial philosophies of history.

The *State*, in its historical development has most frequently served as having a leading value to historians and to philosophers of history; or, historians have most frequently been guided by a purely political philosophy of history. The state appears in such a view of history as the real agent, since it is a whole people unified, and by virtue of its unity, enabled to act as a responsible subject of historical decisions. The unification of all activities of life in the protective shell of laws, enforced by the state, gives to the state the same importance internally towards its members which it has externally towards other states. In both cases the state is a subject of historical decisions participating in a struggling historical life with other states.

Unity of power and authority backing its laws, appear as its central functions; they are characteristic of both small and large states; of states unifying people of the same blood and language, or people of different race and culture; of states ruled by one, by many, or by "all"; of "religious" states and of "non-religious" ones, of states at peace and of states at war.

The state is a valuable category for the understanding of historical developments. History may be considered as though, from this political-legal angle, it would gradually move towards an organization of states which would preserve the benefits of law inside, with the benefit of security between, the states. If such an organization is the meaning of political history, then it certainly is not brought about by reason or good will, which are values which no state as such can legislate or necessitate, but because the disagreeable consequences of the competing pursuit of power, which is politics, may make such an international organization more practical than its absence. And even if such an expansion of political-legal security becomes reliable fact, the problem of history—what mankind shall be?—is not solved, since no one can tell whether man in a universal confederacy will not degenerate.

Other historians are not so much interested in the state as in culture. *Culture*, then, becomes the leading value-category directing the selection and construction of historical data. We then have a history of culture as the essential history. Culture transcends the state and its political necessities. Political totalitarianisms demonstrate what happens when the political power-interest of the state tries to impose its yoke on culture or will permit culture only to the extent that it may be useful to the state.

Culture is cultivation of free and self-chosen tasks, and is therefore inseparable from free individuals. It may be intellectual-scientific, contemplative (Philosophical-aesthetic), or practical culture of craftsmen and industry. Cultural *historia* leads to stories interested in the growth of reason and of enlightenment; to social-practical progress in the cultivation of nature by hand or by scientific techniques; to artistic histories enjoying the wealth and colorful spectacle of life in its free communication and interplay of all faculties in the arts of living. Creative enterprise and the cult of great individuals lends itself to the favorite kind of biographical history.

If this aesthetic interest in culture does not balance the scientific-intellectual interest, the latter is likely to fall into the fallacy of irresistible "progress," confusing the progress in scientific techniques and particularly the progress in applied natural sciences with progress in human culture. If the aesthetic interest in culture, on the other hand, dominates, it may evaporate the seriousness of history into a brilliant show-piece, as if history were there to be enjoyed like a theater-show. A balanced interest in culture will see history as an educational process of man who learns to liberate and to cultivate all his faculties. History then becomes a major discipline of liberal education intending to make man permanently human in subjecting him to the discipline of learning what he has been and what he might be. History as one of the liberal arts expands provincial horizons, makes the student a citizen of the human world, evokes his own potentialities by inspiring memories of the past.

Such education should terminate in and be guided by the ethical respect for every man as an end in himself, and not merely as a means of natural necessities or as a puppet in some providential plan. This is the center of morality and moral existence, the positive meaning of which is the perfection of all human faculties in the interest of a free community of life, and the integrity of a well rounded and balanced personality.

Culture seeks the meaning of life in life itself. In this search life is ennobled. The search is inseparable from undogmatic freedom. Culture is heroic in risking existence for ideals, adventurous is exploring the unknown, enthusiastic in its dedication to truth and freedom. Its conception of the self is that of a becoming self—life is an educational task. It unfolds in three main directions: the human person is to realize itself as subject of knowledge, as socially responsible, and as artistically creative. Sometimes in a tension, sometimes in harmony with faith, this idealism of reason is the main line and the foundation of the historical civilization of Europe. It has made of Europe more than a geographical location. Europe is by virtue of this philosophy not merely a place but an ideal of world-wide radiations.

Aesthetics has given to European art its independence and its autonomy. Art is empowered by this philosophy to "see life steady and see it whole." Religious and secular values, moral conflicts, psychological situations, and natural phenomena are encompassed in imaginative unifications. The world is intuited as a spectacle and actualized in imaginative symbols. Through these works nations and epochs are realizing themselves in a common image. And generations form a continuity of an aesthetic community, sharing a timeless beauty and a probing vision of life's truth.

Man proves, in creating this art, that he is a creator himself. The idea of unity, wholeness, and perfection is the artistic ideal of aesthetic idealism. Art is meant as a monument of immortality. And this form is imparted to the manifold movement of life presented in this form. In identifying himself with these living characters—designs, melodies, stories—the creator subordinates his own will to the will of his characters, who must behave according to their own laws, which are not the law of the artist himself. But in unfolding their own potentialities, the figures in the artist's play nevertheless contribute to a vision of a conception of wholeness which the spectator and receiver of the art must reconstruct. The idea returns to its own wholeness through its embodiment and lives as a common experience in all those who participate. Idealistic or classical art makes creation concrete. Life is celebrated as an eternal and fulfilled Now. The pressures and miseries of life are overcome in a symbol. In losing and forgetting oneself in it, one is reborn and comes back enriched and purified.

Ethics makes practical-moral life independent and autonomous. Moral problems are human problems, regardless of religious creed on the one hand or natural race and color on the other hand. The moral law is its own foundation. Obligations to one's family and one's neighbors and the virtues of truthfulness and honesty remain objective tasks in all circumstances; they remain obligatory whether one lives up to them or not.

Ethics discovers the identity of the moral law in individuals and in societies. "The state is the individual writ large" (Plato); psychological tendencies in the individual appear in magnified form in the social movements of organized society. In distinction from the aesthetic form of wholeness and perfection in the artistic symbol of life, practical unity always remains a task or imperative, an unfinished but going concern of all. Individual responsibility for self-improvement and social responsibility are not separable. The individual must trust and hope that the community will not fail to carry on in the future what the individual can never finish by himself.

The state was thus conceived as an instrument of justice to all functions of the soul. The state as ideal expanded in the Roman Empire to comprise all nations in a family of nations, equal before the law. And this legal equality before the law was again expanded in the abolition of slavery, whereby social equality before the law was established. The same ideal of social justice is at work now to solve the problem of economic injustice. The problem was beyond solution in the time of economic poverty, but its solution is in sight with machine production making possible an economy of abundance.

Practical and aesthetic culture, however, are only applications of *Logic;* of the *logic* of reason, or the theory of ideas. Logic understands ideas as founding not only aesthetics and ethics, but all knowledge. It lays the foundation of the sciences in the pursuit of truth. Truth is the central norm to which all propositions concerning all aspects of reality ought to conform. The subject of knowledge is responsible for the propositions which he holds to be true or false. He should at any time be able to account for them. Truth is the ultimate authority of all theoretical culture. Philosophy in this sense is the conscience of culture.

Logic is the unity of the various natural, social, and theological sciences. It shows that no object can be truly said to be real, independent of its relation to truth. The object is real and reliable insofar as it is apprehended in logical form. *Knowledge does not consist of the data of experience, but of propositions, which alone can be true or false.* What we call objects are data of experience made into logical concepts and relations. The term "object" itself is such a general logical class or universal. The natural sciences owe their progress to this logical method of formulating mathematical hypotheses which are then indirectly verified by experiential evidence. Such logical forms are not, in turn, things or entities in themselves, but forms of unifying our experience. An idea, accepted as a practical, aesthetic, or religious postulate by a culture, makes that culture coherent in all its activities and understandable in its meaning or character. And since all ideas converge on man as their subject and focus, philosophy of culture understands itself as self-knowledge and self-criticism; it is the foundation of the historical civilization called European.

The third power making history and directing its scientific construction, is *religion*. The most basic issue, the one which produces the most incisive distinction in historical cultures, is the religious demand on, and explanation of, the world. Cultures differ mostly in affirming or denying a religious world-view. They are either religious or anti-religious. From this angle history is a struggle between faith and unbelief. Western civilization, for the last four hundred years, has been increasingly anti-religious, a development which has come to a provisional climax in the replacement of God by the worship of national and racial values in national socialism and facism, and by the worship of economic and class values in capitalism and communism. The other predominantly anti-religious civilization was the one of the last four or five centuries of the Hellenistic empire.

There are radical distinctions in both the religious and the irreligious world views. Confining our attention to the major world religions, we find two fundamental types, each subdivided into many modifications. In the West we find what we call "prophetic," or "revealed religions," balanced in Asia by a group of mystic or contemplative religions. The religions of the Western group all originated in the Middle East, among Semitic peoples. Their common root is the Biblical tradition of the Jews, modified on the one hand in the New Testament of Christianity, on the other hand in the Koran of Islam.

The three revealed religions have some principles in common: God is an absolute subject. He is not to be found in this world, because this world is His creation. It is created not in time, but in eternity, out of nothing, as a temporal or mortal creature. Having a beginning, middle, and an end, it is not an eternal nature but a transitory history. Man is created in the image of God, as the subject of his actions and responsible for them. God speaks to him, revealing Himself. Man's response to being addressed by God, is faith. By faith he participates in God's blessed life and becomes an initiated co-worker or participant in a divine providence. Apart from God, turning a deaf ear to revelation, he falls into nothingness and sin. His existence then, is meaningless.

The Biblical religions differ in the interpretation of their common principle of revelation. In Judaism, God addresses the Jews as His chosen people. He is the guarantor of their national existence. In Christianity, the chosen people becomes the Church of those who believe. God speaks not only through prophets, but his word becomes flesh. He speaks Himself in Jesus Christ. The virgin birth, crucifixion, and resurrection of the Lord are essential parts of the revelation of God, demonstrating His otherness, His loving participation, and His transcendence of this world. In Islam, the chosen people are also those who believe. But God speaks only through his Prophet, as in Judaism. Judaism, being restricted to a national group, is prevented from missionizing, except in the form of natural propagation—God says to Abraham that his seed will fill the earth. The two other Biblical religions are missionizing, activistic religions: Islam conquering the Near East, half of Africa, part of India and of the Philippines; Christianity conquering the West, but split into three major subdivisions. The Greek Orthodox church maintained from its inception that revelation is to be understood in *ikons,* that, properly interpreted, the truth of the logos revealing itself, and the truth of the logos interpretating the revelation, are one and the same truth, that faith and reason are fundamentally identical. The Roman church, mainly Mediterranean and Latin in support, made the revelation continuous with the church and distinguished between natural religion available to reason and revealed

Christian religion guaranteed by the authoritative tradition of the church. The reformed or protestant church, mainly Northern and Germanic in its origins, separated faith and reason, reason being competent only in secular matters, faith being evoked by the Word of God over which the church had no jurisdiction.

If we now turn from the West to Asia, we find four world religions, which are in agreement on their main principles, and are, as a group, diametrically opposed to the main principles of the Biblical religions. Whether we look at the "Central Harmony" of Confucianism or the "Silent Way" of Taoism in China, or at the "Brahman" of Hinduism or the "Nirvana" of Buddhism in India, we discover no God in the Biblical sense.

All Asiatic religions are, in terms of the Semitic religions, godless or atheistic. When they speak of gods, and Hinduism has innumerable gods, they refer to them as mythical images, and myths are known as symbolic, penultimate forms of truth. There is no transcendent God, breaking through his creation in personal revelations addressing man, because in the Eastern religion God is the unity of this world, and man is identical with God. "That art Thou." Man therefore needs no revelation, but must by introspective contemplation find this divine identity or harmony within himself. And as God is not a person or absolute subject, so man is no self or subject called upon to dedicate himself to absolute causes or to make everlasting commitments. What he calls his self, is an endless variety of fleeting experiences and perspectives. If he takes one of those moods and moments seriously, he is lost and falls to the misery of delusions and sufferings. The goal is selflessness and the way to this goal is a steadfast practice in learning to see that what we call evil is always tied to some particular want. As long as we want something as good, we create the evil of being frustrated in what we want, because the end of all wants is certain. The horror of the Oriental "to lose face" is the shame of having committed himself to something as certain which he ought to have known to be uncertain and relative. To rely on the uncertainties of experience and images is equivalent to losing your mind, your peace, your balance, your harmony, your spirituality, your religion. In the eyes of the West this is a negative and passive attitude. But in the eyes of the East this attitude is the acme of activity, which is the activity of contemplation, whose aim is to resemble the divine principle. This principle is the absolute unity of life, which is the core of reality; it maintains itself in unbroken peace in all the myriad ripples and vicissitudes of a changing appear-

ance. Any man-made unity, any program of action, any legally established harmony, is at best an imperfect analogy to the absolute, eternal,
and pre-established harmony of Being. But if the man-established
unity is taken seriously, as if it were ultimate, then it becomes the
snare of illusion and the cause of miseries, unnecessary sufferings, and
wars. The East, therefore, has never known religious war, which sounds
to it as a square circle does to us. Western dogma is, for the same
reason, foreign to the East. Dogma means an intellectual fixation,
a conceptual determination of religious truth in definite propositions.
For the Eastern religions all such fixations and determinations are
negations of the fluid continuum of the divine life, which allows an
infinite and indeterminate variety of symbolic expressions. This means
in practice an open and absorbing tolerance of all religious symbols,
including those of the West. Mythical and artistic symbols take the
place of revelation of divine truth.

Whether the Western aggressive activism or the Eastern patient tolerance and compassions will "win out" is a typical Western question.
Since they are both human, it seems more reasonable to assume that
they will come to recognize one another just as man and woman need
and complement each other. The East may learn that the Substance is
also a subject, and the West may learn something concerning the value
of symbolic-mythical thinking.

History, from the religious point of view, appears as a struggle of
faith and worldliness, as a procession or a pilgrimage in search of
salvation from the absurdities and contradictions of this world. In the
Jewish-Christian-Mohammedan traditions, God himself is the subject of
history. He sets its beginning in creation and its end on Doomsday of
the Last Judgment. He has designs and plans with men, He chooses
peoples and individual prophets to guide its course, or He steps into
history in person to bring a fallen mankind back to His love and His
wisdom. Those who believe form the church visible and invisible, the
city of God mingled in time with the worldly city of man, and in
combat with the "City of the Devil" (St. Augustine). The latter's aim
of earthly peace and legal justice is the weak and secondhand analogy
with the peace and justice of God, whose way is not our way, but may
become our way in faith.

The religious philosophy of history may become, and has more than
once become, totalitarian also, rigidly subordinating political and cultural life to its all-absorbing metaphysical vision. Its weakness has
always been the identification of a visible and quasi-historical set of

symbols and stories with faith itself. If the Absolute walks into history to become a party therein, the rest of the profane history is necessarily emptied of value and significance, either as preparation and prophecy, or as apostasy becoming "the Antichrist" and "Satanic." If God is the subject of all history, then it is hard to see what sort of reality the profane history, in opposition to the sacred or holy history, can have. This difficulty can be overcome only if the religious symbol or myth, which is believed intellectually as an object, is seen through as myth and as symbol of faith. But then religion ceases to function as a particular and positive and revealed church, and passes over into a philosophy encompassing religious metaphysics. We then enter upon the task of thinking a comprehensive philosophy of history which is not partial and is not an absolute party in conflict with other parties.

HISTORICAL IDEALISM, REALISM, INDIVIDUALISM

History proper emerges from the prehistorical levels of anonymous social structures when man begins to understand himself. And man understands himself when he formulates ideals, when he embraces them existentially as his own, and expresses them in his attitudes, procedures, and institutions. Man is historically understood when the ideals are understood for which he lives and dies.

Ideals are answers to opportunities and questions, they are the creative attempts of man to do justice to what is. They are not prescribed or given in the geographical and social circumstances occasioning them. The same American nature, for example, evoked opposed answers from the native Indians and from the immigrating Europeans.

Idealism is the key to history. No intelligible history of art, of religion, or of politics could be written, if there is no intuitive-essential and logical understanding of what constitutes art, religion, or politics. Ideals cannot be taught by experience, if the investigator does not have a logical hypothesis in mind guiding him in his selection and in his attention to what is essential and what is not essential to the history he studies. Every induction rests on a logical hypothesis which can be verified or refuted by experience, but which cannot be given or furnished by it. To assume the latter is the well-known inductive fallacy of empiricism.

But while idealism is the key to history, it nevertheless becomes a hindrance if it is dogmatic and not critical. Dogmatic idealism assumes that ideals determine history. But ideals do not allow us to deduce the why of historical rhythms. If it were sufficient to understand ideals, then the historical life would become indifferent as a mere byplay or a gallery of illustrating examples. The theology of Calvin in Geneva in the sixteenth, and the theology of Jonathan Edwards in the New England of the seventeenth century, may be almost the same. There is nevertheless a world of historical difference between the activity of Calvin and the resulting Swiss church, and the activity of Jonathan Edwards in the New World. The identity of ideals is radically different from the concrete historical continuity of historical life. The decisive historical success or failure cannot be predicted from the worthiness of the ideal itself. The resistance against it, or the fact that people get tired of it after having achieved a victory, the sudden appearance of competing ideals are irrational elements which cross the idealistic interpretation of history.

Historical *realism* or traditionalism, therefore, keeps to this real or active cohesion and tradition of attitudes and procedures. It takes ideals for granted and turns its attention to forms and institutions which are developed, preserved and gradually altered by their representatives. The rough and actual interrelation of individuals representing the same objective *res*, or cause in concrete situations, is the object of historical realism.

It will tend to overrate the institutions which must be preserved in their purity. For a Confucian, or a Roman Catholic theologian, or a classistic aesthetician, the history of their causes is less a creative development than a preservation of the given achievements which must be protected from deterioration. All "reformations" mean to cleanse their traditions from corrupting innovations. The ideal is not a norm of timeless value, but rather a ground on which to build, an anchor to hold on to.

Realistic traditionalism will also follow the migration of formed values from their origins to new places, times, and environments. The migration of the Roman law, of Greek art and logic, of the Christian charity, are examples. Such migration includes the movement of symbols or vehicles of meaning, the "signs in which to conquer," the style of structures and of tools.

Realism, like idealism, is an impediment for the understanding of history, if it becomes dogmatic and treats of its objective institutionalized forms of life as if they were self-moving. A history of art-styles without artists, or a history of economic forms-of-production without individuals creating them, illustrate such realistic dogmatism.

Historical *individualism* corrects this error of traditionalism. Life is never life in general but rather, it is exclusively life in individuation. And every individual shape of life is unique, one member of its own class, unrepeatable. History ultimately depends always on individuals and their decisions in an infinite mutual limitation of give and take.

Attention to this irrational and unpredictable play of individuals makes *historia* intuitive and brings it close to art. It also emphasizes the great man in history, without whom the world would be poorer, without whose transformations and crises, history would lack a colorful and outstanding leader.

Great individuals create environments through their presence. If we assume, for instance, that the author of the works of Shakespeare, lived in Stratford-on-Avon, then Stratford became through him an "environment"; without him it would have nothing to "environ." Great historical individuals receive traditions in their own inimitable way and absorb influences organically and in line with their own form. If they belong to the great actors of history they are impatient with traditionalists or "ideologues," because as actors they know that decisions are there and have to be made in situations so concrete and unpredictable that no general theory could ever do justice to them. The historical individual is open to the exigencies of the day and of the hour and proves its worth in being fruitful in concrete actualities. The genius of practical men is compromise. It is the individual who is responsible for the shape history takes, not general institutions or traditions. And individual details and descriptions of fateful minutes is something *historia* could not do without. The advantage of this historical individualism is its closeness to life, its biographical color, its richness and dynamics. Its disadvantage is the danger of an utter relativism and loss of common-social powers in trivialities.

If the ideal unity is overemphasized, which gives meaning to the believing, knowing, acting, and artistic creations of a civilization, then all its individual participations and institutions are in danger of losing their concrete historical actuality. They are mere fragments of a confession, inadequate imitations of the eternal value. If on the contrary the overwhelming power of great causes and traditions is stressed, all individual and creative responsibility is dimmed. If the irrationality and unpredictable novelty and uniqueness of individuation is in the foreground, then continuity and unity of life is in danger.

THE HISTORICAL WORLD-VIEW

Neither the political, cultural, religious values, or their naturalistic negation; nor the idealistic, realistic, individualistic *historia,* can render account of history as a whole. Each of these views has a truth of its own. To deny the power of the factual and irrational nonsense of history would be a shallow optimism. To force the political fanatic into the categories of culture would be as artificial as to force the liberal philosopher of culture into the categories of a prophet or an apostle. History is the dialectical tension of values against the irrational threat of their destruction, as well as the struggle of different fundamental values with one another. In his history man makes the experience in which he is constantly contradicting and opposing himself. He experiences his freedom from and against nature, for and against values, as his inescapable destiny, as his own existential time. This freedom is the value of history as distinguished from all the many and conflicting values in it. History is the processional human verification of the world as an interplay of opposites.

History draws all value-polarities into its open and dynamic process, in which they are molded, filled, and emptied with ever renewed content. Every value is a problem seeking form and solution. We mention a few of those value tensions: on the vital level, life is healthy or sick, strong or weak, pleasant or painful, agreeable or disagreeable, rooted in familistic organic orders or uprooted and displaced. On the political level, persons or actions are powerful or impotent, purposive or pointless, ordered or disordered, efficient or inefficient, just or unjust. In economic culture, enterprises are profitable or unprofitable, useful or useless. In artistic culture, periods are ugly or beautiful, creative or imitative. In education, individuals are informed or uninformed; in manner they are tactful or tactless; in morality they are good or bad; in legality they are correct or wrong. In religion, man is sinner or saved, blessed or damned, holy or profane. And all levels are animated by love for, or hate of, values, which evaluations constitute the universal process of history itself.

History is the whole man, sensual, passionate, acting, moral, artistic—religious creator and destroyer of symbols, seen in the collective process of deciding and shaping the range and constellation of his values. This collective and dramatic formation and transformation of values is, as history, man's shadow. He is more than the shadow he casts, because he cancels and preserves his past as his own perennial potentiality, but he is also more plastic through his shadow:—he is what he has been. The historical process is distinguished from a circular and meaningless natural change through its irrevocable value decisions which give it "direction"; it is distinguished from "progress" because the gain of every civilization in one direction is sure to be its loss in another direction, and mainly because there is no final or providential determinism in evidence.

History presupposes the world as tension which makes it possible. History is the essential inner aspect in which the ontological constitution of the world becomes evident in its human modification. Living reality is the reason for there being a history, history is the reason enabling us to see through it the dialectic of distinct levels and directions, the one and the many, of being and becoming, of freedom and destiny.

History is dialectical. It exists in the contradiction of natural resistance and indifference against the civilizing will, and civilizations exist in the contradiction against the Absolute envisaged and betrayed in the ideals—the Absolute wherein the storms and stresses of civilizations break as waves of time on the rock of eternity. History is dialectical in itself in that the values of the state, of culture, and of religion, limit one another in a ceaseless struggle for supremacy, and in that the good of today is the grave of the good of yesterday and the cradle of its own enemy of tomorrow. Dialectical is the dynamic flux and rhythm of historical life, in which individual subjectivity faces the stern objectivity of the idea, natural constancies are disrupted by the discontinuity of freedom, traditions handed down meet the will of organic wholes to maintain themselves against migratory influences, and where the freedom of the one is the slavery of the other.

There is one guide in these perplexities,—and that guide is philosophy. The history of philosophy is also the philosophy of history. Philosophy thinks what is, and philosophy also unifies its time in thought, the one implying the other. Philosophy in its "world sense," as Kant called it, reflects reality in historical existence, it is the spirit that builds and animates the mentalities and works of civilizations. Philosophy in its "school sense," that is, in a technical, professional and logical form, reflects on historical existence in reality and makes it articulate and explicit—

And so ties the beginning to the end:

History, emerging from Nature, expresses philosophy and is as much a self-searching, self-defining process as a dialectical struggle between contrary values and of values with their own contradictory negations in existential times.

Knowledge and Wisdom[1]

> "*Philosophical critique is based on the faith that true philo-*
> *sophical knowledge is possible . . . it requires a standard which is*
> *as independent of the judge as well as of that which is judged.*
> *Without this idea of philosophy as its own condition and pre-*
> *supposition it would be condemned forever to be nothing but an*
> *opposition of one subjectivity against another subjectivity.*
>
> —HEGEL
> (W. I. 173, 188).

KNOWLEDGE

We define: Knowledge is a communicable logical apprehension of reality (X), by existing subjects.

If the ontological value of X is "given-in-experience," we attain the concept of object-experience. If this experientially given is a sensuous, external image we have "physics." If we interpret such images in terms of psychical functions as their apparent expressions we have psychology. Both together comprise the whole of natural-historical object-experience. Its truth lies in the agreement of those who investigate. We call this scientific kind of knowledge, *immanent*.

If we define the ontological value of X not as given, but as giving (for example: the act of logically or formally apprehending logical and formal apprehensions), then we attain the concept of a formal knowledge, which is not experiential. We have to think in order to know what thinking is. The laws of thought are valid if we think. We cannot find thinking outside of its actualization. More: the logical principles, through which all that which is given is logically organized, are the same forms through which they themselves are apprehended,

---

1 Presidential Address by author, Southwestern Philosophical Conference, 1947.

as such organizing forms. Identity, for example, is that which logic thinks and it is also that by which it is thought. The "logos" distinguishes itself from itself and remains the same in its self-distinction. We call this kind of knowledge, *introscendent*.

If we define, thirdly, the ontological value of X as neither given, nor as formal, but as an absolute whole of reality, as Being which contains both what is given and what is enacted, we develop *ontological knowledge,* or a theory of Being. The terms "soul," "world," "reality," are such ontological symbols of the absolute whole. The faith that there is reality, although it is never given, is to be logically elucidated. Reality is as correlative to faith in it, as the color red is correlative to the act of perception. We call this kind of knowledge, *transcendent*.

Philosophy, the love of wisdom, is not confined to any one of the three kinds of knowledge. Philosophy knows that all three kinds of knowledge participate in the common task of logically apprehending reality. The universe of philosophy is the totality of what is factually given, formally possible, and transcendently necessary. All three ways of apprehending reality terminate on the one hand in man, on the other hand in that which is, in Being. Philosophy must think Being in human existence, and human existence in Being. We call this all-comprehensive wisdom, *dialectical*.

If knowledge thinks itself as all-inclusive, then knowledge becomes wisdom. Dialectical wisdom itself distinguishes within itself three different apprehensions of reality: Knowledge is a communicable logical apprehension of immanent, introscendent, and transcendent reality, by existing subjects. We now ask: What is the relation of dialectical knowledge to its own apprehended immanent, introscendent, and transcendent content?

The given and immanent, as well as the giving, and the transcendent reality, is in each case a non-logical content to be grasped and constructed in logical forms. Wisdom is in all three levels of knowledge a dialectical unity of the opposites of logical form and non-logical as well as logical content. Knowledge is a dialectical unity of opposites, because form as well as content cannot be reduced each to the other; they are inseparable, but the one is not what the other is. Intuition of life, absorption by tasks of the spirit, religious visions of the absolute Being, are fused with the logical concept into a dialectical process which is the love of wisdom. In this process the logical form can transcend itself. In grasping its own logical activity it establishes at the same time the inalienable right of its own non-logical "other." We shall demonstrate this dialectic first for immanent scientific knowledge, and then for introscendence and transcendence.

We subsume both the external, sensuous as well as the internal, psychical objects under the term "appearance." The scientific intellect intends to comprehend appearance. It clarifies and orders appearance by abstractions. Its concepts are products of abstraction—and are abstract themselves. The abstract concept isolates an aspect of the object—and disregards the rest.

Every such concept thinks a something (X) in the logical form of identity and universality. Before it is so thought it is not known, but only met with or experienced. "Identity" means that a thought content remains unalterable, eternally one and the same. Without identity no content is intelligible. The concepts must be identical, if they are to be repeated and used as condition of all human community and communication. Only identical concepts can be affirmed and denied in judgments, and the principle of non-contradiction that "A can not be both affirmed and denied," is unconditionally valid for them. "Universality" means that a concept is valid for all members of its own class. The extension of the class implies logical quantity, i.e., degrees of generality. The least general universal is the *individual* concept, valid for all members of its class consisting of one member only, "Julius Caesar," for example. All historical concepts of individual persons, events, and collectives of persons and events, form the logical character of historical sciences. *Particular* universals are valid for some or many cases of their classes. They prevail in descriptive and generalizing empirical sciences. *General* universals are, like individual universals, valid for all members of their classes. Our term "appearance," for example, is valid for all objects of all empirical sciences.

Universals do not exist in the spatial and temporal appearance, which they comprehend. They do not appear. They are not events and do not succeed and throng one another successively and simultaneously. They subsist, i.e., they have their logical location in judgments; something (X) is apprehended and thought in the relation of concepts. The concept is logically demanded (founded) by that which is to be known. The judgment further subordinates one concept as species under its genus, and coordinates one species with other species under the same genus. (For example: physical and psychical data under appearance.) The judgment is formally valid, according to whether such sub- and co-ordination is logically demanded by the X to be known. The judgment: it must be so and not otherwise, is itself so and not otherwise, demands a definite logical decision, a "yes" or "no." This decision that such is the case, that that which is, is—is itself the logical quality of all judgments.

The logical concatenation of judgments yields systems of knowledge. The principle of this reasoning is the logical demand that all true judgments cohere. This coherence rests on the one hand on the principle of non-contradiction, on the other hand on the verified validity of the judgments which are to be united. Since every concept is identical with itself and different from every other, it is possible to combine judgments which share identical concepts.

The scientific intellect, thus constituted, intends to fix the fleeting world of appearance in lasting structures. It assumes that his own unity may be verified by the appearance. Under this assumption all object-sciences try to organize the data in unified systems of knowledge. Given events, and psychical or living functions, are rationally apprehended if they can be reconstructed in coherent wholes. Logical identity functions in the repeatability of experiments and in the comparison of what is similar.

Scientism, in distinction from science, operates with abstractions as if they were general intellectual objects, confusing its logical constructions with the irrationally given reality, which is to be constructed by means of logical operations. Scientific objects are falsely identified with their phenomenal data. An object-"metaphysics" or "realism" invents a world which seems to be independent of knowledge. Such pseudo-absolutes always run into self-contradictions and inevitable antimonies, because they contradict the concept of knowledge. They leave out of their "picture" both the knowing subjects as well as the non-logical appearance of given events.

This pseudo-metaphysical confusion of scientific object-systems with life is particularly dangerous in so-called scientific constructions of social machines, totalitarian shells, guaranteed against all uncertainties, crises, and dissatisfactions.

THE DIALECTIC OF IMMANENT KNOWLEDGE

Appearance in opposition to logically constructed scientific objects is irrational. Nothing is identical in pure experience. There is no reliability. The appearing x is an everchanging flux, other and other amongst its rivulets, "pushing" and "pulling" one another in a myriad of unforeseen spatial and temporal changes, each event split in an infinite variety of aspects, which influence each other, confused and confusing, the realm of the completely inconstant, passing, transitory, surprising mortality—seat and center of all incomprehensibilities.

If we identify the constant conceptual, universal law with "being" intended by knowledge, then its opposite, the irrational becoming would be its "non-being." And the comprehension of this non-being, the judgment, "Appearance is an irrational flux," is in itself an eternal, identical, and universal truth. The logical concept thus passes into its opposite, establishing it as its own logical requirement. Logic transcends itself by making evident its own negation as the opposite of itself. In "becoming," dialectical logical unity and its negation are thought as a concrete dialectical whole. The *ordo et connexio rerum* is not identical with the *ordo et connexio idearum,* but that non-identity is eternally identical with itself as this concrete wrestling process of both partners. Appearance behaves neither as species of genus, nor is it (as it appears) universal, abstract, identical. Concepts, on the other hand, are neither spatially or temporally located, lack intuitive content, shape, and presence, are discrete and discontinuous against the qualitative continuum of appearance; are united according to logical rules. ("Syntax.")

INTROSCENDENCE

This dialectical negation makes no sense within scientific thinking. It is wisdom, or learned ignorance, as introscendence.

Negation within object-thinking merely distinguishes either some partial content from some other partial content, or distinguishes an abstraction from that which is disregarded by the abstraction. Immanent negations can therefore also be stated positively. That there is no king of America is equivalent to saying that all Americans are busy otherwise. If an object statement "A is B" is denied, then this denial does not mean that there is a negative entity "not B" in experience. An object-negation is a positive statement, with which a denial is incompatible according to the principle of non-contradiction.

The dialectical negation, however, radically introscends the scientific realm of object-thinking. The intention to know objects cannot, for its purposes, bother about the irrationality of appearance. It does not want to know that. But *this* "not wanting to know" conceals and reveals the dialectical negation. Object-thinking is infected with it, without confessing it. It is infected with wisdom and hates to admit it. If this logical self-knowledge and self-introscendence is denied, a "blind spot" for dialectic bars the way to a critical philosophy.

Object-knowledge as dialectical process is known to intend logical clarity and order without being in a position to reach this goal in its purity. But not only that. The logical postulate of clarity of the concept, truth of the judgment, and coherence of reason, believed, and directing or regulating the scientific intention, as supreme value, at once creates problematic uncertainty, error and untruth, as that which should not be. To keep exclusively to finite appearances in their utter relativity and subjectivity as the only possible content of knowledge, to wallow in immediate impressions, to insist on arbitrary and partial perspectives, to pretend that given experiences is all there is—all such finitisms lead to that desperation of knowledge, whose name is nihilism. In judging and condemning the opposite of logical reason as unreasonable, reason establishes its own opposite as such. In pursuing its logical ideal, knowledge is getting wise and now knows that it seeks certainty and truth in a treacherous and lying world of its own making. Knowledge as dialectical battle establishes its own battleground. It could not be this struggling reality if the irrational partner were not as necessary as the logical will to truth.

But even when this introscending self-knowledge is absent from the mind of scientists, its dialectic is nevertheless present in the experience which the scientist makes with the history of his science. The history of the sciences teems with errors, which were believed to be truths. Again and again that which was established is established as not established. Again and again world constructions, seemingly independent of knowledge, are discovered as incompatible with other equally dogmatic constructions. The products of the "abstract understanding" are time and again dissolved by the same intellect that produced them. The first and exemplary discovery and dissolution occurred, when Gorgias demonstrated, that the different "natures" of the natural philosophers contradicted themselves and each other, if they were confused with nature itself.

The scientific situation of today, having learned from its history, is such that a more and more perfect logical organization of experience is counterbalanced by a keener awareness of the irrational character of given events. The scientists seem to be satisfied with statistical averages and probabilities. Every construction is known as resting on hypotheses of greater or lesser generality, so that many hypotheses have room side by side. There also seems to be a growing insight into the inseparability of scientific object-construction from practical and theoretical selections based on needs or interests on the part of knowing individuals.

Returning to our dialectical unity of opposites and to knowledge as a dialectical process, we find in it a first example of a non-given introscending kind of reality. Knowledge as dialectical reality is not given, but is being produced as act of the knowing mind, as an intersubjective, struggling communication of truth. Logic, in transcending and limiting itself, proves the possibility of self-knowledge which is not knowledge of given events constructed into scientific objects. In the history of philosophy this dialectical introscension has been formulated as certainty of the uncertainty of object-thinking, as indubitable necessity in doubting the necessity of given facts, as that truth which limits factual truths to be related to appearance with which they are not identical. If we admit this, and only if we admit this, have we reached the point where we can turn to the question of what is the logic of philosophy as a whole. A critical philosophy of science is the first and preliminary step towards wisdom.

TRANSCENDENCE

Philosophy, like all other sciences wants to know reality. But its reflection on a non-given reality renders wisdom dialectical from the beginning. Reality, the absolute universe of philosophy, cannot be thought without including the thinking of it as its own constitutive member. Or, the other way around: in philosophical reflection as act, reality itself is being disclosed, gains subject-existence in the thinker. Man in philosophizing is himself an existing or existential world-conception. This is so not with reference to his empirical appearance and contingency, not with reference to his private states of mind and passions—the psychical is always the private—but it is so with reference to his forgetting his private self in philosophical thought. To be absorbed by a reality which is not disclosed outside of being-thought, is equivalent to saying, that reality gains in philosophy a subject-consciousness, it undertakes to become conscious of itself. The philosophical concept is not an abstract concept, but it is a concrete attitude of existence, a living world-shape.

Philosophy, in other words, cannot be derived and understood out of abstract generalization about things in the world, but must be instituted as a personal existential communication of world-itself. Philosophical systems neither prove themselves nor disprove one another. No system is ever proved for another system, and no system is able to disprove another system. Transcendent reality—Soul, World, the Absolute—are not open to a common and public inspection, so that all who investigate may come to a reasonable agreement or to a factual truth. Still less is reality a private psychological affair relevant only to private individuals as their dream-worlds are. Philosophical systems are engaged in a never-ending dispute concerning an ultimate and true reality, and must therefore meet in a dialogue. They understand each other even in profoundly misunderstanding each other. Philosophy's existential actualization of reality prevents any system's claim to be the universe which it represents. Each becomes a living symbol of the universe. None is this universe as such. Transcendence maintains itself.

PHILOSOPHY OF CULTURE

The logical function of philosophy, its truth-claim, is embedded in the concrete and living whole of philosophical existence. This existence is inseparable from a social-cultural matrix. Philosophy, therefore, becomes a symbolic gesture, an expression and a testimonial of human culture. Man expresses through the medium of logical statements how the world is treating him. Art does the same in images, what philosophy does in logical reflection. The philosophical thought has this advantage over the image of art, that it transcends itself, that it reaches over and thinks its own living essence in the mirror of the arts. Art is in philosophy, an essential part of its universe, and philosophy is in art. And as art creates many shapes and styles, which replace one another, without cancelling their ever living significance, in the same manner the classical *gestalten* of philosophy go on living side by side, unobliterated and unforgettable, because they all relate themselves to the same absolute universe, which relates itself in and through them. Those formations and transformations of philosophy are necessary, because the universe is too rich to be paid out in one kind of coin only.

What is true for a philosophy of art is true for all non-logical values of life. Philosophy, as logical reflection on the meaning of human existence, assembles all values and unites them in its own dimension or medium. In reflecting on the meaning of practical existence philosophy becomes ethics. It formulates in universal form, and thus brings to self-consciousness, the motives and actions of practical life. Just as something becomes a theoretical-scientific object, if it is apprehended by the subject in logical forms, so something becomes value when it is related to and subsumed under the practical needs of the subject. Philosophy of practical values grows out of feelings of respect and disrespect, out of general ends and purposes, and becomes ethics in reflecting on the fundamental principles of law, morality, and politics. Things, persons, teleological institutions are related to men willing or not willing, for whom they assume the value of urges, purposes, life-justifications. Philosophy thus expresses the self-consciousness of a social and existential time or age. But in all those ethical problems it maintains its very own interests, which is man himself as acting existence. It defends the dignity of man in his practical systems. What we have seen in the scientific world as necessity of error, recurs in the practical world as necessity of evil. Man creates evil in wanting the good. In discovering the meaning of his practical existence, he at the same time covers it in an infinite practical confusion.

In the whole philosophy of scientific, practical and artistic culture, human unity is revealed as a unity of tensions. This unity is broken, when one or the other of the poles in this many-dimensional polarity prevails over other poles. Philosophy mediates, checks, and balances by virtue of its *Logos*. Since all those modifications of human existence are logically clarified, man comes to understand himself as a whole, and in a whole. The function of philosophy is to harmonize the disharmonious; to think, and to be, existential unity.

It can never be more than a unity of tensions. In those tensions we have to distinguish a double dialectic. The "objective" truth, the practical good, the aesthetic beauty, are equivalent contraries. In the cultural value dimensions of existence, however, there is also a dialectic of contradictory opposites. The scientific, practical, and aesthetic norms make possible and necessary their own negations. Here one side exists only in overcoming and denying its own opposite, judged to be that which should not be. The good, for example, lives as much on the overcoming of evil, as evil lives in the act of breaking down the good. We have found the model of this dialectical struggle in the dialectic of scientific knowledge as process.

PHILOSOPHY OF RELIGION

Man creates his own existence as a problematic existence of tensions. In recognizing and acknowledging this, he enters religion. The confession of sin is the origin of religion.

Philosophy meets in religion that transcendence which is present in faith. Even in the nature-religion transcendent powers are worshipped, which are not created by man, and which are not objects of knowledge, but *numinosa*, on which man depends. He expresses this dependence in fear, joy, and thanks. Without this absolute feeling of dependence he would not be human.

In the world-religions this dependence is enlarged to comprise his cultural values also. They are experienced as flowing from an absolute and divine source. The Platonic term for this is creation (*Philebus*, 26). Existence together with its values are created. The problematic human tension is thereby transcended, justified, and reconciled.

In so far as philosophy itself is also open towards transcendent reality, it will recognize in religion a concern similar to its own. In reflecting on the meaning of religious existence, it will logically apprehend and penetrate this similarity and difference from itself. This task is both facilitated and made more difficult as religions themselves produce theologies, in which they claim truth for their particular form of religion.

Religious life is expressed in imaginative symbols (such as heaven, hell, angel, devil) whereby human existence is tried in the absolute. Trying decisions are occasioned by them. Concrete religious communities are assembled in such "names," and live their faith in the transparent symbols of prayer, cult, sermon. Practical religions embrace man in unconditional love as fellow creature and in compassion as fellow sinner. Religious practice reconciles the plurality and tensions of human culture value in the absolute. Sin is forgiven, if man ceases to falsely absolutize his immanent and contingent values. It includes ethics, but does not replace it, because the human-practical sphere produces its own "objective" situations and tasks flowing from them, regardless of religion.

Philosophy, as philosophy of religion, functions in the same manner here as before: Logical reflection understands and justifies the religious form of existence and of symbolic thought. The impartial emptiness and wideness of formal logic makes possible a reflection, in which all dimensions of reality, as they converge in man, are elucidated. Reasoning man keeps them and keeps himself in an open balance.

KNOWLEDGE AND WISDOM

THREE METAPHYSICAL POSSIBILITIES

If we subsume the philosophy of scientific, practical, artistic, and religious culture under the three levels of immanent, introscendent, and transcendent knowledge of reality, then we have the following three possibilities of ultimate or metaphysical orientations.

The first we call *empiricism*. Empiricism mistakes the one realm of given experiences as the world. Science replaces metaphysics. Positivism is a negative, discouraged empiricism. As "logical positivism" it is reduced to talk correctly about correct talking, without any reality whatsoever to talk about. As pragmatism, empiricism is all out for practical manipulation of things, in order to install a paradise on earth supplied with all the latest and most recent gadgets of comfort, convenience, and time-consuming, time-saving machinery. Empiristic art is sensualistic, sensational. Empiristic law is primarily concerned in the protection and organization of material interests. Its anthropology dissolves values and ideals in psychology and pathology. Its ethics is hedonistic and utilitarian, in its extreme the attitude of a clever beast of prey. Its wars are carried on for raw-materials and markets. Its philosophy sees in all philosophies, ideologies hypocritically veiling that "which is in the senses—*"nihil est in intellectu quad non fuerit in sensu."* A victorious empiricism reduces man to an object, theoretically as well as practically. Man can be managed. But its victory is also its end. The treacherous nothing of all which is finite and mortal, is being experienced as self-annihilation and nihilism. Life becomes hectic and boring at the same time. Its convulsions and spasms recur in ever shortening cycles. The metaphysical lie—to absolutize the relative and the finite—needs stronger and stronger injections to maintain as well as to conceal itself.

The second possibility is oriented in the existential center of knowledge. We call it objective, critical *idealism.* It is interested in the ideal norms which become human reality in being actualized by culture. Idealism is *paideia:* it desires to ennoble life in dedicating it to the realization of ideals of knowledge, practice, and art. Its art presents life as heightened, idealized appearance. Its law protects the inalienable human rights, the dignity, responsibility, integrity of the individual person. Its anthropology reconstructs the soul from the values pursued and from objective teleological wholes, in which the soul participates, for which existence is risked. Its ethics is educational. Religion is interpreted as service to purely human ideals. Its philosophy justifies the right of ideal forms and norms not to be derived from experience, as when Leibniz replies to Locke's *"nihil est in intellectu quod non ante fuerit in sensu"* with *"nisi intellectus ipse."* The world becomes here "the material of my duty." Idealism is at home both in a personalistic-moral philosophy of freedom and in a contemplative aesthetic philosophy of a festive life. Its limitation is its own dissatisfaction with the obstacles which it creates. Disappointment and exhaustion threatens it with dissolution of its enthusiasm.

The third possibility is oriented in transcendence. It seems to become event and possession in all *religious* metaphysics. The all-embracing one and unique universe of Being, the Absolute, is becoming transparently present in all other beings which it is not. A *is* Non-A, is the formal expression of its dialectic paradox. Experienced appearance and actualizing existence are media and means, through which the transcendent absolute is honored. Religion prevails in a transcendent culture. Its art is symbolic, it is not created to seem blessed in its own noble perfection, but to point towards a beyond. Its law protects this sanctification of life and punishes blasphemy. Its wars are religious wars. Its anthropology sees man in an absolute decision between damnation and salvation. Its philosophy is a rational formulation of the superrational. Its limitation lies in the impossibility to embalm the absolute in experiential and existential shapes. It is wisdom to know that the absolute is never caught and ascertained in human institutions. This wisdom is one with the love of wisdom. All three possibilities constantly threaten one another. Their struggle is the metaphysical basis for the rhythms of history. History is the shadow cast by human metaphysics. Philosophy is this dialogic, and this philosophy occurs twice: one time in its "world-sense," as Kant calls it, as the totality of a world view and evaluation of life, and again as its technical self-consciousness in a logical reflection, its "school-sense."

DIALECTICAL WISDOM AND FORMAL LOGIC

All three major metaphysical possibilities are true in the sense that each truly formulates an aspect of reality. According to formal logic, however, contradictory systems cannot be true.[2] If one is true the others must be false, or all must be false. If it is true that reality is

---

[2] "If philosophers have produced a great many contradicting systems, all except one must be wrong; and it is even probable that all are wrong." Hans Reichenbach, *Proceedings, A.P.A.,* Vol. XXI, 1947–48.

the sum of experienced appearances, then it cannot be true that the world is disclosed in an infinite ideal task of existence. And if this is true, then it cannot be true that it is an eternally perfected absolute Being. This formal contradiction is valid if we keep only to the logical formulation of philosophical systems. From the point of view of an existential dialectic, however, the formal contradictions merely serve to make real distinctions, self-differentiations of reality, articulate. The fundamental logical postulate of unity not only transcends and preserves the formal contradiction, but needs it for its own self-realization.

No one-sided world-view corresponds to the full circumscendent concept of wisdom. And the concept of circumscendence cannot be developed outside and apart from a clear articulation of all opposites within it. Those opposites, which are abstractly excluding one another, are in reality engaged in a concrete dialectic. They talk together and against each other. But philosophy itself and as a whole, consists precisely in this dialectic. In it it approaches its own ideal of concrete thinking. It functions in the critique of abstract or one-sided standpoints, in recognizing their right as well as their limitation. As many specialists are needed to approach a concrete knowledge of an organism in its totality, so many abstract world-views are needed to approach the knowledge of a concrete absolute.

"Concrete" is derived from *concresco,* and means a "growing together" of many functions into a living "organic" whole. Each philosophical constitution of world and existence, embodied in works and social habits, expressed in symbols, and formulated in thought, is a concrete universal, a unity pervading all of its members. One who thinks such a concrete universal, is in turn absorbed by and in it. Philosophical contemplation, dialectical synopsis, as Plato says, makes of the individual an organ of an "objective" state of affairs, analogous to an artistic identification with a work of art, or analogous to a religious reverence.

But one concrete universal becomes abstract again, when it is seen in relation to other historical formations of philosophy. History of philosophy demotes each of its shapes to an abstract side of its whole movement. Philosophical thinking grows more and more concrete, as it becomes more and more flexible. National and epochal styles of philosophy, supplanting one another, are nevertheless participating in one common concern with reference to a one and common reality, to which they all contribute, and which they all enrich.

History of philosophy teaches the same lesson that we learn in our life, at least if it is maturing towards a greater concreteness. I begin somewhere with a simple philosophy, endeavoring to get settled in it with my few possessions. But then I meet you, who has a different perspective. We are obliged to listen to one another. Our starting-points get changed in the process. A becomes (A in B), and B becomes (B in A). In letting you in, my own life is altered. This is the simple and fundamental law of dialectical growth in the history of philosophy as well as in the history of individual philosophers. At first this dialectic is confusing and disquieting, but then it is hardening. We become "hard boiled," as we say.

The concrete universal grows richer in proportion to its growing extension. This is the reverse of the abstract concept, which grows poorer in proportion to its greater generality. The more things its abstract unity denotes, the more details have to be dropped from it. The most exact and general abstractions are almost completely empty of content.

Hegel speaks of the self-movement of the concrete or speculative concept. Feuerbach and Marx misunderstood this and flattened it empiristically. It should be interpreted in this way, that human knowledge produces human history as an existentially real world-formation (*Weltgestalt*). Man produces himself as human in producing knowledge. In opening reality, reality itself becomes articulate and actualized. However, it is by the same act also limited and made finite. In making reality definite and finite, philosophical knowledge puts itself in contradiction to the intended Absolute. The Absolute appears to it now in the form of a dialectical negation. Man cannot cling to any one system, without engendering an opposite, with which his own position is fraught. The absolute transcends and circumscends any immanent fixation and forces it into a dialectical process.

The growth of philosophy is not merely a gain, but also a loss. On each level we meet a genuine human claim of truth, which is engaging our soul. Each transition is therefore also a crisis. To the impossibility to exist absolutely, corresponds the possibility of not existing as we do. The existential thinker produces himself as one whose existential possibility is always in danger. What I may become is never a fact of object-thinking, it is an open problem. Everything that has become might just as well not have become. Existence is contingent.

The concrete universal, the dialectical negation, and the dialectical process as self-movement, is not only the historical law of philosophy, but it is the logic of philosophizing itself. Dialectic is the logic of philosophy. It does not guarantee a straight progress, but reveals a tragic rhythm.

In the mighty procession of centuries, philosophizing humanity moves from achieved metaphysical systems through the violent crises of doubt and break of tradition, into the new serenity of idealistic freedom and synthesis; from there it moves in tiring and slowing steps to the anti-synthesis of empiristic civilizations, ending in the convulsions of despair, greed, and nihilism. It then repeats this rhythm in a new and enhanced modification.

This procession is perhaps a divine spectacle, which the blissful and eternal perfection plays with itself; perhaps a suffering and struggling God wrestles with its own creation for his deliverance; perhaps it is nothing but a flaming up of illusions and disillusions in front of a black foil of nothing and of death—the views of transcendence, introscendence, and immanence.

Be this as it may—all knowledge, of the given as well as the non-given x, believes in truth; in the logical apprehension of truth lies a possibility of an ever-to-be-renewed reconciliation: The absolute is both revealed and concealed in all dimensions and directions operating and functioning in it. Among them is man. In thinking a universe he awakens to his own historical existence. This existence, in turn, has no ground without object-sciences concerned with the past—with that which has become. The three levels of knowledge are inseparable aspects of wisdom. And in this correlation rests our hope of harmony, balance, and peace. For if we do not find unity of opposites in ourselves, we can never expect to find it in the world about us. And what we find in us now is the seed of things to come. The thought of one century becomes action in the next.

Summing up: The dialectical unity of reality is the criterion of truth. It is the ground of immanent, introscendent, and transcendent knowledge.

By virtue of the logical unity of all thinking man is enabled to harmonize his scientific, practical, creative, and religious life. Truth is the foundation of a viable inter-subjective community.

Reason is unique in the sense that it alone can distinguish itself from itself and remain identical in its self-diremption. It enables man to find agreement with reality as his own other, as himself, and as transcendent whole.

But it is also true that man cannot help missing truth, because he cannot help having finite, one-sided, and limited perspectives. Dialectic is the logic of philosophy in comprehending the necessity of opposites and in absorbing them into a growing concreteness.

Freedom and Human Destiny[1]

*Every system is a system of freedom and necessity. . . . The
Absolute cannot be thought in one of those categories as abstractly
opposed to the other. . . . Truth as concrete spirit is destined to
realize his freedom . . . and his freedom appears as necessity when
realized in a world.*

—HEGEL[2]

HISTORICAL EXCURSION

In early Greek philosophy necessity is earlier than freedom. A
mythical and divine world-order, a fatal destiny, lies back of the short-
lived and illusory appearances of mortals. By their death they pay a just
tribute to it. Even the Gods, personified impersonal cosmic forces, obey
the law of *Moira*, a world-forming and world-destroying order of time.

In the corresponding archaic Greek art, man is bound by the un-
changeable forms of the material, which imposes its own geometric law
upon the human figure that is not allowed to move freely according
to its own potentialities.

The first conscious philosophy of freedom, on the other hand, is discovered by the *Sophists*. Man, as political being, is found to be independent of divine, natural powers, as well as of socio-political institutions. *Free* means, not bound by any given tradition. This indeterminism goes hand in hand with a destruction of religious reverence for
the laws of the *polis* as ordained by the gods. Laws are conventions of
the strongest and most clever will, which is individual and selfish.

---

1 Knoles Foundation Lecture, 1951. Published by the Pacific Philosophy Insti-
tute, Stockton, California.

2 *Werke,* Froman, Stuttgart, I, p. 136; X, p. 382; XVII, p. 55.

The next step is made by Socrates, Plato, and Aristotle. *Socrates* shares the sophistic position that the meaning of human existence cannot be stated in terms of nature. Man is essentially subject, responsible agent of his own actions; and in this sense independent or free from natural necessity. It is not the mechanical necessity of bones and muscles that prompts Socrates to stay in his prison, but it is his own free will to do so. However, and this is the anti-sophistic turn of the problem, this free will is not arbitrary. It is motivated by "the good." The will is free in proportion to its being determined by the good, unfree in proportion to the absence of such a determination. The good once understood irresistibly moves the will so that no good man can voluntarily do evil; when he does evil, that evil appears to him as good in the moment of doing it.

This Socratic discovery of ethical freedom is developed by *Plato*: The human soul mediates between the two realms of being, the floating, physical world of sense on the one hand, the intelligible world of universal essences or ideas on the other. For the world of sensuous objects, Plato's logic demands hypothetical laws and causal connections. Its quality nevertheless remains that of irrational instability, vagueness, and indeterminateness. To participate through sense-impressions and through the corresponding appetites in this world of free chance and contingency, means at the same time *ethical* slavery, determination by external and unknown "pushes and pulls." It is the state of ethical unfreedom of the captives in the cave. Participation in the world of logical order and ideal essences is emancipation from that slavery, ascent to freedom, and self-determination. This freedom demands that man shall determine himself through that which in itself is necessary, universal, validly appearing to man as an "ought," a norm. Real life thus is a mixture, a dialectical tension between fact and ideal; it is free on the one hand in the sense of being free—from norms or values; on the other hand, in the sense of being determinable by rational ideals, without ever being ideal itself. The soul is not ideal, but is like an ideal in that it is a necessary and inevitable presupposition of all its actions, an existential foundation without which there is no experience. It is the soul's own responsibility whether it turns towards ideas or not. It is rooted in a self-moving, eternal soul, which is not exhausted in its actions.

Your "character" is your own choice and your own responsibility, but how then, does it come about that many seem not able to let themselves be determined by the good? The religious idea of a predetermination appears. No one can be more than what the gods have allotted him. That some see the light of valid ideals is a grace of the gods. In this religious hope, facts and values merge.

Ethical freedom, according to which it is each man's duty to act as if the whole and full responsibility and risk of choosing the right and the wrong laid with the soul, is thought together with religious determinism, according to which none can transgress the limitations which are set by the gods.

Aristotle specializes and amplifies the problem. Praise and blame, reward and punishment, reveal the voluntariness of actions contrasted with involuntary actions on which are bestowed pity and excuse. Rational freedom and happiness are opposed to coercion from outside, from passivity, and from sorrow.

The will is not free to create the values which it affirms. The freedom in this sense of creativeness is denied. Values of sensuous pleasure as well as values of an ethical character are not in our power; we cannot make or unmake them by an arbitrary fiat; it is equally ridiculous to ascribe the good to ourselves and to ascribe wickedness to external circumstances. The goals or objects of our evaluations are either eternal, like the cosmos and its laws and God, or merely contingent and factually occurring. Neither the ideal necessity nor the occurring contingency of values are in our power. In our power is only the act of preferring and rejecting among given ends. This decision or choice *(prohairesis)*, is the essence of the will, the source of actions. It is governed by what we think is good. After we have thus chosen our end we are also to a limited extent free in choosing the means and methods to achieve this end.

The execution of the will or the freedom of action is restricted although not frustrated by the conditions of the materials. But since these materials are mostly other individuals, they are actions always containing both freedom and unfreedom. They are compromises of varying degree.

To embrace seeming instead of real goods is evil. The reason for such a wrong choice is ignorance. Lack of knowledge is the principle of all moral evils. It may be voluntary; in this case volition can be repented and repaired. But there is also an ignorance, which is not voluntary, which remains nevertheless an evil.

Unfreedom may also be acquired. If an undesirable value is allowed to become habitual vice it may become so entrenched that a return by free will becomes impossible.

To sum up: Aristotle approaches the problem from the point of view of the individual. In thinking what is true and necessary and universal this individual realizes his own nature as a rational being and therein finds his freedom and happiness. But in finite and conditioned action this freedom is in many ways conditioned. Freedom is a compromise, a struggle to become free by more and more adequately comprehending values.

The post-Aristotelian or Hellenistic philosophy enriches the problem by new motives. The *Stoic* determinism expresses resignation. Everything is what it is. It is identical and thus logically and unambiguously fixed. This is also true for future things. An omniscient mind could predict them and our partial predictions rest on the same principle. In other words, the stoic philosophy looks on the world as if it were a given finished world of objects, a "block-universe." If all rebellion against reality is eliminated, man may find his happiness. For the wise and happy man no real evil exists, because value-distinctions are meaningless, if they cannot alter the situation. Man is in the situation of a prisoner who can ease his lot by fulfilling his duty in complying with the rules of his prison.

The antagonists of the Stoics and the protagonists of freedom are the *Epicureans*. The same desire to achieve peace and serenity of mind in a meaningless world that led the Stoics to the denial of the reality of evils and to their determinism, led Epicurus to his indeterminism. The world as well as man is masterless. His task is to free himself from childish fears and authorities lurking in anthropomorphic religion, and to maintain his personal integrity and independence from fate "called by some omnipotent master." What these "some" call necessity is blind chance. The very atoms move arbitrarily and by freedom. Necessity is only a name for an empirical generalization. We live in a whirl of unstable and transitory chance-events. The less we get entangled in them and subjected to them by foolish ambitions, the freer we are, the more we remain master of our happiness.

In *Christian* philosophy from St. Augustine to the Reformation the question of freedom and determinism becomes one of predestination and theodicy, i.e., the justification of the fact of evil in a divinely governed world. God is the absolute being. He is the creator of this fleeting world, which has no independent existence outside and apart from the creator. God is omniscient, omnipotent, and the highest good.

No freedom of will seems to be possible under such circumstances. St. Augustine (especially after his struggle with the moral indeterminism of Pelagius), and the Reformation hold that man is responsible for the evil in the world originally created as a good world. When God created man He knew that he would fall. He chose this and thus also chose evil. To deny that man is the source of evil is sin. The sinners and the elect are equally predestined. The only mitigation of this dogma lies in our ignorance concerning whether we belong to the realm of perdition or salvation. The all too subtle distinction between permitting evil and effecting it, only pushes the question back a little without altering the fundamental fact that the permission of evil belongs to God's absolute goodness, wisdom, and power.

Man is unfree both in good and in evil; in evil—for after man's fall it is not possible for him not to sin *(non posse non peccare)*; God's "irresistible grace" saves him with or without his own will. Free will in the moral sense is also God-given and in this sense not free; *liberum arbitrium a deo motum,* as St. Thomas puts it.

The secularization of religious problems since the *Renaissance* naturally leads to the rediscovery of ancient positions. In order to protect man from the church, absolute authority is transferred and bestowed upon the prince and the state. In order to emancipate man from God, omnipotence is ascribed to a mathematical mechanism. Later liberalism breaks with the absolute state and at the same time with deterministic philosophy. In the name of creative self-expression and individualistic self-expansion, of self-government and creative evolution the victorious liberalism erects its trees and statues of liberty. Marxism, on the contrary, develops a deterministic philosophy as its weapon against the humanistic liberalism. The proletarian, according to *Marx,* finds himself estranged from the social means of economic production. He is dependent, and like other wares, subjected to the fluctuation of the market. He is powerless as individual and strong only in masses that are thrown together by the same necessities. Unlike the stoic resignation, this determinism is the flag of revolutionary action. The free will of the "bourgeois" is seen as a tragic irony. He believes to further his own creative initiative, but in reality he is digging his grave, through his will but, at the same time, against his will.

Leading thinkers of this epoch illustrate those changing positions. They explore and amplify the problem in its different dimensions.

For *Machiavelli* and *Hobbes,* man is a given quantum of natural forces of egoism. They allow him to calculate his actions in analogy to a physical parallelogram of forces. Left alone or "free" they would produce a war of all against all. This would be the greatest evil for egoistic interests themselves and so they develop the power of the state, where no freedom is left. Back of this political theory stands a materialistic and mechanistic cosmology, whose mathematical determinism is reproduced in the social realm.

For *Spinoza*, to know is the only activity which can be exerted on all things and all experiences. To know means to understand by necessary and logical connection. This is happiness. If anything refuses to be drawn into that logical nexus, happiness would not be possible. Consequently, if will were free it could not be made the object of logical understanding; it would be unintelligible and so would disturb the happiness of the wise man. Any act of will is determined by a motive as its cause which again is determined by another motive in an endless series of causation, which fundamentally is the same as the logical connection of ground-and-consequence. This is similar to the stoic argument. But it expresses a passion to know, alien to the stoic resignation but fundamental for this modern will to identify human "reason" with the world.

Descartes' system is full of contradictions. He regards physical bodies to be causally determined, including animals which are machines. Man's soul, on the other hand, is determined by the highest good, or God. But who is God? He seems to be little more than a guarantor or an exponent of the rationalistic faith in the ultimate rationality of reality, rationality understood in terms of mathematical logic. If the soul misses this goal it is unfree in its hasty and turbulent actions. Where does this disturbance come from?

Leibniz solves the problem by introducing into it the equally complex question of appearance and reality. It is necessary that we act as though our actions were imputable to us, and we, as free agents, responsible for them. This is a necessary human illusion. It is the illusion of a finite being with finite perspectives. If we could see ourselves as God sees us, we would realize that we fulfill a role assigned to us in His world plan. This, however, does not imply a being determined from external causes. All so-called external influences are, by virtue of Leibniz' pre-established harmony, at the same time inner changes, self-changes. All reaction is also action, following no law except the law of self-determination. The law of "sufficient reason" is also "the law of the best."

For *Kant's* moralism, free and unfree are other names for moral and amoral. Nature, as object of scientific understanding, is amoral and determined by laws, which are indifferent or neutral to moral distinctions. The moral law is an added determination, following which man becomes free from natural laws and compulsions. Unfreedom is moral incapability or insanity, which is the same as saying that man is determined by natural laws alone without the added moral determinant.

Fichte restates the dualistic position according to which man can choose between these two worlds; for his active nature the choice is at the same time one between moral activity, and passivity. And *Schopenhauer* transforms Kant's two worlds by placing freedom in a metaphysical world beyond experience. We choose our character without knowing, whereas in experience every action grows out of determining circumstances and inherited traits. We feel responsible, he says, for what we are, although empirically we might explain it by antecedents and environment. This feeling of responsibility for what we are is an index of our metaphysical freedom.

For *Hegel*, freedom and necessity form a dialectical unity of opposites. History is an emergent evolution of freedom from nature and for human values and ends of life. This evolution is necessary as actualizing absolute reality, whose necessity as well as freedom, are both objects of its self-determination. Reality is and does what it pleases to be and to do. There is nothing outside or apart from it to compel it. The totality of *all* conditions is unconditional or free.

Reality eternally *becomes* what it eternally *is*—also, in, through, and against, our participations in it; through our consciousness in us it is both *in* and for itself— it is as such, an "in-and-for-itself" dialectical *(absoluter Geist)*. If it becomes what it is against our will, we call its sovereign freedom our necessity; if it becomes what it is through our will, moving in the direction of our choices, then we call its irrevocable development our freedom.

In history, theoretical, practical-moral, aesthetic, and religious liberations of man from his immediacy, are at the same time liberations of man for,—and to, himself. History, thus, is a dialectical battle,—dialectical reality actualized and transparent, and "progression in the consciousness of freedom."

The history of the problem shows that we must distinguish different levels. First there is a cosmological level; its question is whether given, empirical, spatio-temporal phenomena are dependent on other or previous appearances and calculable by this relation. This is the causal problem, usually discussed from the point of view of physical sciences. The second level would be the axiological problem, whether man is free to realize or to create values or whether he is determined by values without his will. The solution here is partly dependent on the solution of the first level. The third level would be the question of a religious metaphysics concerning divine providence and predestination, where it is particularly necessary to draw the line against the axiological problem sharply in order to avoid confusion.

DESTINED TO BE FREE

Man is distinguished from other creatures in that he can say: I am, I exist. In this act he identifies his true self with his being. He is conscious; he is a witness of himself. He protests his being and his self-consciousness in one and the same act. He posits himself as the living center of all his activities.

"I am" excludes "I am not." I cannot think of myself as a dead, inert, inactive object. I cannot think of myself as a Not-I. When I say "I am" I give utterance to my thinking. It is I who does this thinking. I am, in thinking that I am. "I am" is inseparable from "I think." I identify myself with this pure activity; and I cannot identify that which I can observe in my body with myself as subject, because it is the subject which does this observing.

But, paradoxically, I am as certain of my non-being as I am of my being. I am dead-sure of my death. I am, but I am also limited. The thought "I am" and the thought "I shall die" are both *a priori* certainties. Both are unavoidable or necessary truths. Both are logically prior to any experiences. I cannot experience anything if I do not exist. I cannot experience my death, neither when I am alive nor when I am dead. Death liberates me from the illusion that I can identify myself with an organism whose biological passing I can describe, or with any external possession, as if they were eternal. Death thus purifies my self-consciousness; it prevents me from identifying my true self and my true being with any experienced embodiment of myself. My being and my not-being meet in saying: I am, but I am limited. My whole finite becoming is enclosed in the *a priori* limits of existence and death.

To become one with yourself, to try harmony and agreement with yourself, is peace and freedom. To become truly yourself is the meaning of human existence. Self-realization is the goal which all training and education envisages. This education for freedom excludes any totalitarian claims which train men for ends outside of and external to themselves. True education is the unending progress towards my own freedom, away from illusions and prejudices which prevent authentic existence and truthful self-expression.

But this progress cannot be achieved alone and in isolation. The "I am" is a paradox. I am alone and unique. I cannot be born for you nor can I die for you. I am individual; life is individuated; there is no life in general. I can never say "I am" for you, as you cannot say it for me.

But I nevertheless recognize in you the very same meaning of life which I am. I interpret your empirical and observable bodily appearance in analogy with myself. You are my *alter ego*. I interpret your ability to say "I am" as strictly identical with the same act of my own self-consciousness.

"I am," then, is both individual, unique, identical, and universal. I am this dialectical meeting of opposites. Such a recognition of yourself as one with myself we call love. The progress in the consciousness of freedom is inseparable from my self-realization in a community of love, of mutual respect, and of helpfulness. Love wants to be one with another. To love is to care for you as I care for myself. Individual self-realization is impossible without a human and universal community of love. We can only be free together. We can only preserve freedom by deserving it.

This may all be very neat, many will object, but look at the world! Natural sciences demonstrate how man is enmeshed in blind and brutal irrationalities, how life is an accident on an insignificant planet amidst spatial immensities of star clusters, how organisms are incomprehensible combinations of an infinite number of atoms, how man is conditioned by causal antecedents of his environment and his biological inheritance. Historical sciences record the whimsical ups and downs of nations and of cultures. Arnold Toynbee, for example, tells us that there have been twenty-six civilizations, of which twenty-five have died, giving the twenty-sixth, our own, only a slim probability of survival. What good is this culture and self-realization you are talking about when we are victims of natural and historical determinisms? As Dante puts it in describing the sovereign play of *fortuna*:

> That she might change at times the empty treasures
> From race to race, from one blood to another
> Beyond resistance of all human wisdom.

Beyond human wisdom! We remember the Spartans came too late for the battle of Marathon, because they had consulted the divine oracle, and the divine oracle had revealed to them that the moon was not right. The fatalism of divine oracles beyond human wisdom has accompanied mankind. In the Christian period it took the form of a providential plan from the day on which God had created the world, through his self-revelation in the New Testament, to Doomsday when Christ would return to sever the sheep from the goats. The so-called Enlightenment secularized this oracular revelation. Following this tendency Marxism provided exactly the providential plan: Man fell from original communism to the daemon of private ownership; the world-revolution and the dictatorship of the proletarian class will restore the lost value of man in the millennium of economic communism. In the West similar fatalists trust the "law" of an invincible progress-in-general.

The human freedom to be responsible for yourself, to become what you are, to cultivate and to realize yourself in a community of love and mutual educational help—this human wisdom is pitted against three conceptions of natural, historical, and theological fate. The question of human destiny requires us to choose between freedom and fate. This is a metaphysical decision beyond momentary political constellations. What is the relation of freedom and nature? of freedom and history? and of freedom and providential plans?

FREEDOM IN NATURE

When I see, hear, or touch you I am immediately aware that I am the one who does this perceiving. I am the subject of all my activities. They all are inseparable from my active self; they are I-existent states of mind. But my seeing cannot be seen, it has no color; my hearing cannot be heard, it is not loud or soft; my touching is neither rough nor smooth, it is not tangible. The subject proper cannot be objectified. The active self is not a thing but is a condition, *the* condition without which no things can be experienced.

But when I have trouble with my vision I go to an oculist. He examines not my seeing, but the bodily organ of the eye, which can be seen. It is an object like other objects having color, shape, texture and other sense-qualities.

If I know myself as object, I am not aware of my real self. Rather, I experience an embodiment, a body, which is as strange to me as any other object. I then know myself in the form of alienation. To take anything in this form of objectivity is again an act of my own thinking. "Objectivity" is a category, a universal meaning, under which I can subsume all contents of my external experience, usually called nature.

My knowledge of natural objects or objective nature is ruled by the logical postulate of consistency or non-contradiction. It demands that all such objective contents of my experience be thought in a coherent, unambiguous or identical systematic unity. It is not logically possible to deny this principle of consistency: to deny it I would have to utter an incoherent, self-contradictory proposition, which would be no proposition at all.

My own logical ideal of order is sought and carried out on many levels of scientific abstractions. There are many types of order, from perceptual descriptions to very general laws. The most general law is known under the term of causality. It has given rise to that naturalistic determinism which is supposed to be incompatible with my freedom.

Causality is rooted in the logical ideal of ground and consequence, the principle of all deductions. If verified premises are given, certain conclusions follow. A thing becomes thus an object of scientific knowledge, when it can be logically linked with other known systems of experience.

The logical principle of ground and consequence is transformed into causality when it is applied to objects given in temporal succession. Proposition B is *implied* by proposition A, becomes a *causal* relation if an objective state of affairs is predictable in time. If every time when A occurs B is predictable, and when A does not occur, B does not occur, then A and B are causally related.

Perceived events become objects of causal-explanatory sciences if their changes are known in constant and uniform relations. Ice, water, and vapor, for example, are different perceptions with different qualities. If they were assumed to be independent objects then it would take magic to transform one into the other. But if their changing appearance can be correlated with a change in temperature, a calculable causal sequence is discovered which makes them phases in a causal knowledge. Their causal connection is reliable beyond their occurrence in many perceptions.

In other words, if we expect determinism in nature, we expect it because we ourselves as thinkers make such a logical demand on our own experience. We can think reasonably only if our thoughts are in an orderly sequence. The logical demand of consistency and necessary implications is an ideal postulate according to which we ought to think, if we want to make true and not false objective statements. Or to put it negatively: If we expect determinism in nature, such an expectation is not a given fact, it is not derived from objects or from experience, but from our own soul. Nature does not enter into our thinking-establishment with a visiting card labelled "determinism."

Has our logical postulate been verified by the sciences? If any science has approximated this verification it would be mathematical physics. It has succeeded in stating causal relations in exact quantitative equations, on which all our industrial machinery relies. This technical success has dazzled and frenzied the many, so that they are ready to throw themselves gladly under the crushing wheels of an idolized juggernaut. It is therefore most important that there be sober analysis of this metaphysical self-surrender.

We call "physical" that which is strange to us. You are physical to me when I know nothing of you, when you are given to my senses as a complex of color, shape, sound, temperature and so on. Sensequalities are a complex of appearances correlated with my ability to respond to them. My activities respond to an external challenge. My seeing and hearing you are selective functions which let me see and hear that which I am attuned to seeing and hearing. If I were a flea, my perceiving you as a field of activity would presumably be quite curious. The world *qua* physical perception is relative to the many subjective centers of reactivity, to whose different organization it is adapted. On the other hand you cease to be merely physical to me, when I begin to understand you, when your life, your tendencies and interests and ideals begin to be interpreted as partly analogous to my own. But this is not the way of mathematical physics. It eliminates everything that can be understood and keeps to the observation of external appearances stripped from all teleology. It is satisfied to find regularities in the behavior of externally noticed "masses." Those regularities are the more exact and the more reliable, the more individual differences and individual expressions of life are disregarded.

Appearances are formulated in exact formulae if they can be observed under exact and rigidly controlled conditions. Mathematically constructed laboratories yield precise results; at least the results are precise enough for practical applications. For example: We want to know how large a stove we need to heat a room of a certain size, satisfactorily. To be scientific we must disregard the satisfaction part of the question, because what is satisfactory to one may be most unsatisfactory to another. The question then reads: How many calories are needed to heat a room of a given size to a given temperature? A measured quantum of energy in the fuel minus the quantum of energy transformed into the heat of the stove plus the quantum of warmth in the room, can be stated in an exact equation, such as "100 minus 50 equals 50." If we have used half of our calory units in the fuel we should find the same amount in the room, provided the room is constructed in such a way as to make it impossible that any units escape—which is, of course, impossible. There are no exact laboratory conditions in reality. They are abstracted and artificially constructed limitations. *The extent to which mathematical-physical sciences can formulate causal relations is limited.*

Every natural event, as it appears to my perception and is transformed by my mathematical and logical construction into a scientific object, is never completely identical with the law in which it is formulated. Natural laws are general possibilities of how observed events *may* behave in quantitative equations, but not a single event occurs because we know it in such laws. If I catch malaria because an anopheles has stung me, that event does not logically follow from the general truth that all anopheles may be carriers of malaria; and the happily functioning mosquito is really quite indifferent to the general truth by which it is known to be a member of a causal relation.

Every natural event is different from every other natural event. All such empirical events are single, singular, individual, and unique. Logically it does not matter how small the difference is which distinguishes one event from a preceding one. To the extent that it is actually different, just to that extent it is not merely a statistical number or a sample-case of a general law, regardless of whether this law is more or less exact, more or less statistical. The general statistical expectation that there will be a probable number of suicides does not oblige you as an individual to commit suicide in order to fill the quota.

Events can nevertheless be thought as logically identical or counted in numerical units. But those logical or mathematical determinations must be understood as partial determinations. Furthermore, it is very important to understand the difference between logical identity and mathematical equality. Scientism, following Descartes, tended to confuse logic and mathematics, because it was so eager to prove a determinism which was supposed to be both mathematical mechanism and "rational" at the same time. But the *mathematical* space-time unit, symbolized by "number 1" is *logically* one and the same or identical unit, regardless of how many times it is counted. Mathematical units can be infinitely repeated, but their logical identity remains the same and can neither be increased, decreased, multiplied or divided. Logical concepts, furthermore, are thought in dialectical relations of opposites.

"Difference," for example, is just as valid a logical category as "identity." Difference is a category because it is a class so general that a no more general class can be found to include it. It is an ultimate logical concept. It is the opposite, the "other" of identity; identity and otherness belong logically together. In other words it is logically possible to think the non-rational, non-mathematical event-character of reality, logically. That all actual events are individually different is logically true.

And this truth prevents any determinism based on the methods of the sciences. Their particular laws, observed regularities of "mass" behavior, depend themselves on freedom in nature. A law applies only, and is valid, *if* that individual event has happened whose general behavior pattern it formulates. Newton's law of gravitation, to quote this rightly celebrated scientific achievement, is valid only if planets and moving bodies have occurred to which it can apply. It is an abstraction from a historical becoming. The constant proportion of quantified mass, distance, and velocity is neat; but this neatness does not give or guarantee the actual existence of those things whose behavior it formulates. After you have observed events to have happened to you, then you also can find general relations in them and conditioning them. The actual event of your appearance, however, remains irrational and contingent.

The freedom of individual becoming limits the law of observed and inferred object-constructions. Human existence, considered as an event in this individuated life of an historical nature, is thus partly free and partly determined. We exist as this crossroad of freedom and law. To exist in such a tension of conflicting tendencies is our destiny.

This destiny is veiled if we forget ourselves in our object-sciences. Man can make himself the object of his own sciences. He then splits his own physical appearance into a variety of contradictory objects— contradictory if they are falsely identified with his existential destiny. Existentially, man is not known in his own object-sciences, because he is the living and active source and center of them. He does not know himself in them, because he knows them. In this scientific enterprise he transcends nature. The scientific, human enterprise is not among the data which it formulates. In following his own law of logic man becomes free from nature; he emancipates himself, because this law of logic bids him to agree with himself. If we want peace and harmony with ourselves we must be consistent and truthful in our thinking. Man is striving towards logical consistency and clarity about himself, without being consistent and clear. The tendency towards unity and system in nature as well as in man is never identical with the individuated life, of which, or in which, it is a tendency.

We now leave the analysis of science and the hopefully struggling scientist, and turn to the larger conception of cosmological determinism.

FREEDOM FROM NATURE

Cosmological determinism does not confine itself to some selected areas of regional experiences in which the scientific conception of causality alone can operate. Its principle states that "nothing happens without a sufficient cause." The reality of anything is defined by the causal conditions through which it is linked with all simultaneous and past events. To isolate any event from this universal nexus would be to annihilate it; an isolated event is declared unreal. The present state of the world is the outcome and necessary result of its whole past and contains the possibilities of the future. If we reward and punish, praise or blame, we do so because we thereby want to educate, motivate and influence. Our own actions and valuations thus are drawn into this universal causation as links in the chain. I may imagine or dream that I might have a different heredity, environment, antecedents, and motivations than I really have. But this is an illusion; such illusions too are psychologically motivated, determined and caused. If this cosmological determinism were true, then our destiny would be to submit to a fate; it would not be the crossroad of liberty and law. Our situation would not be one of real and responsible decisions.

The worldview of cosmological determinism, especially as represented by such a great thinker as Spinoza, radiates a religious serenity and calm. Everything is eternally in order. There is no sense in wishing reality to be different from what it eternally is. There is a logical truth in this view which Immanuel Kant calls the regulative idea of reason. Every moment and passage in universal life is absolutely that which it is at that moment. It is qualitatively determined, it is itself and not some other moment. Being cannot *be* other than it actually is, and it cannot be *thought* as other than it is.

But what Hegel has said against Spinoza is equally true, namely that reality cannot only be thought as substance, but must also be thought as subject. This means that reality cannot be thought from the standpoint of a fictitious observer outside and above that which he is observing. Reality is not given and finished, but it is also giving and actual in our own approach towards it. We have constantly to decide anew what conception of reality we are going to adopt as true and valuable. But those decisions are in themselves real decisions; they do not occur apart from the reality which they are trying to formulate. Reality could not be what it is without our uncertain involvement and decisive participation. It is therefore impossible to close the book and to predict a final sum.

World-as-totality is incomparable. There is nothing with which it could be compared or by which it could be thought conditioned. If the world is thought as the completed totality of all conditions, then all conditions are in it and of it. Or, if everything is determined, nothing is. To say that reality is completely determined is to say that it is determined by nothing but itself. But absolute self-determination would be identical with absolute freedom. Cosmological determinism, thought to its own radical conclusion, passes inevitably into its own dialectical opposite.

In other words: Reality is only partially an object of scientific knowledge. Only objects can be known; reality as subject of its own activity cannot be known—but it can be thought. Logical thought is wider than scientific knowledge. Or, if you prefer to retain the word "knowledge," then we would put it this way, that self-knowledge is not a knowledge of an object, but a different knowledge in which I am aware of my own meaning and activity. I then think of myself as representative of an absolute subject. Self-knowledge is then thought of as analogy to the absolute subject in its own self-manifestation.

The objective appearance of reality may be thought of as the appearance of an individual totality of all the creative activities of the same reality. If we thus think of the world as subject, we think of it as that incomparable, indivisible freedom which is totally present in all of its individual self-manifestations; just as I am present in all my activities. The world and individual then are, as Josiah Royce has so well formulated it, not external to one another. Reality is a self-representative system; it is individuated, and each of its individual constellations is at each moment the present step or decision of the world-soul. The world as subject has no environment or circumstances external to itself. What appears to each individual agent in it as a separate and external object, is at the same time in the life of the whole just as much an internal self-modification as is the individual who views the other as its object. My environment is both over against me, and also in me. My own reaction to it at the same time makes an environment my environment. Viewed internally, "I" is no more and no less real than "you." Both together in our mutual active-reactive life constitute the individuated will of the total reality at that moment.

We thus participate in the freedom of the whole. What becomes motive for my action or what I decide to become is inseparable from myself; I can become only what I am. What reality wills is precisely this continuous, never settled freedom for new decisions, new individuations, new existential experiments. There are no absolute substances or absolute stabilities in this life of the whole. Every relatively stable organization or institution of life is engaged in a constant self-modification, is constantly dissolved as well as re-formed in favor of a new and varied mutation.

Human destiny, cosmologically considered, is the dialectical interplay of freedom in causality and of causality in freedom.

Causality in freedom means that life tends towards stabilization, leans towards unity of organization, attempts to be consistent and to settle down in fixed habits and routines. We partly alienate ourselves from reality as if we could hold it over against us in order to catch it in our nets of objectivity. We partly will the stabilization of our own creativity. But this act of self-alienation is an existential act of reality. It is a creation of our own selves; and this tendency towards reliable forms we also and at the same time, counterwill and frustrate ourselves. And so, what we really are and will is to remain unfixed, to constantly balance between our decisions and indecisions, to stabilize the flux of life without sacrificing this fluidity. The position of stabilizing tendencies is just as real as the opposition against any final settlement. New decisions are made on the ground of conditions brought about by previous decisions. But the new decisions are caused and conditioned by the previous state of affairs only in the sense that we grapple with them and change them, no matter how slowly or imperceptibly this may be. We have to decide on the direction from given starting points, "from here on out." And since both the new decisions and the old conditions are equally expressions of the same cosmic life in all of them, they are in their entirety the expressions of its freedom to become what it decides to become. If reliable knowledge *should* be the goal and ground of our discourse or dialectical reactivity, for that very reason our discourse exists only as a struggle for that which it ought to be, but is not.

Freedom in causality means that the universal interconnectedness and reciprocal conditioning of all events exists nowhere outside of individual agents of all this activity. There is no activity or life in general.

Life is active only and exclusively through its individuations. The universal coherence and continuity of life is established through unique and individual events. Causality is not a law outside of ourselves commanding us what to do and what to be. What we are and what we become is not predestined beforehand. Reality does not know what it will be until it decides and becomes that which is going to be through the ever renewed individual change of its own self. This growing cohesion of individual shapes of life is the freedom in causality. Life continually wills to be different and is thus always its own whole and indivisible self at each moment of its self-becoming.

This dynamic rhythm of self-alteration and self-fixation, causal order in free creativity, free activity in a totality of conditions, is the cosmological basis of our freedom, which is also our destiny. Reality in and through us wills at any moment its self-realization, and always brings about that which it wills and nothing else. It cannot will to be bound forever by a past decision. And so in us: To realize yourself and to be free are identical. If we seem to be or to will something which we do not actually realize, then we deceive ourselves concerning our real will. We may regret and change our past deeds, but then this new act is a new act and a new turn of events, which cannot undo what a past deed and a past turn of events were.

We now turn from those cosmological considerations of freedom and human destiny to the moral and historical aspect of the same problem. Freedom in nature, unpredictable individuality, is the basis for a freedom from nature or a freedom for human values; above all, for the moral value of personality and its pursuit of the value of truth.

If man were nothing but a part of nature, the peculiar human question of freedom could not arise. This peculiar human question is a question of the value or meaning of human existence. Axiological determinisms either maintain that man is necessarily too depraved or impotent to be good; or on the contrary that he is necessarily good, that he is "good by nature." Axiological indeterminism rejects both those contradictory determinisms. They are rejected on the ground of truth. I can prefer truth to untruth. The statement that man is necessarily depraved or cut off from truth would have to be a truthful statement, a statement intending to be true. The statement, that man is necessarily good or "good by his nature" is not only in conflict with the experience of evil, but it also would have to maintain that man cannot but be truthful. It would not allow or explain the indubitable presence of errors and illusions. Man may prefer untruth. The pessimistic determinism, on the other hand, would reduce man to an unthinking criminal, who could not even understand the value-question which he is supposed to deny as valid choice for himself. The optimistic value-determinism clashes too violently with the historical experience man has made with his own value-assertions. What is imposed by me on you as value, may be rejected by you as valueless. There is too much egotistic stubbornness in this historical embodiment of values to allow of any uncritical and extravagant optimism. We are not irresistibly determined by values, we are not puppets in a final determinism, which would prescribe our meaning or our part in a great finalistic design.

No, we are free to accept and to reject values. We may reject true values and embrace illusory ones. Man may ruin himself. That choice between values is our own responsibility and freedom. We hold ourselves and we hold others responsible for their choices. It is the fight over such choices of values which constitutes human history. History in this sense is the appearance of axiological freedom in the natural world. This axiological freedom is our human destiny. We cannot but be free and hence in a constant disagreement on what we should agree.

Value is anything which I need for myself. Value is anything (X) appropriated by existing subjects in their purposive functions. Absence of value, deprivation, evil is anything which frustrates me in my human functioning. The difference and hierarchy of values, then, depend on the kind of self and the kind of his needs or functions.

Physical appearances such as light, air, water, and earth are not merely valueless stuff; this would be a scientific abstraction leaving out their value in their interaction with my needs. You need only shut them off to become aware that they are value-vehicles or goods. In the scale of goods they are low but strong, as they administer to my biological survival. The highest good for man, however, is the human self, personal existence, since it gives meaning or value to everything else. It only must not be confused with its temporal and bodily appearance to itself and to others. If you identify yourself with your biological or practical-political embodiment, death will remind you of the non-finality and unreliability of such valuation. But since all values are values to myself and of myself, the Platonic and Christian principle that every human soul is of an infinite and irreplaceable value is well founded. It also is the axiological reason for saying that man is by his own nature good, since we cannot have any value or meaning which is not a value or meaning to and of myself.

But this absolute self, this ultimate "I am" is hidden. Cosmological determinism which sees man as a machine transforming energy into mechanical output, or as animal determined by hormones and genes and vitamines, is hiding it. But why, we ask, is this naturalistic mechanism so meaningful or valuable to the naturalist? We answer: His faith in the value of exact knowledge is the ground of his devotion to that pursuit! He says that we ought to know the causal mechanism of phenomena in order to improve health, wealth and social welfare; which is saying that we ought to learn in order to further values. His own freedom for values motivates his scientific enterprise in order to emancipate man better from nature for the sake of greater freedom. He sees nature in the axiological light of a task and a responsibility; habits of nature, formulated in statistical laws, are thus embedded in a wider, more complete teleological and living actuality. Without his own will and choice to pursue scientific truth there would be no science. Man in his own enterprise determines himself by the value which he needs in order to be his own true self. And self-determination is freedom. But values are not irresistible determinants. Devotion, enthusiasm, dedication, commitment to values, are not self-evident or automatic. They need education, persuasion, example, and encouragement to implement them. A decision between high and low, peripheral and essential, between right and wrong values, is a constant struggle. Self-realization is a human problem, not a foregone conclusion or necessity. I may become what I ought to become, but this is not written in the stars.

Human freedom, personal-moral freedom means decision between values, which therefore do not determine us irresistibly. We are in existential uncertainty and anxiety in making our decisions. We are convinced that there ought to be a best, a right solution in any given concrete situation, which nevertheless remains ambiguous. Our freedom then implies a constant unclarity of our will. That we ought to be good means at the same time that we are not good, because if we were, we would not need imperatives. The freedom for the good is also and inevitably unfreedom for the good. Not even such values as pleasures of the senses or health is in our power. And our highest and best intentions may lead to cruelly ironical outcomes. Our moral situation never becomes straightened out in a finality, it continues to be problematic and demands new decisions and new efforts every day. And yet we insist on this our problematic freedom, and we refuse the illusion of any system which seems to have all answers or promises a final and unproblematic security, because such claims simply are not true to our human nature. We are destined to be free.

It is this our struggling freedom which prevents us from being determined either by natural or external compulsions or by our own values. Since we recognize values essentially in the form of duty which we ought to do, we thereby show that we will it and that we do not will it at the same time. What we really or existentially want to be is what we really and existentially are:—this struggle, this dialectical whole, of will and counterwill. Our freedom is identical with our imperfection and our finitude. Our imperfection is the relation of conflicting purposes and desires, and is the essential unclarity concerning the situations in which we decide to act. We make ourselves responsible for our own conflicting tendencies and for our own limited insight. We could not reproach ourselves for having followed a lower purpose instead of a higher one, if we did not ascribe both conflicting purposes to ourselves. We always exist as such conflict and struggle on any level of culture. The perfect saint and the perfect criminal, the angelic or the satanic being, man depraved by nature, or man good by nature, are fictions.

Cosmological and axiological indeterminism demand and complement each other; cosmological and axiological determinism exclude and contradict one another.

TRAGIC FREEDOM

Freedom in nature, freedom from nature, and freedom for and against values, constitute the threefold human destiny. It is destiny because man cannot choose not to be free. He cannot avoid living the dialectical struggle of his freedom. If we understand and accept our problematic freedom we call it destiny; if we merely suffer and endure it we call it fate.

Nothing—neither pessimistic resignation and lament, nor optimistic action and reform—can alter the real human destiny that we exist as human in our contradictions.

If we now look out upon the sad and bloody tragedies and the amazing upheavals and always surprising turns of human history, we see destiny at play. But it is not a theatrical spectacle because we find ourselves involved. World-historical powers appeal and repel us and engulf us in their rhythm. The collective political powers embodied in states; individual education and enterprise, embodied in culture; religious metaphysics embodied in churches vie with each other for supremacy—a battle of the immortal gods in which there is no final victory! World-historical individuals smash age-old institutions, or institutions survive while individual agents come and go. History is a mixture of nature and values, causal conditions and accident, luck and misfortune, chance and merit, catastrophes and triumphs, sharply accented by our hopes and regrets. We applaud and we revolt. We participate in our common human destiny, which is none the less real because it is not an object of any science. Human destiny is revealing our being in the world and the world being in us. It can be deciphered by a logical reflection as our "cross" of freedom and unfreedom.

The real complexity of our historical destiny is frequently veiled by violent speculations, which claim to have an overall blueprint for it. Various religious as well as secular totalitarian systems have inspired their advocates with their panaceas. Augustine knew that the meaning of history was the city of God which he identified with the spread and victory of his church. Islam and Calvinism believed themselves to be agents of predestination. Secular systems knew that the meaning of history is an invincible progress or an economic communism realized by the world-revolution of the proletarian class. Such beliefs do not only explain, they also make and complicate history with their incompatible antagonisms. A sober logical analysis of our situation should make us immune against such vague and sweeping generalizations, which hide from us our limited and existential responsibilities.

Man is a temporal creature who lives in remembered continuity with his past, in anticipated continuity with his future, in actual decisions concerning the present. The past is irrevocable, unalterable; the present is factually given; the future uncertain, possible. We must distinguish from this historical possibility of a real future the natural possibility of general laws, as found in books on physics. That water must boil if there is a certain temperature states a causal if-then relation. Logically speaking all such laws are general possibilities which may or may not be realized. The boiling water does not depend on the law only, but also on various actual contingencies, whether I have water, pots, matches, kindling wood and the will to make the experiment.

The logical analysis of historical reality into unalterably real, factually real, and possibly real, is furthermore intersected by the teleological analysis of actions. A purpose may or may not become actual. Think of the seeds in the Biblical parable. Some seeds fulfill their potentiality in actually becoming plants; others suffocate in weeds, dry up on the road, or are picked up by birds. From the bird's point of view the seed fulfills its potentiality to become bird-food. From the seed's point of view the outcome is a frustration of its own potentiality. This omnipresent possible frustration of purposes we call contingency. Contingency is the always irrational, unexpected, unlooked-for uncertainty. The lack of matches may be the contingency which keeps the physical law of boiling water in the realm of general possibility, as the action of the bird is the contingency which prevents the potentiality of the seed to actualize itself in a plant. The contingent floats between possibility and impossibility; it is the doorway passing through which something becomes real or is prevented from becoming real.

We exist in the present, in actual decisions. Once they are made they become necessary in the sense that we cannot wipe them off the record regardless of whether anyone knows about it or not. And we can never repeat the same decision a second time. Alternatives, which seemed possible, but which our decisions excluded from becoming real, are relegated to the limbo of impossibilities of missed chances. Impossibility is a negative necessity. As the poet puts it:

> The moving finger writes, and having writ
> Moves on: Nor all your piety or wit
> Shall lure it back to cancel half a line
> Nor all your tears wash out a word of it.

"Possible" is that which may, or may not, become real. We talk of unlimited possibilities which the future may hold in store for us. But of these one, and one only, can become real. Leibniz expressed this by saying that from the infinite number of all mathematically and logically possible worlds only one can at any moment become the actual and real world. Really possible is only that which actually becomes real, and this depends on all the past conditions which must be given to allow our new decisions. If only one condition is not present at the right moment, the thing which seemed to be possible turns out to be impossible, unreal, negatively necessary.

The logical possibilities and the teleological potentialities have to go through the ordeal of the contingent. Passing this test the possible becomes real, and the real becomes unalterably real or necessary. If it fails, the possible becomes unreal and hence is forever unreal or impossible. The teleological will, our purposive activity, is one of the factors which may help in bringing the real conditions about, without which our intentions remain illusions.

Our destiny is to live this dialectical tension between the necessary condition of the past, the undecided contingency of the present, and the ideally possible future. We exist as crossroads between a negative impossibility, a given necessity, and a limited potentiality. Between plan and fulfillment, between reality and ideality, falls the shadow. If we accept this destiny, we accept a limited responsibility in a limited and dialectical situation.

FREEDOM AND PREDESTINATION

This act of accepting our threefold freedom in nature, freedom from nature, and freedom for values, as our human destiny, is a religious act. Faith accepts our human destiny as posited in the eternal necessity of God's will. In the Christian language: we take the cross upon ourselves. In other words, we are not free to deny our freedom; we cannot will not to will, we cannot choose not to choose. We may refuse to choose between two evils, but this choice not to choose is itself a choice. Our human destiny is identical with a religious or absolute predestination, which expresses the absolute self-determination or sovereignty of the Absolute. This religious truth cannot be canalized, or appropriated by anyone particular religious institution. Infallibility is an attribute of God alone and not of a human representative or institution.

Lack of faith, irreligion, consequently consists in a refusal to accept our freedom as our absolute destiny. This refusal takes various forms: Either man is seen as determined by a blind deterministic or mechanical natural fate, which drags him against his will and excuses all calamities; or, in contradiction to this, man is victim of caprice and irrational accidents, of an irrational whirl of arbitrary chance constellations. In the realm of axiological freedom irreligion either denies the responsibility of our choosing between good and evil by saying either that man is naturally good, irresistibly determined by values, or, in contradiction to this, that the human world is so full of moral evils, that God cannot possibly have anything to do with it. Man hates, in this case, his own moral incompetence in the moralistic image of a tyrannical deity, who imposes moral imperatives, although he knows that man is not able to live up to them. This anti-religious moralism does not understand that the moral law is not the end for which man is created, but merely an ideal orientation by means of which man becomes aware of his dialectical struggle, inevitable for a being which strives to realize moral ideals without being wholly determined by them.

This dialectical struggle is ontologically founded. It is posited in the ultimate reality. We are the living focus of causes and values, of possibilities and necessities. But what is tension for us and in us, is no tension for that Being in whom all those dimensions are internal distinctions within its own unbroken unity and wholeness. Being has no other outside of itself. The universe is always what it wants to be, and it wants to be itself and nothing else.

For us, the possible and the real always fall apart. We are, we exist as this falling-apart ourselves. It is our destiny. But this falling-apart in ever conflicting modalities is no problem for the universe which maintains its own unbroken unity and its everpresent self in all those different modes of our existence. There is no ontological sense in opposing that which factually is given, with that which ideally ought to be, because that which ought to be, is truly that which it is; namely, this moral orientation towards a unity or harmony of finite wills.

Being *is* equally in all parties, in all polarities, crises, and catastrophes of history. They are crises in it, not of it. If we thus realize this blessed and undisturbable peace of the eternal, we participate in this eternal peace in the midst of the dreadfall uncertainties of our existence. As Spinoza put: there is nothing given in ultimate reality (which he means by his term "Nature"), that could be an opposite to this intellectual love of reality (*Nihil in natura datur, quod huic amori intellectuali sit contrarium*).

Greek tragedy celebrated human destiny as a struggle between nature and spirit. Man finds himself involved in natural and ideal determinations and affirms both as belonging to himself. He assumes full responsibility, both for the causal determinations and chance events of nature, as well as for his own ideal striving to be free from nature and to achieve a rational order of life. Making manifest in human suffering the divine justice of a blessed being whose wholeness and holiness is not

soiled or spoiled by our blindness, the tragic Muse purifies the heart.
As Aeschylus puts it:

> Unknown the future
> The mind of Zeus unfathomable
> Ask not too much in things of Heaven.
> Content with better than evil
> Mixed
> May conflicting rights
> In accordance with my prayers
> Attend the course of divine justice.

(End of *The Suppliant Maidens*.)

Language and Imagination

The poet hands over his wealth of visionary images, his luminous dreams to the artist in him. The artist is a critical craftsman who has to bring order and intelligibility into this overabundance of poetic invention. He must render them communicable. He must eliminate and clarify. After he has done his work the poem is ready long before a line of it has ever reached ink and paper. He hands his product to the writer. Alas! Ask a painter whether he would find it natural to reproduce the vision which he sees by means of ink and grammar! But the visionary images of the poet are essentially not different from the visionary images of the painter. No, language is not a natural, but an unnatural, a quite horrible means to "tell" the poetic vision of a moving life.

—CARL SPITTELER
Gesammelte Werke. Artemis, Zurich, 1954. Band VII. Aesthetische Schriften. "Wie dichtet man aus der blauen Luft," pp. 57-74.

LANGUAGE

As the sun rises, talk awakens. As soon as people have yawned themselves back to consciousness, their interminable chatter begins in innumerable languages, dialects and jargons. Thundering avalanches of words pour from printing presses over the continents. And while housewives go silently about their work they listen to their talking-machines. In classrooms, lecture halls, and assemblies, on stages and in "talkies," public performers hope their audiences will like their expert speeches as much as they do themselves.

In this ever present verbal fluidity there are a few hard islands—works of great literature; they endure through the centuries. They *seem* to share the medium of language with all other kinds of talk; but what, then, is the secret of their perseverance? Why does Homer stay with us although no one speaks his language?

All other arts have a medium of their own. The noises of the world are not the musical tones woven into perfect musical compositions; the colors of things, seen in nature, are not the colors on the flat canvass through which the painter expresses himself and forces us to believe in a world of his own making. The sculptured stone ceases to be an inorganic block and seems to live although it is not alive; and the living body of the dancer is not the body of the dance integrating remembered gestures, expressive movements in space-time patterns. Only architecture is like literature, subject to a similar misunderstanding—there are many buildings but not much architecture, just as there are many books but not many poems; by "poem" I mean any literary work of art—the English language has no word for it!—and by "poet," likewise, I shall mean any artist who creates a work of art in the medium of words, regardless of whether it is in verse, prose, or dialogue.

Some poets have bestowed the most meticulous care on the choice, the sound and cadence of their words—but others have written like volcanos. Mere carefulness does not make a language poetic. Demosthenes wrote his political diatribes with scrupulous attention to effect and delivered them with emotion and conviction; Cicero's legal speeches against Varro or Catilina are famous for their well-groomed periods—but neither Demosthenes nor Cicero have therefore created poems. Their language points beyond itself to practical objectives to be achieved. Poetic language does not intend to be effective in such limited temporal situations. But this mere negation (that it does not refer to objective situations or practical purposes) does not say what it is. It only says what it is not. To deprive the poet of the language of scientific information or of moral character would reduce him to a childish babbling—"da-da-ism." No great poet has played with language just for the fun of playing with language. Great poets are not childish. Poetic language is neither scientific, nor practical, *nor* is it an end in itself.

Poetic language intends to create a symbol of life in its entirety. To achieve this ideal it makes full use of the ordinary informative and practical usages—but it does this by taking them out of their own temporal context, by de-realizing them while at the same time preserving them, heightening and intensifying them. Poetic language blends all other languages in a powerful potion; transfigured, they yield *levels of meaning* in the complete poetic symbol—"symbol" means literally a "together-throw."

We distinguish, then, the following six levels of linguistic meaning:

1. *The Physical Language:* A system of formed sounds appears to the eyes in script and to the ears in speech. It is the one and only aspect of poetry that is empirically real and can be recorded. Vocabulary and grammar is shared with all other non-poetic uses. No other art suffers under such a painful barrier. It confines the poet to a narrower or wider linguistic community in which alone his communication is understood. Physical language is *objective;* it is a shared appearance; the poet has to learn it and there is no end to this learning. But it is also *subjective;* each poet speaks it in his own individual way and he transmits his peculiar intonation and his preference for certain words to his writing. He makes the most of the musical potentials in language, paying attention to sound-effects, melodic "ups" and "downs" or pitch-sequences; to intensity, rhythm and tempo. This attention, particularly when it is heightened in the musical structures of the verse, announces already poetic intentions and begins to differentiate poetic language from an inattentive use, where only *what* is said matters, not *how* beautifully, freshly, originally it is said. The tone in which I say something may be more important than the word use. 2. *The Symptom Language:* This is mainly a preverbal, non-verbal language of life itself. Life communicates itself through symptoms. Organisms respond to symptoms of danger or of lure. However, if I say that "he speaks like a teacher, a sailor, etc.," I value his manner of speaking as a symptom. Red dots of the skin are a symptom of measles and a baby carriage a symptom that the young woman pushing it is the mother. Poetry extends the symptom language to inanimate nature: "The "same" snow may be inviting to sports or may be a "threat" to my bones; the "same" cloud may be a symptom of a devastating storm or of a beneficial rain. Poetry uses words to make you perceive such symptomatic situations. These situations are infinitely individualized, they are relative to the interests and roles of the individuals involved in them. There is no "sameness" ever, the language of life is surprising, unexpected, in one word, *irrational*. Each symptom is new and different in an everchanging individual experiencing. Poetry creates the impression of a unique and individual life acting and reacting within equally concrete and unique situations of immediate experience. This symptom language of life is stronger and more convincing than any

mere verbal signification. "Deeds speak louder than words." If you see an actor on the stage say to a petitioner that his documents are nice, very nice indeed, and then see that they are thrown into the waste-paper basket, you believe the symptom, not the verbal assurance.

Through the medium of the first empirical-physical level of language a second level of images is conjured up. You are led to perceive the images of things, objects, persons, situations, landscapes, rooms, streets, public places and so forth, which are symptomatic of the life that goes on in them; the landscapes and portraits of life are filled with symptomatic expressiveness. This second level in poetry is analogous to the *sujet*, the "subject-matter," in painting. Pure music and abstract painting skips this level, while program music may vaguely contain it in its reference to "pastoral scenes" or "scenes from a market place," etc.

3. *Sign Language:* Theoretical intelligence comes into play! The sounds of language become signs, when they stand for and refer to any multiplicity of instances. They are possibilities. A railroad sign points to the possibility of trains coming through at this point. Experience is widened and exhibits what is typical, what is repeated, what is the same and recurring, "always and always and always." Poems may include vast theoretical awareness of scientific structures of the natural and the social world. Situations and actions may be significant for all of us at all times. *Fabula docet.* Without involving such general possibilities literature may be entertaining and amusing, but not significant; the general significance of signs widens our horizon. Essential structures of life are no less important than individual events.

The second and third level of language together comprise the language of object-experience in its immediate and mediated or rational aspects. The third level of general and typical significance appears through the second level of symptomatic situations, gestures and events. And both of them appear or shine through the objective physical appearance of sounds.

4. *Self-expression:* Poetic language not only points to an imagined world in perceptual presentation and conceptual representation or comprehension, but it also expresses how the poet feels about his imagined world. The basic expressive language are ejaculations, the "ahs" and "ohs" of life. I express how I feel the world is treating me. The object-contents become the media of subjective attitudes, moods, emotions, feelings. Appearances are charged with the feeling-tones of

agreeable/disagreeable, hostile/friendly, inviting/repulsive. But in distinction from existential communications of defeat and triumph, the poetic expressiveness is projected into the impersonal illusion; it is not feeling but a make-belief of feeling. The poem may express sadness, but it in itself seems to be sad—the poet personally may be very merry after having written it, or a humorous poem may be born out of personal gloom. It is a profound misunderstanding of poetic expressiveness to infer the personal-psychical privacy of the poet from it. What he feels personally or privately is at the very most an occasion, a spring-board, a raw material for the expressiveness of his poem. The poem in itself is evocative or appealing to existential feeling in anyone who can read it with "empathy." Its emotional quality must appear in the tones, colors, cadences, rhythms, of the words and their objective contents. The hand that trembles with fever and rage can not be the writing hand. Poetic passion is unimpassioned in its expression and performance. The actor choking with emotion is not able to convey the emotions in his lines. Expressive language is "emotion collected in tranquility."

5. *The Signal:* Traffic lights are not only artificial, conventional *signs,* indicating general possibilities, but they are also and at the same time *signals,* which tell you what to do or not to do. Signals express practical directives, they are imperatives. The most elementary practical signal-language is contained in the imperatives "do" and "don't." Practical life is at its thickest in war—and all military movements are directed by commands which are signalized.

The signal may be hidden as in clever propaganda. Its intention is to direct your will, to condition your practical attitudes, but intention may come disguised in the form of little stories which seem to be merely informative. The signalizing intent is veiled by factual object-language.

Again, mere existential self-expression would not be very significant without also and at the same time signalizing an orientation in practical life. The poet is involved and fascinated by the universal moral problems of individual and social decisions.

On this level we find the central moral problems of humanity, the struggle and battle for and against values, those which are held to be worthy of sacrifice and love. To portray the moved image of self-sacrifice, for example, is infallibly moving.

The practical signal-language of imperatives, again, is de-realized, taken out of its own context, pealed off and preserved and presented in its purity, in its essence. The ever problematic struggle for values, embedded in the social conflicts, becomes the non-problematic image in which friends and foes are treated with the same aesthetic love.

The poet may hate his villains morally, but as an artist he loves his character portrait of his villain dearly. His characters signalize their will; their actions involve them necessarily in the consequences of their poetic destiny.

Existential self-expression and practical-moral signal language are the two subjective levels of language again blending and appearing through the symptom and sign language of the two objective levels. The four levels of meaning together accomplish a symbolic fusion of world and soul.

6. *Ceremonial Language:* A ring on a finger may be interpreted as a symptom that the wearer is married. In the religious marriage ceremony, however, it is meant to dedicate a holy union of two lives to God. The ceremony points beyond this life to an eternal and absolute Beyond, in which this fragmentary and questionable existence finds its ultimate ground and justification. Religious myths, legends, prayers, cults, constitute a ceremonial body of expressions, repeated and traditionally adhered to. If the poet makes use of this religious side of life, he takes into the poem an absolute dimension which becomes a part of the poetic symbol. He may be an irreligious writer making use of ceremonial forms, or he may be a religious writer without using traditional ceremonial forms. It is sufficient when his characters move, speak and behave in such a way that the reader is aware that they are relying on an absolute ground of their faith beyond human practical power and theoretical knowledge. Purely irreligious writers are working without this dimension—there is no transparency, no leaks, no cracks, beyond the appearances of this world; they are on the contrary closing in on us as ultimate and sufficient in themselves.

7. *Irony and Dialectic:* The poet may be conscious of the poem as symbolic fusion of all those different functions of language. He then is not only a poet and an artist of words but also an aesthetician. Philosophical language enters his art. He knows what he is doing when he is doing it. He is aware of the distinctions which we just made. He holds them together in the wholeness of his creation; he knows that his creation both reflects the whole of reality and is, at the same time, only

a symbolic mirror of it. A divine comedy; a spectacle, but alas! only a spectacle! The philosopher in the poet knows the power but he also knows the limit of his artistic-poetic language. In art itself the aesthetic world-view is portrayed and contrasted with other world-views such as the religious, the moral-practical, the intellectualistic and the vitalistic. Over-all metaphysical orientations make use of the language of philosophy in the poem. Philosophical language selects essential "realms" of experience and refers through them to a whole of reality. Philosophy *in* literature is in harmony with the philosophical reflection on the value and limitation *of* literature. The poem then speaks the language of aesthetic irony. It is aware that aesthetic reality is real in and for itself and irreducible to other realms of reality, which are used and fused; but which on the other hand nevertheless maintain their own right in their own domains.

> Life like the dome of many coloured glass
> Stains the white radiance of eternity
> Until death tramples it to fragments.
>
> (Shelley)

IMAGINATION

Poetic language is a whole of many levels of linguistic meanings which all are necessary; they all shine through one another; one is both itself and at the same time the condition of the appearance of the others. The philosophical-aesthetic meaning of a poem is appearing through the presence or absence of mythical-religious language; moral-practical and expressive-existential language is made apparent through the object-meanings in signs and symptoms, and all these levels are carried by the actual physical shape and music of the physical sound-systems. The whole poetic symbol is built up by de-realizing all other linguistic meanings, by taking them out of their own real context, but preserving and heightening them in their new role as contributors to a new kind of reality, the aesthetic symbol. Symbol of what? Symbol of imagination! Without imagination, without the vision of levels and essential values of life as a whole—no poetic language and no poetic symbol! Poetic language is the outer appearance, the appearing body of life as imagined. Poetic language is imagination itself as appearing to others, imagination in the outward form of self-communication. The levels of linguistic meanings are interfused with the levels of poetic imagination which does the de-realizing and synthesizing in order to communicate to others itself, the vision of life as a whole in all of its facets. There can be poetic vision without poetic language, but there can be no true poetic language without imagination—although technicians may learn a good deal from the linguistic bodies of genuine poems and may learn to handle poetic language as if it could be learned. "The third inspiration and frenzy from the Muses seizes a tender and sacred soul agitating and elating it to make appear a beautiful whole in festive hymns or other works of poetry; celebrating innumerable (thousand) deeds of ancestors it (this soul) cultivates posterity. But he who enters the precinct of the poetic temple without this mania of the Muses, with the opinion he could become a poet through technique only, such a one is unauthentic and his learned art will be put in to shame by the creation of the inspired." (Plato, *Phaidros*, 255.)

Poetry is the art of imagination. The words merely serve to evoke imagination in the hearer or reader. It is indirect communication. It can not be said directly. If it could be said, then the poem would be superflous. The direct, literal meanings of the words only serve to make appear the invisible reality of the soul. This letting see the soul through the cracks between the words and between the lines is the function of imagination, is imagination. Imagination is what it does—and it does this: it lets appear a totality of life, the soul.

How? One can approach the answer to this question by paying attention to various well-known psychical functions which are approaches, pre-conditions, avenues, to poetic imagination.

1. *The Dream*. Poets proverbially are dreamers. Dreams are spontaneously emerging images. They only seem to refer to external experiences, from which they take their "raw-material," their "face-values." At the same time these images from external experience are de-realized, they are taken out of their normal, logical context and are absorbed in the subjective context of the dreamer's situation in life. They are I-existent. They express how I find myself situated in life. They *symbolize* my moral status. They are, as Freud has taught us, expressions of wishes, urges, and appetites which are not satisfied in waking life and clamor for fulfillment. But they are also censored by my logical and moral conscience, which distorts them and renders them ugly and monstrous. They are compromises between the turmoil of my vital-spiritual conflicts and my need for rest, for sleep. They may reveal in a flash of insight what it might take a long time to explain

rationally. They may rise to poetic intensity and telling beauty—and may actually turn into a poem, if the dreamer can retain and tell their tale. In that case, the dream ceases to be floating and private, it becomes enduring and shareable. Poetic imagination as embodied in poetic language, is the dream made essential and universal, stripped of its mere psychical and private momentariness.

2. *Day-dream.* The psychoanalytic method uses the day-dream by inducing the individual to associate fancies with given stimuli. A word, an ink-blot is given and the individual associates anything that may come to his mind with the stimulus. His fancies are led and fed by his inclinations, tendencies, interests, and thus produce a self-portrait of his state of affairs. In the ordinary, unguided daydream the day-dreamer projects himself into situations, he anticipates situations in which he plays a heroic role. He indulges in the sweet illusion of projecting himself as the center of his own scheming. The transition from this to poetic imagination is to retain the ability to project and construct essential and vital situations, but stripped from ego-centricity.

The poet may tell his story in the "I" form, but the "I" of the story is a role, a character-mask which has his own will—the poet is not free to let the "I" of his story say anything that comes into his, the poet's mind. He must be true to the character which tells the story. This is analogous to the transfer of spatial orientation from psychical to mathematical coordinates. The psychical center of our spatial orientation is placed between our eyes: from the root of the nose out we call something right or left, up or down, behind us or in front of us. Geometry replaces this private orientation, in which right becomes left as I turn around, with an abstract and arbitrarily chosen point, from which other points can be measured to be so many units out in fixed dimensions. The poet, similarly, projects an objective, communicated "I" in an objective, communicated situation with relationships that are seen as necessary and contributing to an understandable whole.

3. *Memory.* In the Plato passage quoted, memory of an important past is the condition of a cultured future. Poetic imagination needs a rich and vivid memory of the past, constantly ready to stream into the present creation. Aeschylus calls "Memory *(mnemosyne)* the mother of the Muses." Past experiences are not only gone but are also retained and stored for re-employment. Memory balances the anticipating projection of the daydream. Poetic projection at the same time feeds on memory. Vivid impressions are charged with sympto-

matic, emotional, theoretical, and moral significance. The time elapsed makes little difference. Freud has shown that very early experiences are still effective in late neuroses. The same holds for poetic imagination. Memories of forty years standing are still "standing by," and may all of a sudden contribute to a poem. There are many amazing stories of the tough retentiousness of artistic memories: for example, the story of Mozart who, after having heard a fugue of nine voices went home and wrote it all down, accurate to the last note.

For everyday efficiency this leakiness of the poet, this openness to the treasures and threats of his subconscious soul may be very inconvenient. All of a sudden he is "off" and not "here and now." His vastly expanded presence of mind seems to others absent-mindedness. Carl Spitteler's novel *Imago* pictures the devastating effect of a remembered past, idealized and glorified in imagination, upon the factual and present actuality of practical existence. On the other hand, the more exciting and disdainful the experience, the more worthy of telling in the safe distance of memory. (The theme song of *Dionysos* in Spitteler's *Olympic Spring*.)

5. *Suggestion*. When I was a boy I had a tame crow, named Chäred. Chäred loved a little glass of cognac after Sunday dinners. He spread his wings about, staggered, his feet turned inward, rolled his eyes so we could see the white, crowed softly and voluptuously. In short, he was in a "rosy glow." But once we gave him dark tea in his cognac glass. He imagined it was cognac and produced all the effects as if he had actually drunk cognac—and not merely the tea. Such is the power of suggestion. Animals have imagination which transforms ordinary perception into something which they are not—prosaically speaking.

Poetry may be regarded as practicing this power of suggestion. We are forced to see things, events, characters, plots and human destinies which never existed in practical actuality—but which seem more real and more concrete than the scattered and ever-changing experiences of life. The Muses, Homer says, grant us the vision of life as it really is; apart from them we know nothing—only rumors and opinions. Polonius sees in the clouds, camels, or weasels, as imagination suggests.

But poetic suggestion is not a practical delusion. It makes clear that its suggestion of reality is and moves in an ideal, de-realized realm of its own creation. It sets man free, it does not misguide him to a foolish confusion of practical actualities with its imagined life. Aesthetic distance allows us to identify ourselves with the suggested life which we know to be a spectacle for us.

6. *Occasion*. The external, unforseen occasion is as important for the poem as an acorn is for the existence of a mighty oak tree. Goethe says that all his poems are "occasional" (Gelegenheitsgedichte). The occasion for his *Faust* written in sixty years, was the puppet play which the boy saw on the market fair in Frankfurt. The occasion for *Werther,* written in four weeks, was a newspaper item: "I heard the news of Jerusalem's suicide . . . and in this moment the plan for Werther was found, the whole shot together from all sides and became a solid whole, as water in a vessel on the point of freezing can be brought to crystallize in an instant through a minute shock." Occasion for the Gretchen tragedy in *Faust* was his love for a girl whom he felt he had to abandon—the guilt reaction had to be transformed into imaginative atonement.

Occasions are meetings, unexpectable and uncontrollable; external circumstances act like catalysers in a chemical process. Hence the seemingly vague hunts of poets for such occasions; the often desperate waiting for a fruitful moment or "stuff." Poets read other poets, not to find out what they have to say, but to find occasions for their own creativity. They seek adventures in strange social and geographical environments, where impressions are new and fresh and challenging. like Melville's "whaling" and Jack London's "bumming."

When an occasion presents itself it must be recognized as such, must be grasped, jumped upon. Hebbel was told the story of Herod and Mariamne in the afternoon—and in the evening the main scenes of the tragedy were feverishly put to paper. Examples are endless. Aesthetically they tell us that imagination must meet the actual world in order to be and to become its own best and ideal self. However, the occasion need not be external, they may lie in the poet, his own "trauma" or "neurosis" may become the fruitful source of "seeing" the world and the ambiguities of life.

The occasion fuses with the other conditions of imagination. It is used like a scaffolding which is removed upon the completion of the building. It becomes indifferent after it has served its involuntary purpose. Thomas Mann has portrayed the tragi-comic misunderstanding of such an "occasion," Mrs. Kästner, model for the girl Lotte in *Werther*—who forty years later comes to Weimar to remind the poet of his indebtedness to her. But aesthetic love does not mix with practical ties and obligations.

7. *The Creative Mood*. All forms and phases of imagination must work together and be actualized in the moment of creativity, of imaginative synthesis, which we call the creative mood. It has often been compared with the moment of sexual orgasm. There are many descriptions of this moment of the poetic mood. Hebbel told his servant who announced a visitor in such a moment: Go tell him that I can have no other visitors when I am visited by the Lord.

I try a very general account: In the poetic mood the difference between I and other-than-I is obliterated in the feeling of sameness or oneness. The other than I, the image is grasped and is transformed into an expression of myself—but this self is not an individual or merely psychical I, but that I who can see in the other its true and essential, its inner and living character. Or: Imagination lives in an original unity, in an essential kinship with a beloved image of the world, which in turn expresses what the imagination is and does. It is the moment when the interplay of all faculties, as Kant called it, becomes event. The impact of occasions, the freshness of intuition, the warmth of feeling, intellectual and moral values play together to produce the totality of an ideal whole—which is the poem. The poet finds himself in his imagined world and the world in turn expresses and contains his self. "Objects" are freed from their conditions and are transfigured or "saved" in being imaginatively recreated. "The poet gratefully gives back to nature a truthful image of a second nature which is felt, thought and filled with human significance." (Göthe.)

8. *Levels*. The levels of linguistic meanings in the poem are complemented by the levels of imagination. The poetic symbol needs both the clarity and mastery of the linguistic medium as well as the leveled reach and richness of imagination. Both scales start with the physical sound through which all other levels are made to appear.

The first level of imagination makes visible the image of natural and social scenes, milieus, moods together with the image of persons, their movements, deeds, plots, long range actions and conversations. Beyond this level the entertaining literature does not rise.

The second level of imagination makes visible the inner character, the intelligible essences of events and persons. Corresponding to essential and inner character-motivations is the destiny, the understandable coherence of their interactions. We are not merely entertained, but get involved ourselves.

The third level of imagination gives us the feeling that we have here a world-mirror, in which nothing human is absent. These are the enduring world poems belonging to world literature and to all ages and races. They are the appearing wholeness and totality of life.

The fourth and final level is philosophical. The work of imagination gives metaphysical guidance and orientation. Ultimate world views are contrasted and embraced in that aesthetic love which is the counterpart to a mature dialectical unity of opposite world views. But the philosophical poets express it in terms of the preceding levels, in the language of life itself.

The dialectical nature of reality is made manifest in the poetic symbol of imagination.

Metaphysics and Epistemology

The Absolute produces itself in philosophical reflection for consciousness. As dialectical struggle it becomes for itself an objective totality, a whole of self-knowledge, an organization of cognitive spheres. In this organization each part is at the same time the whole, because it exists only through its relation to the Absolute. As a part, which has other parts outside of itself, it is limited and is what it is only through this not-being the others . . . If unity of a world-view is accomplished only by denying one of the opposites, then it is irrelevant whether we deny the subjective as real or whether we deny the objective as real. Their oppositeness is in our consciousness and reality is thereby just as much in the one as in the other.

—HEGEL
(W. I. 74, 87)

REFLECTION ON REALITY

Philosophy defines itself as the reflection on all meanings of human existence in reality. If we bracket the middle part of this definition: Philosophy is the reflection on (the meanings of human existence in) reality, we think philosophy as reflection on reality. This "bracketing" does not mean that we forget or disregard the human center. This would be the fallacy of all naturalism, which posits reality as that which was when man was not or as that which will be when man may have disappeared. This is a fallacy because it does not think reality as we know it to be and to manifest itself; and it is a fallacy because it leaves out the knowledge from what is known; "nature" is not known in abstraction from our perceptual and mathematical knowledge.

The reflection on reality distinguishes philosophy from other "social sciences," in which man makes himself an object of partial observations. Philosophy means reality. Reality is the meaning of philosophy; as God is the meaning of religions, beauty the meaning of arts, goodness in some sense the meaning of all practical life, and the constitution of objects the meaning of various sciences.

All such meanings or (Platonic) "ideas" are "dimensions" of reality. They all are, and meet in being something, and not nothing. They all are, and meet in man as their living focus. And as all converge in being and in man none of them can be ultimate in itself, apart from the others; they all limit each other. The whole of reality alone can be the truth of reflection, and it exists in man realizing this. Meaning or value and reality are equivalent, inasmuch as a both must be thought by living individuals,—must exist in life.

Reality which is the "problem" of philosophical reflection, includes all approaches to it, all formulations of it; they are "qualities" characterizing reality. Philosophy, in reflecting *on* reality reflects the ultimate character *of* reality, it articulates reality as that which reflects itself by reflecting on itself. The reality which philosophical reflection discloses is such that the meaning of human existence becomes intelligible in it.

The reflection on ultimate reality is that function of philosophy which is traditionally known as metaphysics. It is the battleground of the most important and decisive philosophical decisions. The "culture-mentality" of whole nations and historical epochs is determined by what they believe to be ultimately real and important.

What do we mean when we think reality, and, what does reality mean when it becomes conscious of itself in us, are the two inseparable and central metaphysical questions.

PARADISE LOST

Man has tasted the fruits of the tree of knowledge and henceforth is cast out of paradise. He has lost the naive and unbroken unity with things, which he cannot restore. He only remembers it.

Man is born to think. Logical consciousness distinguishes him from the vegetable and animal, where "thinking" is an instinctive reaction to stimuli or a "phase of action." His occasional longing to return to the innocence of the beast is vain. When he loses his logic he does not regain the happiness of animal existence, but here he merely becomes a deranged and insane human.

Consciousness, or more accurately speaking and in order to avoid psychological misunderstanding, logic, frees man from the narrow confines of biological-experiential environments, from which the animal cannot escape, and opens his "vision" to a world-whole. This world-whole or universe is a logical idea, which is not given in or to any experience. Experientially there is no such one and common and same world for all; there are only different distorted worlds for each experiencing individual.

The logical idea is any content in the form of universality and identity; its universality means that the idea signifies or formulates any number of instances of its own class, and identity means that it is the same for all who think it. The content in logical form may be the idea itself. When I think the idea as anything in the logical form of universality and identity, I refer to the idea itself. The idea is thought by itself, refers to itself. And because idea can know itself, man as logical thinker can know himself, he is conscious of himself. Logic is the basis, and the only basis, of a community of self-conscious beings.

In distancing himself from a fixed biological environment by discovering the universe as the logical idea of a whole, which is given to no experience, but which is eternally prior to any experience, man is enabled to criticize what is given to his sense experience and to make the "object" a problem of scientific investigation. And since nothing is exempt from the universality of logical reflection man may turn upon himself and make himself his own problem of knowledge.

To be an object of knowledge is to be a problem for knowledge. A problem is anything that is questioned. Objects of knowledge are problems because they are confronted with the logical question: What are you? Such questions can be asked from various points of view, on many levels of intellectual interest, and they bring the object in question in many relations. The object is always incomplete because it is not one with my understanding. And this unity is never completed because the object as other-than-I is never identical with the object in the form of being known by me.

One truth only is certain, that to know something is to be uncertain concerning its reality. If we were certain of reality we would not desire to know. But to have problems is to be problematic. To doubt something is to be in doubt. This being in doubt is the signature of man thinking.

This is doubly the case when man makes himself the object of knowledge. By making the given nature an object of knowledge he has estranged himself from nature, but in making himself an object of knowledge he inevitably testifies by this act that he is estranged from himself. He is in doubt about himself. As object of his knowledge he is a problem; and as being in doubt about himself, he is problematic himself. Logical reflection creates the object as problem, and man as a problematic being. All experiential uncertainties, doubts, and problems are existentially certain and indubitable. In thinking, man affirms this existential uncertainty as his own indubitable truth. To doubt it is to repeat the act which it intends to deny or to question.

Man cannot think himself truly as unthinking. Logical reflection, then, has at once two directions. It is at the same time transitive and intransitive. As transitive, it reflects on or about given objects in experience, subjecting thereby experience to critical scrutiny. As intransitive, reflection reveals what man-thinking existentially is. Logic is the medium through which man expresses his problematic existence. That he is truly and indubitably problematic, that he lives in self-created tensions—is what he is. He can humanly exist in no other form or mode than in the form of being logical and therefore problematic, certain of his uncertainty. Thinking is both the ground of his experiential uncertainty and of his existential truth.

Such is the fruit from the tree of knowledge.

DOGMATIC AND CRITICAL METAPHYSICS

Thinking does not go on apart from the thinker. The above reflection on logical thought also reveals the thinking subject of that thought as a being seeking clarity, certainty, and truth concerning a reality which is confused, uncertain, and dubitable. The two opposite sides belong inextricably together. Nothing can be judged to be uncertain unless I want certainty and refuse confusion. Untruth and error do not exist in themselves and independent from the logical demand which seeks their elimination and by this demand, establishes what it wants to overcome.

The thinker finds himself as existing in this struggle. He is this struggle. In his uncertainty he grasps an existential reality which precedes any scientific statement concerning any object. Self-reflection and self-knowledge reveals reality as existential dialectic.

Metaphysical knowledge, however, is not satisfied with this reflection on the real nature of the thinking subject. It wants to know reality as it is "outside." The existential reality of reflection seeks its place in a larger whole. It asks what we mean when we say that something is real. The search for an ultimate reality outside of the thinking subject proves that all given and experienced appearances are suspected of being only provisional or questionable.

And there we have reached the battleground of dogmatic metaphysical "standpoints." A standpoint becomes dogmatic when it does not realize that nothing can be posited as real abstracted from the logical judgment which claims truth for its position, and secondly when it does not realize that it absolutizes an aspect of reality in opposition to another aspect which it denies. Critical metaphysics, on the contrary, knows that any abstracted aspect of reality is at the same time a logical hypothesis (as Plato teaches), and that any position which not only allows but makes necessary an opposition, is a half-truth which is completed only by that which it denies.

The battle of such dogmatic positions, renewed in every generation is nevertheless both valuable and necessary. It is not as sterile as the snap judgment of layman has it. "Isms" are valuable in sharpening our "vision" for what they "see," and they are necessary as the whole truth could not be thought without them. The whole truth is their dialectical interdependence.

Truth on its formal side, as norm and ideal of all logical thinking, is the idea of an eternal and consistent unity of what is; but since this eternal universe of truth *is* at the same time as a whole of unfinished and oppositional processes and functions of life, truth is never static and fixed. It exists in breaking down errors and provisional positions, just as errors exist as resisting and overcoming truth; as for example when "economic class interests" or biological-racial interests are declared to be truths to which logical critique must submit.

Truth becomes existential in breaking down erroneous positions which it had previously created. Truth lives in the process of overcoming its own deficient self-realizations. In this dialectical process thinking truth matures, and as it matures it will not only overcome positions which were erroneously assumed to be true, but it will also preserve their core in a wider "horizon," because no position can be absolutely false. There is always something that remains.

Dialectic is thus discovered as the logic of maturing. We take a position or are born into one, but in working it out its limitations appear. But the new position gained is not merely negative with reference to the first, because it can gain itself only in the struggle with the position it wants to overcome. The result is finally or ultimately the idea of the whole truth, which whole is not outside or apart from the living process itself; it cannot be stated apart from the opposite positions in and by which it is developed. Each position is transcended because none taken in isolation can adequately represent the idea of the whole, but each is immanent in the whole because without it the whole would not be itself.

The following samples of dogmatic positions are not meant to be historical, let alone "complete"; they merely serve to illustrate critical dialectic.

REALITY IN ITSELF

Empirical knowledge is a continuous process of clarifying and verifying opinions, beliefs, and sciences concerned with given "facts." The "facts" are based on psycho-physical events, which become "facts" when they are selected and apprehended in logical forms such as quantity, quality, mathematical, causal relations, and so forth. The tests applied are logical norms; on the one hand the norm of formal consistency, which rejects contradictory statements, on the other hand the norm of inductive proof, which, at least in the case of general laws can be "secured" through experimentation. But these two poles of empirical knowledge, consistency and inductive proof are never quite identical, because inductive proof is never more than probable. Consistency and inductive proof coincide only in the case of mathematical inductions, void of any *given* content. In historical knowledge it is easy to see that a consistent interpretation of phenomena can never be had, as every new event happening destroys the former certainty concerning the functional meaning of previous events. But even mathematical physicists have recently discovered that empirical observation of events makes an unambiguous or consistent judgment concerning the observed, impossible. This can come as a surprise only to those who have never reflected on the discrepancy between the subjective and objective, and between the formal and empirical aspects of all empirical knowledge.

Metaphysical reflection has repeatedly shown that it is impossible to solve or harmonize those discrepancies. Every attempt to overcome them has ended in necessary self-contradictions.

As soon as man steps out of his paradisical unity with nature, the problem of knowledge appears. A single recognition of a false judgment suffices to set metaphysical reflection in motion. When, for instance, Ptolemaic astronomy gave way to the Copernican astronomy, the stars themselves had not changed their courses, only what was supposed to be a true knowledge of them had been revolutionized, and the question of the relation of knowledge to reality had again become inevitable as it had many times before this particular example. And this should be helpful in making clear that the metaphysical question is not concerned with the correction of empirical knowledge as such. The metaphysical question is untouched and is the same whether the phenomena of astronomy are described by Ptolemy or by Copernicus. A description which is empirically more correct and more consistent in its description poses the same problem of the relation of being in the form of being known to being as being in itself apart from the judgment which thinks what it is.

Let us assume that all error falls on the side of the subject trying to apprehend reality. Reality, according to this assumption, is what it is regardless of whether anyone knows it or not. If it is known, then that knowledge is true when it corresponds with its intended object, false when it does not do justice to it. Reality, in this *"realism"* is both a "thing in itself" and a norm of true judgments. Truth is founded on what is. Judgments are true or false about, or with reference to, that which is, and which they either hit or miss. The approach towards a true judgment is identical with stripping from its intended object all subjective additions or warping perspectives. The true judgment transcends itself, whereas the false judgment has not succeeded in escaping from merely subjective opinions.

The tenable kernel of this "realistic" or "objectivistic" position is, that every judgment intends to apprehend something that is other than the judgment itself. It transcends the judgment. But the standpoint is nevertheless untenable for various reasons.

1. It is not possible to strip the intended reality from subjective forms of apprehending it, such as sensate qualities, comparative and measuring quantities, measuring relations, causal links with the subject, and above all purely logical forms such as identity ("It is what it is"). The thinking subject in his judgment apprehends an "X" which is transcendentally given in logical forms; it still is connected with the judging subject by this very negative relation which says that X is not identical with what is known of it, which negation is also a logical judgment.

2. This standpoint introduces a dualism, which is a self-contradiction. Error, it says, is merely subjective. But as error it exists and is real. To deny that false knowledge exists refers to that which it denies,

apprehends it in the logical form of a negation. It posits false knowledge in the center of its own judgment which splits the reality-in-itself from a reality-for-us, or in-us.

3. If reality as it is in itself is proclaimed to be the norm of true and false judgments, then it is clear that truth cannot be separated from reality. Reality in itself would be neither true nor false, it would simply be what it is. If it can function as logical norm of judgments, then it cannot be independent of judgments, since only judgment can be true or false.

4. But reality as it is in itself cannot function as logical norm, because the judgment would not be able to compare a "false reality" with a "true reality," it could never be sure whether it has hit or missed reality. A "false reality" would be as real as a "true reality."

The attempt to think reality as an "object" independent from thinking is self-refuting. It is limited by the subject experiencing and thinking it, and it is limited by the logical forms in which it is apprehended as the "other." Independent reality is not reality but an abstraction from reality.

The distinction of reality in the form of being known and reality as it is in abstraction from this form, is a distinction which the judgment makes within itself. It is a dialectical proposition. In other words, thinking necessarily makes this distinction between itself and its own other. It thus thinks reality as one and other, as identity and as that whose identity it is, as apprehending logical form and apprehended non-logical content. The dialectic of being in the form of being known, and as that to which knowledge refers, is the dialectic essence of the judgment and of its object.

Thinking breaks the unity of being one with itself. Thinking itself is that model reality which is both being and being known. It is the identity of these opposites in every one of its acts of judgment, and as such a dialectical and living reality it is the ground, the existential and *a priori* ground of all specific or empirical knowledge. It is the certainty of our uncertainties. It is reality lived and living in its own theoretical situation, which is existentially the same and shared by all who think.

The thinking subject seeks clarity and truth concerning its own other, and every form and level of such a consciousness is at the same time a form and level of self-characterization and of self-consciousness. And so, if it violently tries to disengage itself from what it believes to be real, it will not only produce a torn and violent and unhappy consciousness, but will project its own fission into reality, in which "reality-independent" appears as an unrecognized self-contradiction.

REALITY FOR US

Truth cannot be divorced from reality but neither can reality be divorced from truth. This is the thesis of "idealism" opposing "objectivism." It denies all transcendence and tries to identify reality with what we know of it. Reality is what is known to us. It is immanent in knowledge. This metaphysics of immanence absolutizes the subjective side of knowledge. We may call it "subjectivism," which has like "objectivism" many names and levels. Historically it emerges as the Sophistic movement. Protagoras expresses its fundamental theme that "man is the measure of all things," and Gorgias contends that being is not known, and if it were known it could not be communicated. All we have are opinions. All sorts of "subjective Idealisms," psychologisms, pragmatisms, positivisms, and skepticisms have elaborated these two statements. As a one-sided standpoint, and as metaphysical error, it is just as prolific of true insights as the opposite position of various naturalisms, realisms, objectivisms, provided it is dialectically criticized. Dialectical criticism, in developing the ultimate implications of the positions will discover the same self-contradictions and antinomies which lead to the logical refutation of objectivism.

To begin with, we admit that nothing can be known apart from someone knowing it; that in a sense everything stated to be so, is my statement; that there is not sound or color without someone seeing, or hearing it; that there is no measure without someone measuring, since numbers do not add or multiply themselves; that to judge something to be real or existent takes the logical form "reality" or "existence," universal classes of concepts, which cannot be found apart or outside of thinking them.

Truth, then, would have to be found in logical norms of the subject thinking, as his own norms; a statement would be true if it fits into a system of statements which are coherent or non-contradictory among themselves. Untrue would be a statement which would destroy such a systematic coherence of the judgment. Thus we avoid a recourse to a reality which transcends human knowledge.

But who, we ask, is the subject which dares to identify reality with reality in the form of being known? Obviously it can not be the individual subject. It would be fantastic to suppose that the flickering, intermittent images or experiences which the individual has of an other is the reality of this other, that reality would disappear during the night in order to renew itself on awakening the next morning; that the reality of history depends on whether it is remembered by some individual; that the individual itself is not real because it is not experienced but must be rather presupposed before the individual can make any experience.

Subjectivism must find a more reliable subject than the momentary "bundle of associations" of the psychical I, experiencing. This more reliable subject is sought in the collaboration of many individuals. Reality, then, would be identical with what the human race as a whole knows of it. This is an inter-subjective or social subjectivism, real for it is that on which those who investigate, agree. Their agreement is the test of true knowledge. To insure agreement and peace between various disagreeing groups, the agreement further is a standing invitation to join the investigation. Truth thus becomes hypothetical, subject to further corrections. But is reality hypothetical? Does it change when provisional agreements are changed to other provisional agreements?

Social collaboration is an excellent method in handling phenomena; as a metaphysical answer to the question of reality it is as self-contradictory as a psychological-individual "idealism." Its test by which it overcomes the uncertainties of private-sensate experience is merely practical. Its formulation is the formulation of pragmatism. Pragmatism defines knowledge as phase of action, reality as the sum total of practical expectations and manipulations, truth as that which works, and error as a practical difficulty or obstacle not overcome yet.

Knowledge may indeed arise as a phase of action, as a means to remove an obstacle which is felt by the individual or by a group as disagreeable. But the uncertainty to be removed and the problem to be solved are created by the will to remove it. Without such a will there would be no problem and no obstacle. And since this is valid universally, for all practical problems, the truth that life is problematic is an everlasting truth, which cannot be removed. Nothing can "be done about it." Knowledge is not only a phase of action, but action is an aspect of reality and thus a content of thought.

Realities as the sum of somebody's practical expectations, are conflicting. Pragmatism describes the everlasting conflict of incompatible interests. As "sum total" of such practical expectations reality is never identical with the expectations or wishes of anyone of the parties involved in "the making." Disagreements are no less real than the "agreement of those who investigate." The whole of practical reality is unimaginable. If true is that which works, then truth is self-contradictory. What works for me may work against you and vice-versa. Truth is nothing but a species of propaganda, "becoming true" and "becoming untrue" with the changing constellation of events and with what the subjective group interests find agreeable or disagreeable. If error is a practical difficulty not overcome yet, then error is established for good and can never be overcome. The practical obstacle to be overcome is the reality which includes the overcomer and establishes him as real.

If pragmatism were true then we would know nothing outside of our practical agreements how to operate and handle practical situations. Such knowledge would be tied to particular actions for specific purposes here and now. But if we say that all knowledge is that kind of knowledge, then we reveal quite involuntarily the dialectical structure of reality, disclosed in the dialectical structure of knowledge. If we were true to our theory then we should make no such statement concerning the real character of all knowledge, but we would confine ourselves to operating the machinery of particular and practical experience.

If we assume reality to be identical with what is given to me as my private-psychological image or as object of social-practical manipulation, then this reality as object-for-subject is phenomenal, fragmentary, uncertain, problematic. This subjective and partial view of reality is real. It is an undeniable aspect of reality which this immanent and experiential metaphysics establishes as eternally valid. The negation of reality as a transcendent whole exists as real and characterizes that reality as one of its undeniable attributes. The non-given idea of the whole contains this subjectivistic disruption of itself within itself.

Reality thus turns out to be the same dialectical unity of opposites which the criticism of the objectivistic transcendence yielded. Reality is dialectical, and dialectical thinking is real.

REASON AND IMMEDIACY

For "rationalism," real is that which is intelligible. An intelligible are universal structures, patterns, laws, types, which can be thought in the universal terms of sciences. Their system is the system of reason. Reality is the meeting place, the systematic concatenation of such forms. That which seems to transcend thought, reality as an alien and given other, would, if properly understood, reveal itself as a rational system. Subjective opinions and errors would, if logically criticized, be transformed into a true and universally valid science. Being and thought are one and the same reality.

This metaphysical ideal of reason may take care of ideal possibilities, but it does not account for actual knowledge. The mathematical laws, which it takes as its clues, may or may not be verified by experience; "a" plus "b" is always equal to "b" plus "a," but sulphuric acid added to water results in a harmless solution, whereas water poured on sulphuric acid results in an explosion. **Every universal law is a logical** possibility, in that it demands an experiential verification, which may be lacking. It is fine to know that water will boil when you put it on a fire, but this law remains in the realm of ideal possibilities if there are no matches to light the fire.

The stubborn fact that actual knowledge is conditioned by what happens to be given, which demands to be apprehended in logical forms, limits rationalism. The other stubborn fact that knowledge is for vast stretches subjective and practical, also limits rationalism. If it were true there would be no error in the world. The fact that the world teems with errors makes any rationalistic metaphysics a pious dream, which exists only in contrast to the world of unclarity and untruth, from which it strives to escape. Non-rational functions of life, not subject to the scientific ideal of truth, are no less real than it, and limit it on all sides.

To think of reality as a logical construction forgets that reality is presupposed by, and in, the rationalist, to enable him to make logical constructions. It did not have to wait for the scientist to make logical constructions. It did not have to wait for the scientist to be real. The faith of the rationalist in the value of rational science is not scientific, being a belief in a value not yet realized. If only scientific knowledge is true in disclosing intelligible reality, then this metaphysical evaluation is untrue, being unscientific.

Universal forms are forms of a content which is not identical with them and which they do not produce and whose existence they do not guarantee. The law of gravitation unifies our conception of the constant relation between mass, distance, and velocity of moving bodies, but it neither produces the planetary system, nor does it guarantee its continued existence. Its contents are irrationally given and must be given if they are to be apprehended by such a logical universal pattern.

The statement of scientism, which is a "modern" variation of the "ancient" and "medieval" universalism of rational forms, that only the object of science is real, is self-contradictory, because it is not a scientific statement concerning a given object, but an evaluation of the scientific type of knowledge, an expression of a faith. There is, further, no such thing as "Science," there are only various sciences, which select from the psycho-physical "material," patterns of various levels of abstraction, various logical hypotheses, various logical perspectives. The "same Julius Caesar," who is a unique individual actor in the science of history (a "universal class with only one member"), illustrates for the physicist the mechanism of falling bodies when he drops dead, the dagger of Brutus in his heart.

Every universal idea denies the individual and irrational event-character of that whose universal idea it is. The mathematical construction of a straight line is *not* the line drawn to illustrate it, the number two is *not* the sound or the sign "two" which is written and spoken now, the rabbit in the zoology book is *not* the rabbit jumping across the garden lot now. And yet the universal form is never complete without that whose form it is and which it denies in its irrational occurrence. The rational concept is at once that which it is and that which it is not. It is the unity of opposites. It establishes thus a dialectical reality which makes all rationalism impossible. Reason demands its own negation. If we agree, therefore, that reason discloses reality, then this reality stands disclosed as the inseparable unity of irrational content in rational form. And the actuality of this dialectical unity is the struggle and movement of the "non-being" of the irrational life towards the "being" of its rational unity. Reason itself *is* this dialectical movement and is therefore not identical with its own ideal of rational consistency. Historically this is the "position" of Plato's dialectical idealism resulting from his critique of the Parmenidean rationalism, just as it is the position of Kant's critical idealism developed in criticizing the dogmatic rationalism of his predecessors.

Metaphysical *irrationalism*, from Heraclitus to Schopenhauer, Bergson, and William James, has developed the opposite extreme to rationalism in seeking reality in the immediate flux of life. Reason, to them is "abstract" and has to do with the static, the dead, with that which has become and is externally and superficially manipulated for practical purposes. The "abstract intellect" invents measures and logical rules by which to simplify operations, disregarding, however, the metaphysical truth that what seems a static shell is in reality the outward manifestation and gesture of an ever-moving and creative life, given in its fluidity in my immediate, living, and creative experience. In reality nothing is repeated, but every situation is new and full of undecided potentialities, which become actual in and with the decision. The organ which discloses reality to us is not the stabilizing and falsifying generalities of reason, but the actual "intuition," grasping the moment in its new significance. Reality in its concrete and ever individual actuality slips through the net of generalizing reason.

Knowledge, for this metaphysics of immediacy, inevitably must be a psychologism. Knowledge is meant as psychical or mental process, "art of thinking," association of ideas guided by desires, day dreaming and genial intuitions. But mental functions, interests, images, and acts of apprehending, are known in the same way as other objects are known; they are given contents apprehended in valid and universal logical forms. They are referred to and thought about, they do not communicate themselves as knowledge. They are private and individual states of mind, but if they are known as such they belong to the past, the last minute, the yesterday, the last year; as such they are given as objects of knowledge in time, and the subject thinking them as real, is identical with them only in so far as he thinks them to be his own past experiences.

I can take myself as object of my knowledge. In doing this I am not one with myself as I distance myself from myself in order to know myself as my own object. What I share with others is not my intuitions, but I "share" this theoretical situation of splitting myself in subject thinking, and object-thought-about.

Mental processes as such are not knowledge, let alone metaphysical knowledge, because mental processes remain individual, private, incommunicable. Even if, under an excitement exciting many individuals at the same time, there are similar and contagious feelings, this does not sum up to a valid and universal knowledge, but those various excitements remain, as individual states of mind, private, and without cognitive value.

"There is nothing in heaven or on earth," Hegel says, "which is not immediate and mediated at the same time." The truth that in experience all flows and nothing abides is so true that it does not change and abides forever. What Heraclitus discovered to be true was the same and identical truth which was rediscovered by Schopenhauer, Bergson, James, as the "new" process philosophy.

The metaphysics of immediacy cannot state its own truth without contradicting itself and without becoming dialectical.

The logical idea exists in the living subject of all thinking. It is the certainty of its uncertainty. It is the unity of transcendence and immanence, of reality in itself and reality for us, or identity and difference, form and content, One and Many. It is the dialectical unity of necessary opposites. To think is to exist as tension. Thinking makes the world as tension, explicit.

SYSTEMS

Reality is thought in metaphysical systems and nowhere else, least of all in empirical sciences which do not even raise the question of what is real. But those systems clash. Observing this, skeptics have believed that metaphysics has never achieved any reliable knowledge. This belief, though, is itself a metaphysical system, if it should try to become articulate and prove its point by investigating the systems. The change from one metaphysical system to another becomes apparent in profound historical crises, in which the metaphysics governing one "culture-mentality" is being broken and exchanged for a different system. An example of such a crisis is the change from the sensate-materialistic and skeptical metaphysics of the Hellenistic period to the mystic and religious metaphysics of the Christian era. Such revolutions and conflicts of metaphysical systems magnify the Platonic truth that wisdom is present in the struggle for it.

There must be opposite systems, because there are many dimensions of reality and man is not able to see the whole except through one-sided perspectives. The whole of reality has become articulate and explicit through formulating dimensions as conflicting systems. But this does not remove the other truth that it is always the one and same universe which is ultimately meant by conflicting systems. If there were several universes there would be no conflict. There is conflict because there is absolute unity. And this unity is the unity of opposites, it is not a unity as a super-system over and above and outside the systems. As such a unity it would not be an absolute unity, but an abstract, separate, and relative unity.

The system of philosophy is at the same time the way of history of philosophy, and the history of philosophy is in every one of its steps and stations the expression and self-consciousness of the universe. The one universe is *also* the living movement to formulate and express itself, and the metaphysical endeavor is the reflective remembering what we are in reality. The last insight to develop in experience, the idea of the whole, is also the first in "dignity and power." The search for reality is carried by love, the goal of love is also the ground of its being sought. We could not seek reality if we already knew what we are in search of. We seek what we have "forgotten"; philosophy is not wisdom but "love of wisdom," and "reminiscence."

THE UNIVERSE

The universe as a whole of reality is *idea*. It is One, unique, and incomparable. It is ungiven, it transcends all that is given to somebody, and it is immanent in all that is, as its unity and unconditional condition. Its uniqueness is such that all hypothetical forms and relations and comparisons are only "lines" drawn within and presupposing, but not defining it. The idea is radically distinguishing itself from all concepts used in natural or historical object sciences, which always unify their objects of empirical knowledge in comparison and in relations with one another.

Every individuality is unique. As such it is an analogy to the uniqueness of the idea, and has therefore repeatedly been thought as "microcosmos" reflecting the uniqueness of the "makrokosmos" in itself. But empirical individualities are not unique in the sense of being incomparable. They can be compared with others and can be logically apprehended as a convergence of forms and laws.

The idea is all-pervasive. It contains, posits, and cancels our efforts and our approaches towards its comprehension within itself. They are distinctions within its unity, and they are real distinctions. The universe distinguishes itself from itself but remains one and the same in and through its self-distinguishing activity. It is equally impossible to deny that there are such real distinctions, as it is to affirm them as final. Distinctions are real, there can be no valid "monism." The Absolute breaks down any attempts to stiffen experiential distinctions into absolute positions. There are no absolute positions because the universe alone is the whole of all functions and activities. On the other hand, reality is nothing apart from its own distinctions, and philosophy, therefore, is a knowledge of limitations, in which alone there is value and articulateness.

The organism is another analogy of the idea. It also is a systematic whole in which all parts are defined by their function in the whole, and the whole is defined as the totality of its functioning organs. But this too, like the individual, is an analogy only, because the universe has no environment, on which all organisms depend.

The universe is concrete. To think it requires concrete thinking. The universe is the only concrete reality, and philosophy the only corresponding concrete "science." Understanding and transcending ourselves within its being and life is a thinking of concrete reality inseparable from our fragmentary and transitory existence. Dialectical ontology is the foundation of dialectical anthropology.

Philosophical participation in the idea requires the recognition of abstractions as well as their reintegration in the whole of life. The philosophy of science, practice, art, and so on, always means considering an abstract, but as such, real distinction with reference to its contribution to the idea of the whole. The universe is the true measure of all partial and as such abstract truths. Philosophy, further, must recognize irrational aspects within each of the distinguished spheres,— irrational with reference to limited systems of rational orders. The most superficial or momentary level of experience is linked to the whole no less than a deeper and more concrete level.

PARTICIPATION

We return to our definition leaving out the "bracket." Philosophy is the reflection on the meaning of human existence in reality. The philosophizing subject is indissolubly linked with metaphysics. He participates in the idea and the idea participates in founding his existence.

The philosopher finds himself involved in various concerns and tensions, none of which he can choose or affirm as ultimate modes of existence and none of which he can avoid as unreal.

Man exists as organic an "piece" of nature. As such he is a victim of natural forces and their brutal contingency, subject to death, the dissolution of all natural organisms. And although he cannot extricate his existence from nature, he nevertheless rebels against being confined to it. This struggle for the freedom from his natural immediacy constitutes the natural world as a world of tensions for him. Overcoming his immediacy in his thinking natural laws and orders, he is elevated intellectually and becomes a scientist, but his inferred world of impersonal laws and mathematical equations is not the world in which he exists. His experiential construction is in tension with his existential living.

Man exists in a world of culture which he has brought about himself. If he turns away from nature to immerse himself in his own practical-moral concerns, he experiences his will as being limited by counterwills, by obstacles arising within himself and met externally in others. The practical world is a tensional world of struggles and cares.

Man exists as artist. He turns to the world as aesthetic spectacle condensed in artistic symbols. They would be empty if they did not mirror the tensions of the other dimensions.

Religious existence turns its attention to the transcending "beyond." This "beyond," however breaks into "this world" and thus creates the greatest of all tensions, expressed in the struggle between secular and religious metaphysics. The open and transparent symbols and myths, furthermore, in which man assures himself of the religious relation to God, are finite and incompatible and lose their religious value if faith abandons them. Thus they become signals of religious wars.

Philosophy is the battle to remember and to restore, the wholeness and harmony of existence as a harmony of conflicting tensional dimensions. The totality of human existence is the totality of tensions. As truly being, they are foundations of existence. The task of a philosophy of existence is to think the world as tension and the meaning of existence in such a world.

Truth and Reality

If you put a question to a person in the right way, he will give you a true answer of himself—but how could he do this unless there were a commitment (epi-steme) *and right reason already in him? . . . If knowledge becomes evident as follows we call it reminiscence: when a person having seen or heard or used any sense-impression and not only knows that but becomes aware inwardly* (ennoese) *of an entirely different Other, whose knowledge is not sensuous . . . then we judge justly that he recollects the meaning of what he has grasped in himself.*

—PLATO (*Phaidon*, 73)

Logic is the recognition (Wissenschaft) *of the absolute Idea, the concrete Whole in the abstract medium of thought. . . . It is the unison of universal Being, which is* in *itself what it is, with its being* for *itself in this individual subjective thinker, who knows this unison as the Truth.*

—HEGEL
(VIII, §19, XI, p. 54)

TRUTH

When philosophy began to ask for "criteria of truth," it assumed that truth is something which can be investigated, as if it were an empirical object of an empirical condition. This desperate opinion happened in the late Hellenistic-Stoic and Skeptical schools. To question truth misses the "point"—the "point" being that truth is prior to any conditions, which in its "light" are known to be relative and limited. Truth is unconditional or absolute and sovereign. All "criteria" presuppose it. They are criteria used in cultivating truth in experience, but not criteria of truth itself. They presuppose truth in the same sense in which the "truth-tables" of symbolic logic presuppose truth.

These "truth-tables" are elaborate descriptions of *saying* "yes" or "no," without consciousness of the metaphysical presupposition, that world-itself characterizes itself by the "fact" ("factum" from "facere" = deed) that I am free to affirm or deny truth; which original decision and function of my self precedes any "saying." Symbolic logic tends to confuse thinking with a formalism.

One of the "criteria" is supposed to be *consistency*. Judgments are said to be true when they are not incompatible among themselves. But this *logical* principle of identity and non-contradiction is *ontologically* founded in Being, which is eternally that which it is.[1] Applied to experience, however, consistency is merely a norm, which is more or less actualized. Theoretical systems (Ptolemaic astronomy) or practical beliefs (slavery) may be perfectly consistent, but nevertheless false; the empirical fulfillment is not identical with the formal norm. It is not impossible that we are all consistent fools.

To guarantee the truth of the premisses the *correspondence* criterion is invoked. Judgments are said to be true if they correspond to the given "object" *(adequatio rei et intellectus)*. But this assumes that empirical objects are known before they are known; or that they are known apart from any reactions, perspectives, purposes, in which they are envisaged; or that it is possible to compare the judgment with the object as it would be without being judged. This is a realistic dogmatism which is contradicted by the evermoving advance of empirical scientific investigations, which transform the alleged stable "object" into a constantly more intricate occasion of problems. Truth, in other words, is guaranteed neither by formal deduction, nor by empirical induction. The former is, in experience, a formal promise, the latter yields a probability within defined fields of research.

The third criterion, first developed by the second Platonic academy (Arkesilaos), supposed truth to be identical with *success* in handling phenomena. This is the pragmatic "criterion" of control and predictability. This is tantamount to a declaration of bankruptcy: Truth is abandoned in favor of practical efficiency, which does not say what anything really or truly is, but only how it affects me in my practical functions and expectations. The pragmatic criterion is the method to establish disappointment and despair as final.

To give up now, to declare that truth has failed because our "criteria" of truth have failed, to conclude that the quest of truth is a "chase

---

[1] Aristotle, *Metaphysics*, 1005 b.

after the rainbow" or a "tragic realm" (Santayana), is like blaming a man for not finding the black cat that was not in the black room. The black room in this instance, is the place of empirical sciences. Changing metaphors: To expect criteria of truth by fishing them from the troubled waters of empirical data is indeed beginning at the most unpromising end. Philosophy must always begin with beginning: "We seek the beginnings and the ultimate grounds." [2]

Truth is not only untouched by the failure of "criteria," but on the contrary, affirms itself in this very failure. The criteria are false. It is true that they are false. *Veritas index sui et falsi*—truth is the ground of itself as well as of its own opposite.

To ask for criteria of truth would be meaningful only if we assumed beforehand that we would find *true* criteria of truth. In other words, truth is assumed prior to *any* question; it is *a priori*. We could not question all truth-claims if truth were not unquestionably presupposed; just as we could not look empirically for an object, if we did not have a hunch that it existed. Truth, then, is a metaphysical presupposition of all knowledge without which there is meaning to no question.

Or, truth is *intended* by any judgment whatsoever, regardless of the problematic empirical contents or "objects" of the judgment. Every judgment means to state that reality is so and not otherwise. Every judgment intends a "yes" or a "no." The case of doubt, question, suspended judgment, is no exception because truth is also intended by empirical uncertainties and indecisions. "I do not know whether X is such or not," respects truth in its suspension of deciding for or against a "yes, it is so" or "no, it is not so." Truth is the intentional meaning of *all* judgments. It is universal and apodictic.

Truth, secondly, can not be separated from the fundamental *ontological* category, that of Being. Truth says that anything is that which it is, identical with itself and eternally so. Once true, always true, again regardless of the fleeting moment which has passed before I have caught it in my statement. *Ens et verum convertuntur*—one cannot state what truth is, without saying what Being is, and one cannot say what Being is without saying it truly; and there are no "criteria" for Being either.

Truth, thirdly, is inseparable from the *human* judgment. This has given rise to the psychologistic "criterion" of truth, which bases truth

---

on "intuitive evidence." But when I am asked to "tell the truth and nothing but the truth," I am asked to testify to the being of something which transcends my "evidence." "I am" is not true because my existence is evident to me, but because without my existence I would have no referent to which any evidence could refer. Being has not waited for my "intuitive evidence" in order to be. The "criterion" of truth as based on "intuitive evidence" is helpless against any relativistic criticism, which points out that what is evident to you may not be evident to me, or that I have no access to your evidence. Being is not merely my "object of knowledge." I together with my intended objects are encompassed and enclosed in Being.

In the judgment intending truth, Being itself appears, becomes conscious or aware of itself in us. The consciousness of truth is original, prior to any particular piece of information, whether scientific or empirical. Truth is our ontological consciousness; we are beings conscious of Being itself. This truth is as alive in the common man as in the scientist. In truth we originally "know" that we meet, in ourselves, and consequently in all other beings, that which is. We know ourselves as beings "addressed" by Being. And we intend to "respond" justly, fairly, impartially. We do not intend to miss the true otherness of the other which we meet. Our original knowledge: "I meet you" is one with, and inseparable, from the Being of this meeting. Being-conscious-of *(Bewusstsein)* is identical with our human sort of Being. There is no meaning to truth if it does not include the truthfulness of our judgment. The Oneness of truth and of Being immediately implies the manifold individuality, in which Being manifests itself and is met with. I have to be truthful in intending to "grasp" that which you are, and you have to be truthful in "getting" me. Negatively: no individual is what he is without the others which he meets. In making or having you as the "object" of my judgment, I am at the same time the "object" of your judgment. Truth is in this reciprocity of individuals meeting one another. The world in truth is the totality of reciprocal individual meetings. It is the unity of Being in the infinitely changing constellation of functioning individuals. The judgment is the ever renewed logical intention to apprehend myself and my own position and function together with you whom I am meeting in a universal unity and order, together with all others. Judging, I am in truth. Truth judges my being. Being reveals itself in my judging truly.

The relativistic argument against the absoluteness of truth points to the relative, limiting and changing natural, social and historical conditions of "truth." "Truth," it alleges, is *a priori* to us in our culture as water is *a priori* to a fish. This argument is either relative itself, in which case it has nothing to say concerning the absoluteness of truth, the possibility for which is left open; or it is true that all "truth" which is naturally or historically conditioned is not absolute— in which case the absoluteness of truth is that which makes possible, beyond all empirical probabilities, the insight, the true judgment that whatever is relative and conditioned is not absolute truth. The whole argument rests on the empiricistic premiss that reality is confined to that which is on exhibition.

CATEGORIES

Categories are the most universal formal modifications of truth. Negatively, they are those universals more general than which none can be thought. They are undefinable postulates necessary for the definition of any other concepts. Plato has shown that they mutually imply one another *(symploke)*. Hegel means the same thing when he says that every category is incomplete in itself. They are, according to him, self-defining. This expression must be understood in its most literal sense: They express and explicate the self. "The category . . . is the simple unity of Being as thinking actuality, or it is this that Being and self-consciousness are essentially the same . . . the category is the unity of I and Being." [3]

The history of philosophical logic is to a large extent the self-reflection and self-explication of the categories. Here we merely intend to point out the meaning of some categories as formal moments of truth, implied in the dialectical or self-distinguishing unity of thinking and Being.

Being, the supreme ontological category, is inseparable from the fundamental self-"experience" (Er-lebnis); whatever is said to be is correlative to the living center of "experiencing," for whom it is. The living and acting self which is conscious of, or which is in doubt about, an other, is, for us, the archetype of Being seen existentially or from "inside." In "I am," Being and the living consciousness of Being are one and the same act; knowing and being-as-knowing are the same. I am the same in the many and successive functions of myself. In that I distinguish myself from my own past and from my own anticipated future and nevertheless retain my identity in these objectified self-pres-

---

[3] The empirical, observable self of psychology is "the category in its negativity." Hegel. *Werke*, Stuttgart, 1937, II. 185 f, 268.

entations, I grasp in this philosophical self-reflection the category of historical *Substance*. Further, in knowing myself as responsible subject of all my functions I am as *Cause*. As choosing my existence in the choice of possibilities, in which I hope to realize my existence, I am the categorical ground of *Freedom* and *Teleology*. Since my functions and acts of decision are irreversible I grasp myself as *temporal;* time is the category of my existence as historical being, as *space* is the category of my being together with others in a structural contemporaneity.

In the experience of resistance and obstruction in myself as well as outside of myself, lies the spur to "apply" categories to experience in order to "rationalize" the irrational *Otherness* and *Difference* of experience. The category demands its own negation as counter-category. I am myself only in encountering my limitation in meeting the other self ("you") or the non-self ("it"). This attempt to see and cultivate truth in "external" or self-limiting experience becomes a scientific process, which is a "synthesis a priori," or dialectical unity of the *a priori* category and the counter-category ("anti-thesis"): "a posteriori or given content" which is that which I happen to meet or to be thrown against. This scientific process is the practical and therefore never quite successful attempt of a "stranger in this world" to make himself at home.

UNTRUTH

What, then, is untruth and falseness? When do I miss truth? How do I know when I am untrue to my intention to be truthful? In this question, we logically think that which is non-logical or irrational.

We lie when we judge that what is, is not; or when we judge that what is not, is. And we do this every time when we distort the absolute and individually determinate, qualitative order of Being by our arbitrary, subjective perspectives and our "practical" or "wishful thinking," when we "judge" to "suit ourselves." Experience is the seat of untruth. It is false to confuse the ontological "so and not otherwise" with empirical opinions correlated to questionable appearances. There are, however, such dubitable opinions. Falseness must be thought truly, the antithesis, the "non-being" of truth also *is*.

We know that in the changing circumstances of experience, more often than not, we do not know what is going on, as we do not know the cards that are going to be played. After a time the truth of the situation will become apparent, the cards will be played, but in the meantime we fumble around in experiential ignorance. And if we do not use caution and suspend judgments, or entertain tentative guesses ("hypotheses"), we shall make false assertations.

If, on the other hand, we ignore our experiential limitation, if we proclaim experience in abstract isolation to be the fountain of truth, we establish untruth. *Dogmatic empiricism is the declaration of untruth.* It is the great metaphysical lie and self-deception.

Truth gains existence in individuals; judgment is the clearance in Being and the dignity of man. But individual judgments are severely limited, and the experiences met with are never predictable.

I am what I am in and for myself. At the same time I can not be what I am without the other, the partner, the you, to whom I am obliged in truth to do justice. Varying distances in space and time, varying emotional and practical interests, functions, reactions, varying scientific approaches and specialistic perspectives, limit my ability to see the other as he really is. And the same holds for the other. On the one hand I cannot "get out of my skin"; on the other hand I ought to cultivate truth and diminish my "dispositions," my bias and my prejudice, if I want to be true to both myself and the other.

In abstract laboratory conditions, where I can artificially determine some of the factors determining the conditional, selected appearance of the other, I can achieve objectivity, but only at the expense of the ever new and ever changing individuality of events which I meet in life. There I can not determine beforehand what I shall meet and what our mutual reactions will be. In Being, ontologically, we do not determine the unique and individual qualities of our partners, and they do not determine or predict ours. All of which sums up to the ontological truth that the many beings *(onta)* can not see each other in truth and Being *(on)*. Truth is empirically veiled and half-hidden. The Greek word for "truth," *aletheia,* means the lifting of this veil. The absolute truth of Being is not met with in that which is over against me *(Gegenstand),* because it is incomplete without me, as I am incomplete without it.

Truth as the absolute ground of all conscious beings, and of being-conscious, transcends each and every judgment in that we know all of empirical judgments to be relative, tentative; they are not grounded in themselves; they depend on that which is met with. Truth is discovered in the overcoming of the untruth, the illusion, the inevitable error and uncertainty implied in my meeting you. There is no truth "behind" or "beyond" or "apart from" the contingencies of experiential meetings. Truth and Being must be cultivated in the attempts to over-come the errors of all our experiencing processes and nowhere else. The logical task, therefore, consists in *cultivating truth in experience* in spite of all the barriers and difficulties involved in such a pursuit; negatively, this logical culture consists in the *fight against our experiential ignorance;* we ought to diminish our psychological-private per-spectives and "subjective" predispositions.

We now turn to this affirmation of truth in a perennially dubitable experience. The absoluteness and sovereignty of Truth is the ground presupposing which we are skeptically aware of the relativity and groundlessness of experience. Truth, therefore, is the eternal well of an infinite process of investigation and distrust in empirical fixations and pseudo-absolutes.

THE AFFIRMATION OF TRUTH IN EXPERIENCE

The original awareness of truth omnipresent and absolute is a pure *a priori* or philosophical knowledge. Quite different is the scientific, empirical knowledge, which investigates that which is perceptually given. This datum is never true or false, it is that about which truth is to be established; it is perennially doubtful or problematic. Not dubitable is the truth that I am aware of dubitable empirical contents.

Judgments alone, not "things," are true or false; but as indeterminate or "infinite judgments" (Kant) they are questions making that which is questioned, questionable ("*n.* valued logic"). The affirmation of truth and/or the negation of untruth with reference to a given X is the *logical quality* intended but never wholly accomplished in the scien-tific process (probabilities). We now analyze this scientific process as such, i.e., as logicians we are not interested in determining the object —that is what the sciences are trying to do—but we are interested in the logical structure of the process.

Scientific judgments are experiences logically formulated in com-municable propositions. Their logical subject (X) is that about which something is said to be true; but it is, as perceptually given always contingent, irrational, *a posteriori;* this prevents any final logical fixa-tion. The logical predicate is that which is said to be true of the subject (A). "S is P" therefore becomes "X A."

This "X A" (the scientific process) *IS*. In words: there is a never quite successful struggle for truth, a dialectical unity of the irrational X and the rational A. For example: The existential judgment, "This is a rose," apprehends the given this-here-now ("met with"), something, "this" (X) to be a member of the general class "rose" (A). In "These red roses form a part of this garden," the "red roses" are the X and "part of the garden," the A of this further judgment. Likewise, the garden is part of the landscape, the landscape a part of the land . . . until finally we find the red rose included in a cosmological system of planetary systems in star-clusters. In the opposite direction of "intensive analysis" we may think the rose broken up into smaller units and dissolved into its atomic structures.

In this example both directions of extension and intension take place only within one particular system of reference, which is the psychophysical material world. But, a rose may also serve as a token of love in a practical process of sympathies and moral values; or we may take it as a symbol of beauty in aesthetics; or we may take it out of all experiential contexts and think it in the light of faith as celestial rose, or as a religious ikon.

On all levels of the scientific process of affirming truth in a problematic experience there is always the same "X A is." The something given, the X in the existential judgment, is enriched and enlarged by its first "A" and then becomes, together with this "A," the new X of the next judgment. This concatenation of judgments form systems of reasoning called the sciences. In any "X A is," there are always the same three movements: that there is something given (X); that there is a predicate (A), which ought to be affirmed to be true or false of the given; and that this process *is*.

The internal agreement of two or more sets of information among themselves is the immanent coherence criterion of experiential "applications" of truth. The immanent criterion of applied truth suggests *the probability* that the judgment also agrees with that which is given. If two sets of information, derived from different sources agree among themselves, then it is probable that the judgment agrees with its intended and transcendent object; "in assuming hypothetically for each given case *that* proposition which I judge to be the strongest, I posit that which seems to agree with it, as being in truth." (Plato, *Phaidon*, 100A.) The immanent correspondence criterion, on the other hand, is the reminder that the transcendent object "out there" is an always contingent, questionable event, which keeps the process forever unfinished and open.

The Being of the scientific process itself is an ontological truth; it is the appearance of the category in the world. The world is characterizing itself by being uncertain about itself but seeking certainty. This certainty is reached in self-knowledge. It is indubitably the case that doubts concerning my own "other" exist and are enacted in the scientific process. The sciences, consequently, may be evaluated as to their closeness to the original truth of self-knowledge.

Farthest removed from it are the exact physical sciences. Their "other" is an externally given data, the physical X. The mathematical method of exactly imagining their relative positions, motions, velocities, intensive and extensive magnitudes, leads to *mechanics,* measuring strains and stresses, pushes and pulls; to *chemistry,* measuring qualitative processes of change. Theoretical physics uses mathematical equations formulating statistically mass-behavior, mass-fluctuations and energy-transformations. In none of those sciences is there a meeting with a "you" resembling the process itself. This, the genuine category, is absent; Croce's *Logic,* therefore, calls physicalistic concepts "pseudoconcepts."

Sciences, dealing with organized or living "matter," on the second level, are dealing with a "you" which is at least analogous to the life of reason.

In history, on the third level of knowledge, the process investigated and the process investigating are the same sort of process: thought struggling and actualized.

The fourth level, philosophical logic, the category comprehended is identical with the category comprehending. *That* there is logic and *what* logic is, the existence and essence of logic, is the *that* and *what* of logic itself, which understands itself together with its alienations. Logic is self-reflection, it is dialectical self-knowledge.

Before we take up the logic of ascending rationality towards self-comprehension, we return once more to the scientific object—thinking in its relational aspect.

RELATION

We return to the formula "S is P." The copula "is" formally signifies four kinds of relations between the subject and predicate terms of the judgment. Its categorical meaning is: I am relating myself to my functions; or, there is communication with myself and with others; or, Life is universal interaction. The copula "is" here must not be identified with the ontological "is" in the formula "X A is." What makes the distinction difficult is this, that the ontological and the relational meaning of "is" are always co-present; judgment as process *is,* and it is always internally related.

1) The first meaning of the "link" (copula), is known as categorical relation or the relation of inherence ("in," "of"). The predicate here expresses the function of the individual, it is the qualitative expression of the subject. "I am writing," "I am a writer," expresses what I am by what I do. Example of a chain of nontemporal inherences of our concept in others: "If this is a dog, then it is a mammal, then an animal, then an organization of life, then finite or mortal."

2) Secondly, the relation may be an "and"; "I and you are friends, enemies, colleagues, married," etc., are relations of reciprocity or symmetrical relations.

3) The third meaning of relation is that of ground and consequence ("if-then"). The subject here is the condition without which the predicate is not possible. It is also called hypothetical implication. The subject (that of which something is said to be true), is the antecedent; the predicate (that which is said to be true of something) is the consequent. They are ususally expressed in whole propositions. They must not be confused with the grammatical subject and predicate words in sentences.

The relation of ground and consequent turns into a causal relation, if the consequent follows the antecedent in time. "If-then" turns into "when-then." "If and when there is a killing frost at the time when peaches bloom, then there will be no peaches in summer."

4) The disjunctive ("either-or") or conjunctive relation ("both-and"), think a systematic whole in such a way that if one of its members or functions are known, the other members or functions are required to complete it.

All those logical relations are fully treated in logic books. Here we stress their metaphysical meaning. The category "relation" is the universal and formal expression of the truth that actions, reactions, and interactions are functions of the subject—whether the subject is myself or an analogy of myself in external experience; or, nothing happens without a "cause"; or, all individual "monads" in all their functions enact and constantly renew together an irreversible and necessary order.

MEDIATION

We recapitulate: Truth is known unquestionably, indubitably. It is never a problem. What is always a problem is experience. The judgment, subjecting experience to the "ought" of truth, tries to cultivate truth against the resistance of "subjective" psychological prejudices. The affirmation of truth in experience is one with negation of experiential untruth, error, illusion. In this ideal task and "infinite judgment" I am guided by my own category of order or relation. I am more or less successful in cultivating truth in experience. This "more or less" is not meant in a quantitative or mathematical sense, but in the sense of what is traditionally called "modality." The modality of the judgment is usually classified in three levels, that of recording factual meetings (assertoric), that of possibilities which may or may not be verified (problematic), and that of necessary truth, the denial of which is impossible (apodictic).

This classification of modal values of the whole judgment describes a process ascending from experience to absolute reality-as-a-whole. We call it mediation. Plato calls it *Eros*. In studying it we see that the lever of this ascent is negation. Negation is the dialectical method of distinguishing these levels (the one is *not* the other); thus they become articulate as self-distinctions of the whole.

Negation as the negation of empirical untruth leads to progressive levels of the affirmation of logical truth. As we progressively overcome our empirical limitations we gradually ascend from "lower" to "higher" logical organizations of life. Negation distinguishes different levels of generality in the "subject" (X) of judgments, and thus prevents the universe from being a closed system. Stages of a living reality make their own self-distinctions articulate in man. Truth is approximated through negations in ascending logical organizations of life.

This existential self-knowledge should not be confused with any psychological introspection. Judgments function scientifically, if the X to be apprehended is a perceptually given something. Among such appearing data, grasped by science, are also mental processes constructed as objects of psychology. Introscendent logic is not concerned with psychological object-inferences. Temporal and private stimulus-response processes of thinking and learning in organisms is not introscendent logic, which thinks the logical structures of the judgment itself as symbolic expression of the existential subject of knowledge.

To empiricism negation is not important. There are no "negative qualities" in experience. A quality which is "negative" in the sense of morally or emotionally undesirable to me, is still, logically speaking, that "positive" quality which is what it is and not something else. The absence of an empirical quality does not give any clue to the presence of a positive one; one quality merely replaces another quality. But in saying "negation is *not* important in experience," empiricism has made use of a negative judgment which is not empirical, and therefore, stated as true for all experience. This is not an inductive generalization, but a "bracketing" (to use Husserl's term) of experience as ultimate point of orientation.

DIFFERENCE AND ANALOGY

The negative singular judgment ("I am not you; this thing is not that other thing"), declares that this individual here and now is unique, that it is different from every other this-here-now. The individual refuses to be expressed by that which it has in common with others. Negation as difference expresses the negative character of pure experience.[4] If one individual is negatively related to another individual then this singular mutual exclusion in its universal form is the judgment of difference, i.e., everything is different from everything. There are no two things alike or equal (mathematically) or the same (logically identical). It is Plato's *héteron hetérou:* everything is the other of another. Everything is irrational. No science knows why I am sitting here now.

Existentially this judgment expresses that we are alone in this world. Solitary, the knowing subject, being-conscious, faces his uniqueness. The individual negative judgment of difference is the logical expression of our individuation. That inevitability of being alone is the existential barrier which nothing can destroy except annihilation of the subject itself. Related to all other things by such impassibility, the subject records in this its very own negativity. It grasps this negativity in the anxiety of "nothing," dreading certain annihilation if left to itself, discovering its groundlessness in its unique isolation. The logical demand that we must think of all events as different, expresses at the same time the existential truth that we live and die alone. The negative singular judgment in its universal form states our existential-ontological situa-

---

4 Compare William James's *Radical Empiricism.*

tion; the category "difference" is true both for all "things" and for myself.

But if I emphasize my difference from you and you emphasize your difference from me we both think one and the same thought. In thinking this *same* thought, that we are different, we are *not* different. We are identical in being *not* different in our thinking that we are different. Difference is also indifference: your difference is indifferent to me, my difference is indifferent to you. To posit everything else as indifferent to me because everything else is different from me is universally recip- rocal; and this reciprocity establishes the irrational world-process as one in which all differences devour and replace each other indifferently. What we build up will be torn down.

This indifferent difference is also the comedy of error. When Epicurus said that the sun had the size of his thumbnail he identified his error with his empirical standpoint. The individual in his uniqueness must see the things far away from him as small and unimportant. Shifting, arbitrary, endlessly differing standpoints are taken as points of orienta- tion. Internally, the final phase of self-estrangement of the self as radically different from all others and from himself is insanity (schizo- phrenic, schizo-thymic, etc.).

The feeling of lack, anxiety, dread, which is grounded in the dis- covery that I am alone and running towards death, leads to the desire to "do something about it." This logical deed results in *compromise:* Everyone is different, *but* the other differs from complete difference, it is *partly* like the one, it is analogous. The judgment of analogy is the logic of compromise philosophies. It insists that everything is different, but that in some respects and nevertheless, these differences can be compromised. They are *not only* different *but also* partly identical. In some respects they remain different, but in some other respects their difference is partly not different. "The barber's chair is analogous to the dentist's chair."

The thinking in analogy is the logic of magic and superstition, astrol- ogy and other "occult sciences." Ghosts slithering around the grave- yards are partly identical with persons we know.[5]

Hedonism offers a good example of this logic of compromise in prac- tice. The good is my individual pleasure, and the general good is to be gained as the compromise of similar pleasures. The differences are

---

[5] Plato. *Phaidon,* 83.

not really overcome, but there is an analogy of unity built on the fundamental retention of the initial position. In some "respects" egotistic pleasures are compared as alike or similar, and the good of the whole is supposed to result from this prudent calculation; in other respects they retain nevertheless their difference or egotistic pleasure.

In the history of philosophy Anaximenes was the first compromise philosopher, compromising the "water" of Thales with the *apeiron* of Anaximander in his "air," which, on the one hand, was a different element like "water," on the other hand, was "infinite" like the *apeiron*.

THE ABSTRACTION OF ESSENCES AND THE ESSENCE OF ABSTRACTION

I cannot maintain my difference against all others who do the same. But the suffering implied in this contradiction may be the beginning of a higher level of logical organization of life. I may disregard differences and abstract from them that which they have in common. Regarding abstract essence as essential and empirical differences as unessential I have reached the level of abstract essence; it is that which is known as "object" in sciences.

The general abstract essence answers the question, What kind or what sort of thing is this? This essential "thing-in-general" is what individual difference is *not*. Two white balls, for example, are *not* logically identical, they are not the same but different. But the color-class "white" which they have in common is the same general essence "white." It is not possible to arrive at the general essence without opposing it to the individual differences which are regarded as unessential. The identity of a general essence implies the non-identity of individual difference, and the difference of individuals negatively implies the identity of their general essence.

The abstract essence is logically as real as its non-essential opposite. Logically real is that without which no true knowledge is possible. Nominalistic, psychologistic, or empiricistic "logic" denies the logical reality of general essences, because, as Locke for example says, I can not imagine a picture of a triangle in general. He would be right if logical forms were derivable from mental pictures or processes. But all mental processes as well as physical percepts, or words, belong to the logical category of difference. Any two drawn, seen, perceptually given, triangles are different; but the definition of triangle is the same for all empirically different triangles. One may choose to stay within that empirical factual realm of experience if one wants to. But even then one constantly uses general essences, as if they were logically real. Any denial of the logical reality of general essence practices, in this negation, the very essential distinction which it tries to eliminate.

The essence of abstractions is to abstract essences. Rationalism understands that abstract thinking and general essences are correlative. Essences are as evident to abstract thinking as this-here-now color is evident to my now seeing it. But rationalism wrongly concludes that reality is a product of this logical consciousness. It does not understand the seriousness of the negation, which makes it impossible to identify the identity of logical classes with the non-identity of irrational individual differences. They have to be met with in experience. Dialectic thinks the non-logical differences logically; it is the unity of identity and non-identity (difference).

Abstraction overcomes the mere difference of position and opposition by introducing instead the distinction of what is essential and what is unessential. Some essential types are selected as belonging together by virtue of a common quality or a common tendency. This abstract type is considered as their "essence"; individual differences are discarded as not essential. Selected general characteristics of an individual or of a group are preferred to the non-general this-here-now occurring event. Every abstract essential type is determinate, and as such is distinguishable from infinite, undetermined individual differences. Descriptive sciences, such as botany, zoology, sociology, psychological typology, practice this level of logic. Degrees of more or less generality lead to abstract classifications in a double form: 1) In *coordinating* types, one type is opposed to others. All abstract coordinations, therefore, are "some" judgments. "Some S is P" is logically equivalent to "some S is not P." That some people are intelligent also means that some people are unintelligent; logically it is the same abstraction. 2) in *subordinating* less general to more general types, what is essential on one level of abstraction becomes unessential on a more general level.

In general: What is considered as essential in the process of abstraction is correlative to, or depends on, the degree of generality envisaged, and on the cognitive purpose or perspective guiding my abstraction. Thus, for ecological purposes a whale and a fish can be *classed* together while for zoological purposes they are *not* in the same class (species).

All abstraction is negative in that it prohibits individual differences to be considered essential. The abstract class "dog" is *not* this individual dog barking here. The word "all" may occur in such essential abstractions without thereby having transgressed the abstract "some." That all bodies fall within a specific gravitational "field," is a typical essential abstraction which selects a certain group of phenomena and observes it with regard to common and general characteristics.

Abstraction of essential types is the method of all descriptive sciences. If we continue this process in the direction of generalization we disregard essential types derived from, and illustrated in, empirical differences. Thus we arrive at "explanatory" sciences which work with very general classes, such as chemical elements, or atomic structures. Their constant relations are general "laws." They are extracted in order to handle the behavior of "masses." That you can work with a law, that you can predict the mass-effects which you expect, is the proof of the correctness of your abstraction. If an "unusual" instance occurs doing what the law prohibits, then the law must either be reformulated or the law must be admitted *not* to be of the same order as the empirical occurrences from which it is abstracted.

The most abstract of all "explanatory" sciences is mathematics. It has discarded *all* empirical content as unessential and has kept only the pure and universal forms of perception (Kant's *Anschauung*); possible relations of points and moments and their configurations are symbolized by geometrical figures and arithmetical series of "units" of measurement. And since spacetime is the framework of all perceptions or condition of all sensuous appearances, mathematics is the universal and inexhaustible foundation for the abstract measurement or statistical calculation of all physical phenomena. Its equations are comparisons of quantitative "more or less" of changes, motions, intensities. The logic of mathematics is not a "mathematical logic" but says what mathematics *is* and is thus the reflective non-mathematical self-knowledge of mathematics. This is probably the most hotly contested problem of contemporary philosophy; the relation of logic to mathematics would require a lengthy discussion by itself.

What the abstract intellect has thus sundered in its classes cannot be made whole again. We have overcome the position-opposition situation of individual differences, and we have received instead the negative dichotomies of one abstract class which is *not* the other class, or of one class which is not identical with the individual content whose class it is. The individual in its difference does not actually become a general class which therefore is prevented from becoming a concrete and organic universal. It remains a particular itself. Abstract essences remain external to the individual and historical life of reality. This is the negation essential to the concrete scientific process which abstracts generality as essential from (irrational) difference as unessential. Abstractions, because they negate individual difference, remain conditioned by what they deny. They remain negatively related to that which they try to eliminate.

Sociological, economic, and political "systems" present this particular negation in action. General rules, group-conventions, and habits, rule within a certain selected group. This group thereby is opposed and distinguished from other such groups. The individual must submit itself to these "systems," must adjust its "color" to the social, political, and economic "law" of its group. It requires subordination of individual services to group demands. Such partial "rational systems" are abstract and artificial, but they behave as if they were universal and actual solutions of the initial problem of individual difference. They base life on the "in" or "out" of group-solidarities and thus enhance and express conflicts between organized groups.

CONTRAST OF CONCRETE UNIVERSALS

The process of abstraction is a concrete struggle of an existing subject, oscillating between two poles of orientation. On the one hand "abstractions from" are regarded as nominalistic fictions; on the other hand, immediacies are regarded as unessential, as cases of general laws which are essential; on the one hand the existing subjects strive towards clarity, consistency, logical determination; on the other hand the individual and irrational events are remembered as making this goal unattainable. This mutual cancellation of these opposite orientations, establishes the processes as a never-ending, concrete struggle and phase of life. As such it is and makes, history. But this historical process of sciences is not the only historical process and struggle. There are other equally concrete historical struggles for goals or ideals, which are equally problematic in that they do not or only partly achieve what they want to achieve. Such processes are concrete universals which contrast themselves to other equally important concrete universals or whole spheres of activity.

The logical formula for this contrast is: "No S is P." This universal negative judgment declares that both terms of opposed concrete universals are "distributed," i.e., you learn something about each and every member of both classes thus exclusively opposed. We have, then, a total contrast of universals, in which each distinguishes itself from the other, limits itself against the other and knows itself through this self-limitation. Each knows itself by knowing that it is not the other. There is not merely the immediate otherness of another, as in difference, the immediate singular negation; nor the partial otherness of a general abstraction from its singular and external illustration; but in this total negation the relation and unity of the judgment contrasts itself with its own other: "No S is P," is equivalent to "No P is S."

It is a unity of unity and self-distinction, and a self-distinction of contrasting wholes within unity. Contrast is the whole judgment and at the same time one of its own members; and unity is the whole contrast and at the same time one of its contrasted spheres.

Contrast thinks historical life as a whole of such concrete universals. Each sphere as realm completely actualizes its essence in the individual, and the individual finds in the realm of its activity the ideal essence or norm of its existence. The individual which is merely a contingent illustration on the level of abstraction now becomes the concrete representative of a concrete development of natural, scientific, moral, or aesthetic life. Contrast is the logic of the historical battle for truth in all those spheres.

We contrast morality as the sphere of practical responsibility from beauty as the sphere of ideal appearance; or the sphere of political power contentions from the sphere of scientific objectivity. We characterize each by contrast to the other. We know them by what they are not, and we find their values in their self-limitations. At the same time each is seen to embrace by virtue of its universal exclusiveness all the others in its own perspective. Reality is the possible occasion of aesthetic representation, or may be the object of scientific description and analysis, or may be the material of my duty.

As established by total negation these essential and concrete dimensions of history are thought logically, and the logic of universal negations is seen as self-modification or self-expression of reality as history. Each realm demands and posits the other in the universal contrasting negation; each is self-determined and determines each other; all together they are the "circles" and basic disciplines of philosophy, practiced and enacted in historical cultures.

This total unity of the contrasts is not artificially split into its own contrasted opposites: We are not *either* businessmen *or* artists; we are both. We distinguish and contrast the spheres of business and art in our historical existence. We are the negative ground of all contrasted opposites. We move through them and demand knowledge of their limitations for a wholeness of historical culture. This is self-knowledge which transcends the knowledge of any one pursuit and is just to other equally essential pursuits.

History as a whole is not what each of its self-distinctions is, and all of these contrasting wholes are not it, but neither are they outside or apart from it.

But the subject may not understand these necessary contrasts and is free to assert the law of his life at the expense of the rest. He may thus establish a fight in which each partner ascribes right, true, good and beautiful to himself and wrong, false, and ugly to his opponent. Contrasts thus develop into a process of contradiction.

CONTRADICTION AND PROCESS

Difference develops into abstraction, abstraction into self-contrasting contraries. If any phase of this process isolates itself it develops contradictions in developing itself. We now reflect on this principle of contradiction.

Empiricism says that the subject knows *nothing but* experience. This is a dialectical contradiction, because it limits the subject's experience by that which it does not know and that which lies outside of its experience. In order to overcome this limitation, knowledge tries to move the limit. It expands this movement in an infinite task, based on the contradiction between that which has been achieved in relation to the unachieved. The process cannot be halted and cannot rest on a past achievement. This living contradiction between the achieved and the unachieved is the principle of the self-movement of thought. No finite position can be hardened into an absolute one. The judgment "A is not non A" (the subject is not the Non-subject or object) expresses this tension. The object is to be "subjected," is to be apprehended by the subject and organized in logical form. In contrast, each side is left independent in itself, whereas contradiction demands the extinction or the non-being of that which resists.

If we could not declare a judgment to be false, we could not know a truth either. An untruth is not merely a factual error, a naive ignorance or misinformation, but it is an error, a finite position or achievement, set up and claimed as truth. The "non-being" of the untrue is demanded by truth, the contradiction of the negative necessarily belongs to the universe of truth. And this truth, then, defines itself as the overcoming, the negation of that negation which threatens it. Truth is a dialectical movement. And life, as this dialectical movement is the power to produce, to encompass and to stand its own negatives; it is the Heraclitean "war, father of all things." Dialectic is the logic of philosophy, because it expresses this dialectic of movement in the universality of its logical forms. Philosophy is the self-knowledge of this life of reason, "giving account" (Plato's *logon didonai*) of itself.

Existentially, beyond theoretical error, contradiction is known and felt as the core of life and of movement. It is the pain of existence, the lack and disappointment of life. As such, it spurs to action, to the overcoming and removing of obstacles. Life is life only as long as it is able to hold together the contradiction in a powerful struggle. In all privations finite differences and obstreperous contradictions assert themselves against the law or harmony, unity, and perfection. Physical deficiency, psychological forgetfulness, economic poverty and social discrimination; wrong action within the sphere of law are examples of privation.

In the biological organic world, death and life belong together as contradictions. They are not contrasts because they are not independent spheres, but are moments within becoming. They are logically conditioning the non-being of each other.

In the world of morality, the logic of contradiction is everyday practice: virtue is not only externally compared or contrasted to vice, but consists in fighting it. Good as the absence of evil is fighting its own corruption and annihilation. Virtue is noughting vice. And evil, as the absence of good, is not merely a fact to lay hands upon, but *is* only as *actively destroying values* that ought to be. Vice is not only privation, but the active contention of a negation as positive. Every passion is contradictory, lives on overcoming the absence and non-being of its own opposite, joy and sorrow, hope and fear depend essentially on their own destruction which they victoriously overcome. The decrease of pain is the increase of pleasure, and the decrease of pleasure the increase of pain.

REALITY AND THE CONTRADICTION OF CONTRADICTIONS

Being is logically prior to any particular experience. This logical priority of Being is truth unquestionable. Implicit in truth are those logical levels and polarities the denial of which involves absurdity: Everything is something and not nothing; is that which it is and not something else; is related; is different; is typified, classified, generalized; belongs to essential spheres totally contrasted to contrary spheres; is involved in the struggle of contradictions. Contradiction, the logical dissatisfaction with any phase or position of the whole process, in so far as they are fixed and isolated by an abstract intellect, is the spur of the whole movement, and the *continuity* of this logical movement depends, on the other hand, on the *discreteness* or fixation of its "steps."

Reality is the ultimate category of all philosophical logic. The contradiction of contradiction is the self-affirmative life of the absolute whole, present in what is radically other and finite and contradictory to it. The logical formula of reality is the paradox: A *is* Non-A. The Absolute preserves its wholeness in its own negations.

Thinking demands unity as non-contradiction, it excludes and opposes incoherence. But as exclusion of contents which are opposed to its postulate of coherence it posits itself as a contradiction. It contradicts contradiction. The principle of non-contradiction is, then, in itself what it denies. In contradicting contradiction, negation is posited as essential in reality. Or again: Being as non-contradictory unity excludes thinking from itself, because thinking always distinguishes form and content, one and other, etc. But Being, on the other hand, cannot be found except as thought, as logical identity. It cannot be found in experience or as a thing. Being, hence, necessarily is, and is not, unity, is and is not distinction. It is the movement of overcoming the opposite of itself within itself. It negates its own negation, and as such it is positive or self-affirmative Reality.

Reality conjoins all disjunctions, which are its own self-distinctions. It is the unity of all opposites, the *coincidentia oppositorum* (Nicolaus Cusanus).

All errors and illusions, faults and failures, are inevitable because we are finite creatures. All experiential knowledge is tainted with subjective perspectives, private differences, stubborn fixations, conventional formalism, skeptical despair, blinding passions, existential negativity. But all this finite negativity also IS. And this means that reality is not merely Being and Truth, but also "non-being" and untruth. Being posits its own negation within itself. Reality as a whole is this dialectical "synthesis" of one and other, infinite and finite, eternal and temporal, unity and difference, unproblematic truth and problematic experience.[6]

Reality both posits, cancels and eternally preserves and renews finite negativity within its unbroken wholeness. The negations characterizing our finite dialectic are not nothing, but are "living mirrors"[7] of the absolute dialectic of Reality itself. Life as suffering is willed and shared by the absolute, which has given itself to its own finite self-alienation, but which it nevertheless eternally transcends.

SPECULATIVE FALLACIES

Since dialectic is the logic of philosophy, any violation of its principle results in speculative fallacies or dogmatic "isms" which all have been pseudo-absolutizations of any one of its aspects, phases or levels.

If the transcendent and *a priori* unity of truth and Being is isolated and absolutized, then the temporal world of experience and of Becoming is theoretically nothing but illusion and error, practically the radical evil. This is the fallacy of a dualistic absolutism, the metaphysics of a torn and unhappy consciousness. The world-ground is isolated, given a pseudo-independence "beyond" reality, as if the ground of the world would mean anything apart from the experiential world whose absolute ground it is. The unity of reality transcends all and any finite experiences, true, but transcendence is not a "thing-in-itself," apart from the experiences whose transcendent unity it is.

If, on the other hand, the absoluteness of truth and Being are denied, then we have experiential relativism or metaphysical *empiricism* as expression of a logical desperation (despair of having no truth). Since in finite experience everything indeed is perspectivistic, relative and subjective (relative to experiencing centers), reality itself is supposed to be such. This fictionalism always contradicts and annihilates itself. If all finite experiences are relative and uncertain, nothing at all can be concluded from this with reference to reality itself, since reality is not any of those momentary experiences. A consistent relativism, therefore, will end in a skepticism whose whole effort is bent on exorcising the remembrance of that bothersome reality; neither positive nor negative references to it are allowed. The moment of negation is fixed and absolutized.

Thirdly, if the different dialectically necessary "poles" and "levels" of reality are tyrannically reduced to one of them, in terms of which all the others are to be comprised or from which they are to be derived, we have the fallacy of *monism,* or substantialism.

If, on the contrary, the Interplay of Opposites is disrupted into many incompatible and contradictory "pieces" or "fragments," we have a false metaphysical *pluralism*. Reality then is thought to be like a jig-saw puzzle, the fragments of which are mixed from different sets, so that all the ingenuity and patience of the jig-saw puzzler will never find a whole picture. The problem of philosophy, then, remains forever a "world-riddle."

TRUTH AND REALITY

If, finally, the whole of reality is believed to be in the grasp of philosophy, as if philosophy were in a position to pronounce an "asbolute" scheme or providential plan of experience, a final and closed "system," then we have a false absolutization of experience; an illicit generalization from a known part to an unknown whole; an uncritical deduction with unexamined premises and confusion of contingent experiences with necessary Being; or a confusion of problematic scientific object-research and philosophical self-reflection, an "absolute idealism" or providentialism (the philosopher has sat in on God's council table). This is the speculative arrogance of *philosophism*.

SUMMARY

Logic is our self-reflection on truth; as category, truth is the presence of Unity and Being in man, it is our ontological consciousness; guided by truth, logic leads to critical self-knowledge in scientific experience, in historical existence and in reality-as-a-whole (the Absolute), which is the unity of the rational-ontological unity and the irrational-experiential differences; the many disciplines and levels of philosophy, mediated by negations (opposites, polarities), are unified in this self-differentiating process of self-realization; dialectic is the logic of philosophy, positing as well as transcending the various types and levels of special "logics" within itself; the eternal paradox of the Absolute in all our relativities is reflected in it.

6 "Mirror" in Latin is *speculum*, hence "speculation," "speculative philosophy." "Living mirror of the universe" is an expression of Leibniz.

Being and Becoming

We are seeking the principles and the causes of the things that are, and obviously of them qua *being. For, while there is a cause of health and of good condition, and the objects of mathematics have first principles and elements and causes, and in general every science which is ratiocinative or at all involves reasoning deals with causes and principles more or less precise, all these sciences mark off some particular being—some genus, and inquire into this, but not into being simply nor* qua *being, nor do they offer any discussion of the essence of the things of which they treat; but starting from the essence—some making it plain to the senses, others assuming it as a hypothesis—they then demonstrate, more or less cogently, the essential attributes of the genus with which they deal. It is obvious, therefore, that such an induction yields no demonstration of substance . . .*

(Aristotle, *Metaphysics*, 1025b.)

Becoming is interpreted by various regional sciences. The exact sciences, physics and chemistry, interpret the universal ontological becoming within the limited sphere of physical appearance by changeless mathematical equations. In such an equation of quantities of physical magnitudes, one side always balances the other. And the balancing of the equations in one field with the equations in another field is interpreted as the invariance of natural law in all fields. Numbers may be divided or multiplied, they may change their serial positions, but the sum total of the whole equation "conserves" the same quantity of energy. In this manner both mechanical and energy-physics construct changes as a change of positions of unchanging particles in a continuous

[1] With permission of *The Journal of the Philosophy of Science.* Cf. Paul Haeberlin, *Naturphilosophische Betrachtungen II,* Zurich, 1940.

but divisible space and in a continuous but divisible time. Chemistry constructs qualitative change as a change of unchanging elements in finite systems so that the sum total of the elements involved in such transactions is always completely accounted for.

On the other hand, the invariance of mathematical laws, the constants of energy-quanta and the constant of the "velocity of light" are opposite to the variance, inconstancy, and change, of all empirical appearing events. There are no unchanging atoms, and no unchanging chemical elements. Both the physical atom and the chemical element, thought immutable before, are now seen to disintegrate, to radiate, to change their character according to their position in the "field" of gravitation or of energy in which they occur.

Biological sciences, similarly, in the rationalistic seventeenth and eighteenth century perfected useful and universally applicable system of classifications, inherited from Aristotle's Logic and the Scholastic "substantial forms." When this system of classified types of organisms was thought to be about perfect, Becoming entered it and left it in shambles. Species evolve and many are not stable. There are sudden mutations and gradual transitions between them which make it doubtful where a species begins and where it ends. Not even the main divisions of organic and inorganic, or of plant and animal life could be maintained. The vivid "explosive" reaction of elements when contacting each other seemed at least as vital as the dull behavior of unicellular organisms. In the tropics trees were found which actually marched across the country by sending out branches which took root while the old tree gradually disappeared; there were sensitive plants which shrunk back when touched; and others again that devoured insects, although movement, sensitivity, alimentation, were supposed to distinguish animals from plants. On the other hand there were immovable parasitical animals that resembled more a sucking fungus than a "normal" animal. Gradual changes of forms in response to new conditions or sudden mutations or "sports" within the main divisions of organic life destroyed the confidence in the constancy of species even where they had seemed well defined before.

While the biological sciences gave up the constancy of forms but clung to evolution as genetic continuity, historical sciences in the meantime learned to see a serial evolution of forms, similar in structure and function, without a genetic continuity, as you might, on the other hand, find a continuity without finding similar forms of organization. There were gods, for example, who were born, functioned, and died in history, and who could be ordered in a series of evolutionary steps of similarity, without engendering each other in the least; and there were, on the other hand, peoples of the same blood, which produced opposite symbols.

The situation in all those regional sciences seems to contain contradictions, hence problems. The various and sundry images of becoming, evolved by various and sundry sciences, would contradict each other if any one of these interpretations should claim that it is the true image of becoming itself. But none of the sciences can make this claim, because none of them can apply its scheme of interpretation to the field of the others. They are all "provincial." Hence, Becoming in sciences is contradictory if it is not interpreted ontologically.

The *physical* image of becoming as a circular rotation of equated quantities, or as equality of cause and effect, is incompatible with the *biological* image of becoming as an evolution of new forms which are never identical with the previous ones; and the *historical* image of becoming breaks with the genetic continuity which is to explain the similarity of dissimilar forms in biology.

The sundry object-images of becoming are further influenced by practical evaluations and desires. Optimists confuse evolution with progress, while pessimists see evolution as dissipation of energy, as a machine disintegrating and running down;[2] the second law of thermodynamics spells a scientific Dooms-Day. The emergence of man in the evolution of biological species is likewise evaluated either as an apex and a triumph of natural progress from "lower" to "higher," or as a degradation of human values to a sub-animal level. These practical world-views color the problem, which must be analyzed without regard for this complication. The problem is ontological and has its truth regardless of whether we like it or not. The logical analysis of empirical sciences is to clear the way to the ontological dialectic of being/becoming.

THE PROBLEMS

The shock many physicists felt in this century, when their constant world-mechanism threatened to become fluid is similar to the shock many botanists and zoologists registered, when evolution inundated their neat classifications. In either case Becoming was a scandal to a neatly perfected scientific system. Rational systems turned out to be statistical

---

[2] Henry Adams, *The Degredation of the Democratic Dogma.* Brooks Adams, *The Law of Civilization and Decay,* Alfred A. Knopf, New York, 1943.

computations, limited border-cases within a wider and more complex situation; reliable rules turned out to be nothing but methods of controlling sense-data, but ceased to be, or to reveal, the nature of all things.

Historical sciences began at the same time to understand natural sciences as phases in historical evolution. Seen historically these systems were emergents. They characterized the Western civilization at a certain level of its development. And in the historical evolution of human-cultural life, sciences functioned and had their real existence side by side with other functions and other existents and they were impotent to foresee and to guide the future of this historical evolution of which they formed a part. They knew about general and abstract possibilities which they called laws, but these laws would help nothing when it came to guess the shape historical life would take tomorrow. Becoming again was an insult to reason, this time reason as practical intelligence and "control."

Practical men, who believed in the value of their moral systems of life, were dismayed to have these values explained as steps in the immense relativity of historical becoming. A good illustration is the opposition of the church against the discussion of the Bible as a relative and historical document and against the discovery of its gradual growth.

There were futile compromises, to save one part as constant while admitting the fluidity of the rest. Scientists, for example, tried to keep the constancy of laws while admitting the fluidity of content, or they distinguished between "resultants," which could be explained as products of known and stable elements, and "emergents" where the change was radical and new forms had to be admitted with a grudging "natural piety." (Lloyd Morgan) Similar compromises in history are the various "fundamentalisms" to preserve the essence of a belief and protect it from evolution; in art, for example, the classicists tried to exempt what they called classic art from the relativity of tastes.

But such half-way measures and compromises only prevent logical clarity. The radical character of the problem can be thought and faced only, when the all-pervasive universality of becoming is admitted. And it must be admitted as soon as it is clear that it pervades all regional experiences and leaves no empirical science untouched. But if Becoming is thus all-pervasive, then departmental regional images of it will be insufficient to think it as such. It is essential to all appearance; and this ontological essence must be thought in a logical category, i.e., a concept more general than which no other concept can be thought. In other words: to think Becoming is not a problem of empirical sciences.

A *problem* it is, if it is confronted with the logical principle that judgments must not be incompatible. This negative formulation of the principle of logic is better than the positive statement that all judgments must agree, because this latter formulation may lead to the misunderstanding that all judgments must form a factual and closed system, such as, for example, the "conservation of energy," and its derivative, "entropy," of factual and closed systems. Empirical or regional propositions of how evolution should be pictured, are not compatible, if they claim knowledge of reality. What they do know are abstract constructions of the sense data of "X" which appear on different abstract levels in selective logical perspectives. The universal or all-pervasive Becoming is never and nowhere experienced as such. It is an ontological category. The sense-materials are given to the experiencing mind. This being-given is a first selection made by the experiencing organism. Out of this first selection, further selections are cut out by abstraction, resulting in objects of experience. These so constructed models of objects are not thinkable without contradictions if they are identified with reality; the various object-images of empirical sciences cannot be pieced together to form a whole of evolution, let alone a whole of reality.

If we keep this phenomenal nature of object-thinking in mind, the logical problem of evolution boils down to this: if Becoming liquefies and blurs all empirical "constants," then the evolutionists must show how such empirical constants are logically possible. If everything is not only in flux, but is flux itself, then how are even relative or comparative constants possible? And if these should be declared to be illusions, then how is it possible that flux produces illusions which are its own negations? If there are no classes or constant species in nature, how then can one speak of their similarities or refer to transitions from the one to the other? If the static systems are abstractions, isolated from evolution, then how can such an abstraction be made from something which does not lend itself to it at all? And if the evolutionist tries to evade such contradictions by saying that there are no "real" constants, but only tendencies or directions within evolution, then such a constant tendency or direction introduces no less a contradiction, because it also limits evolution and logically prevents it from being all-pervasive. A directing or shaping factor in evolution, making for stability, is just that much and to that extent non-evolution, impeding the perfect fluidity and passage-character of all processes. And if the evolutionist finally seeks refuge in the environment whose constant pressure is now made responsible for the sameness and constancy of forms, then evolution is either cut in two, one-half reserved for the organic world, the other for the inorganic environment—a typical compromise— or the whole contradiction is pushed back to the environment. How can *it* be constant if everything is in flux? If, on the contrary, the maintenance of stable forms is imputed to the participating individuals and to inheritance, then a non-evolutionary check is admitted in the individual, which obstructs the limitless variability of becoming.

Evolution, in rendering all empirical constants problematic has become problematic in turn. The original distrust of abstract reason against evolution, from which this analysis started, is now clarified; evolution seems to contain three self-contradictions: If, A, the original form evolving, disappears in the emergent or evolved B, then it can hardly be said to have evolved since it is now non-existent. If, secondly, A contains B implicitly, virtually or potentially, then B is nothing new, but simply makes explicit in time, what was implicit there earlier; the beginning in that case is so far from being simple, that it contains the whole complexity of the world—but this absolute simplicity which is at the same time absolute complexity is beyond any sort of empirical verification. It is neither given nor evolved. If, thirdly, the whole world is that which evolves, then evolution is only a modification of one perennial substance, whose identity this kind of evolution must presuppose, in order to maintain a variation of it or in it. Variation makes sense only if there is a constancy of the substance whose variation it is.

However the problem of evolution is stated, there is always a contradiction which seems to make a reduction of Being to Becoming impossible. There is always a constancy, and the more radically Becoming is formulated, the more inevitable is also the presence of non-evolution. The logical analysis of becoming, then, results in the dialectical necessity to think both being and becoming together.

We have tried to clarify an empirical situation as formulated in various sciences. The contradictions found lead to the problem of how to think Being compatible with Becoming. This problem is not empirical, but ontological, because it is presupposed by all levels of empirical sciences and their objects. The ontological question is: how can Becoming, be? How can Being be, if evolution is?

THE ONTOLOGICAL UNITY OF BEING AND BECOMING

Everything changes, evolves, becomes. But every changing, evolving, becoming process also IS. If everything changes, then this is eternally true. The truth of change is its changeless being. The self-identity of Being is reflected in the logical identity of truth: once true always true. True being is absolutely identical with itself and is in no manner disrupted by becoming. On the contrary, only if we have a radical and thorough-going becoming, from which no empirical constant is exempt, do we also have as its correlative truth the absolute being of all change. True being is the universal coherence, consistency, relatedness, of all events at all levels of experience. It is never a particular or regional law, which only formulates as an abstract, ideal possibility what has been found to occur regularly together in the past or in part. The unbroken ontological continuity of being joins by one tie all empirical factual changes and the diverse forms of inorganic, organic, and human evolutions. And since it is the absolute presupposition of all events whatsoever, it is neither an event itself nor does it happen or emerge in experience. If we think it, as we think it right now, we merely make explicit that this thinking-event-now also is, and in so doing we make further explicit the eternal truth of all and any events: that they change, evolve, become.

To deny being as absolute world-ground of all experiences is impossible because the denial would neither be itself nor refer to being; it could only "be" or "refer" to "Nothing" as the ontological negation of being. The denial cannot escape this absolute either/or by referring to some experience, because experience as becoming event is, as we have shown, logically unthinkable without reference to that which is, and if an experience is thought to be something and not nothing it is also a being identical with itself. Experiences are in truth only because it is true that they always change. Universal change is truly and not only experientially, because experientially there are many things that appear static. Experientially we experience only relative changes in comparison with relative constancies. It is this impure or compromise character of experience that obscures the dialectical unity of being and becoming.

Perhaps this will be more evident if we try to catch being outside and apart from change; we may do that only by denying that Becoming truly is. We would have to declare becoming to be an illusion, non-being, or error. But if we judge becoming to be non-being, illusion, or error, we obviously refer to something and not to nothing. And this negative something is as such what it is, namely illusion, non-being, error. Being, then, contains its own opposite within itself. Being is also non-being, or non-being truly is. Becoming is ontologically founded.

The attempt to save Being from Becoming is to declare it to be wholly other and uncontaminated by becoming. But this separation is, as Plato has shown, a relation. You have thought a one and another, and you have thought them inseparably related by this negative relation by which you try to keep them divorced. They form a dialectical synthesis, in which either side would be nothing without being a one of another. To separate being from becoming, is just as impossible as to deny that being is, or to deny that becoming is what it always is.

A third attempt to avoid ontology is to call on formal logic for aid and say that dialectic is itself a contradiction, that Being is only Being and Becoming only Becoming, and never the twain shall meet, or else they shall be caught by the principle of identity. But dialectic has no quarrel with the principle of identity. The principle of identity says that things are as they are, but it does not say that they shall never form a dialectical union of opposites. Eternal being manifests itself through its own temporal evolution. To quote Plato again: Being is process, life and knowledge.[3]

Pseudo-metaphysics or scientism destroys the value of particularized scientific experience, by absolutizing it. Since the absolutization of any empirical object-construction is untrue, pseudo-metaphysics always signalizes a potential state of alarm, a fear to be found out, sitting in the untruth that Becoming can be looked at in isolation from yourself. Involved in a turmoil you cannot look at it unaffected. The true character of becoming can be known only in reflecting on how I participate in it. Becoming is not experientially given but existentially lived.

My becoming in the world is an active/reactive struggle. My senses are highly evolved, selective organs which do not copy what is, but which reply to what affects me. They are filters which leave to me only what I am able to absorb and cope with. My becoming is an active reply to my participation in situations which are of functional or becoming significance to me. My touch is a contact-response, as my sight is a distancing response, and what is touched and seen exists for me only as it is my living-world. And I change myself and become a different one according to the ever new active relations I find myself involved in.

But the other individual processes to which I react are active-reactive

---

[3] Against the false but popular conception of the Platonic Idea as static object and as separate from becoming. Cf. Mueller, *What Plato Thinks,* Open Court, 1937, Ch. VI, on "Dialectical Idealism." Jowett's mistranslation, particularly his frequent use of the term "absolute" where Plato never uses it, is an important source of this misconception.

with reference to me as well. My presenting myself to others is at the same time a self-modification co-determined by the others in action/reaction to me. Every change is thus co-determined by all participants, and since all participants are, in turn, linked with still other such circles of reactive agents, it follows that every individual becomes in a universal interaction of all individuated processes. Nothing happens in isolation, or more precisely, there is no isolation in becoming, since isolation is itself a relative reaction in connection and with reference to others. It further follows that there is no safe and isolable position from which becoming could be viewed objectively. It is impossible to formulate a scientifically acceptable and valid interpretation of what happens. Existential becoming is never unambiguous. This is in strict contrast to the logical idea of inference. Logically, if A implies B, and B implies C, then A also implies C. But in existential becoming, A affects B in a different way than B affects C, and this again does not imply anything how C may affect A. In comparison with the neat postulates of formal logic Becoming is radically "irrational." Plato calls it the sphere of the "other of the other."

Becoming is always actual. I exist as active-reactive newcomer in the present. I become in having to react to new situations now. These new situations are never predictable, but they always demand decision. I have to react to them either so or so. A decision taken is irreversible. No step can be retraced. What is so called is in the reality of becoming a new step and a new decision. Becoming, therefore, is the place of responsibility and is "big with consequences," quoting Leibniz's expression.

Every step creates the condition from which a new decision can be made. Becoming is thus not arbitrary, but determined by its own decisions. But this is so only in retrospect. The past creates the conditions for the new decisions, but the new decisions must be made by all individual participants. If the past could condition the future, the future would be predictable. But the new decisions cancel the past condition by restating a new one. Here too the true character of becoming can be seen in contrast to the logical relation of antecedent and consequent. In logic the consequent never destroys the logical antecedent, while in evolution the appearance of the son is identical with the disappearance of the father, a new decision or existential turn cancels the previous one. Further, what has become is eliminated as possibility; it can never recur, and it can never be preserved as actuality. But since the past is also the condition of the present the past is constantly reformulated by the present. The past, or what has become, lives on in the actual shapes and constellations that have grown on it, taking it as necessary condition and starting point.

Becoming thus is a dense continuity of individual and contingent decisions of life. It is always unforeseeable or surprising in its existential individuation. In becoming I never know the future, because I can neither make up my own mind what I shall do in new situations, nor can I know what my partners will do. In addition to this real contingency is the contingency of knowledge, the weakness of the spectator, who is surprised for the simple reason that he can never know all the factors even in a most familiar or intimate relation. Out of this double contingency are born rationalistic dreams to control becoming and outsmart its unpredictability. Many people incline to overlook the existential character of becoming in favor of a simplified image which promises control or predictability. They cling to formal logic as an instrument of object-thinking. They externalize becoming in abstracting types and orders of relatedness. Or they dream morally of a providence, of a world-plan, whose final realization is either "just around the next corner," or immutably revealed in tradition. To distance becoming, to objectify it, is always the first step away from its actuality, and from responsibility.

But if Becoming is the destruction of all "absolute" constants in experience, and if nothing empirical is exempt from change, and if change is the individualized reactive process of existence, then Becoming would destroy, so it seems, all valid knowledge and all ethical judgments. No two people can ever be right or wrong, none can deny what another affirms. We stand at the Heraclitean river into which no one can step twice, because there is no one river to step into.

But we "remember" at this juncture that it is Being which becomes. The more radically you formulate Becoming, the clearer it passes into its opposite, which is Being. The universal relativity of all processes with reference to each other is but another expression for the truth that nothing is in isolation, or that being manifests its unity through the whole of Becoming. If Becoming destroys all pseudo-absolutes or "absolute" empirical constants, what else is this but the affirmation of the one absolute and omnipresent Being whose eternal order is present in the whole of temporal evolution. If it is true that becoming is irreversible, then a true order is thought which is a true order forever, a being order. If our value judgments are necessarily faulty, what else does this say but that the perfection of being is not a task to be brought about. It is not in my grasp, because the perfection of Being is always and indestructibly manifest through the existential and struggling blindness of individual standpoints. Being is the truth of Becoming. To deny this would be to maintain that nothing becomes.

Our problem was to think being/becoming, constancy/change, together. This problem is dialectically solved. They are not merely compatible, there is not merely a compromise; they are dialectically one and the same unity of opposites. Being becomes; Becoming is.

We now return to the theories of experience, from which we started, in order to see what happens to them when they are understood ontologically.

PHENOMENALISM, MECHANISM, AND FINALISM

Empirical sciences look at becoming as if it were given to different impartial observers. They handle, measure, and order object-images. They agree to select them according to certain levels of abstraction, so that one science always leaves out what appears essential to another science. We now compare them with ontology. Their compatibility with ontology is the measure of their truth.

A first level of interpretation is the standpoint of pure phenomenalism. It abstracts from laws as well as from purposes. It sees becoming as succession of images which happen to be experienced. There is no unity in them and there is no reason why we should get just this sequence of images in our experience and not just as well another selection of them. Experience resembles a camera which takes at random whatever happens to cross the lens, and the film shown is a sequence of snapshots with no other connection than the fact of sequence itself. Anything, in this conception, is a series of attributes in succession, as the wax in my hand is now hard and then soft, now square and then round. Becoming, experientially looked at or merely noticed, would indeed appear in some such fashion. Its change is a "passive" change; simply happens to it, not that it changes itself. There is no subject of the change because a subject can never be perceived, since it is doing the perceiving. This Becoming, similar to Aristotle's formless and shifting "matter," is criticized when we understand that it is an abstraction from an experiencing subject which is left out and forgotten, and secondly, an abstraction from forms of order, of relatedness pointing in the direction of being. But change without the one for whom it is change or whose change it is, is unthinkable, a pure contradiction or nothing at all. But as a real illusion or error it is understandable. Its ontological truth, shining through its error, would lie in the recognition of the non-logical individualized event-character of all real processes.

A second level of interpretation is guided by the practical interest and purpose of control and prediction of change. This standpoint of mechanism abstracts both from the irrational helter-skelter appearance of impressions as well as from purposes. The mechanist is unaware of his own guiding purpose. He acts surprised when his scientific hypotheses turn out to have practical applications. Changes can be controlled when they can be repeated. To get patterns of repetition we must disregard the real and individual event and keep to general similarities. Mechanical science, consequently, selects those changes where individuality can be safely disregarded. It studies primitive societies, called physical, whose behavior looks as if it were always the same. At least one can calculate it; it is practically useful. On this level cause always equals effect. The causal relation can be described in exact equations. But what is practically useful and empirically correct may still be false ontologically. The mechanical system is a static abstraction in a moving, historial universe. It does not describe change, but only the traces, the mathematical curves which simple changes leave. Its abstract and regional character becomes evident, when the mechanist tries to apply it to biological or historical evolution. The mechanist is right when he sees the causal relatedness of change, but he is wrong when he misinterprets this causal relatedness of all interacting individual events as a law, which prescribes invariably what must happen. The recent indeterminism principle in physics has recognized this old ontological truth. Mechanical determinism disregards both the unique individuality of all evolving beings and their decisive participation in becoming. Causality only works backwards. After something has happened then we can ask for its real conditions, without which it could not have happened. As long as we deal with simple individualities, or rather, with individualities which look simple to us, we may treat them practically as if they could not surprise us. They do surprise us, though; every time a machine breaks down, the universal inter-activity of all things has played havoc without selected quasi-stable system. The ontological truth of a mechanical world-view lies in its conception of being as unity of all changes, the symbol for which is the "constancy of all energy." The absolute constancy and omnipresence of Being shines through this formulation. The mechanist thinks Being through the symbol of his object-image. Being is the ever-present unity in all becoming processes; it is in all appearances; it is the subject in all modifications of the world.

Biological and historical sciences use ends or purposes in their interpretation of observed or given becoming. *Finalism* abstracts from the irrational event character as well as from mechanical repetition. Cells and organs cooperate in order to serve the idea of the organism as a whole; animal and human individuals cooperate in order to preserve and further the ends of their societies. This level of interpretation is rooted in the practice of the artisan, who gives shape to an idea, which is preconceived and directs his operations. The idea is the organizing unity of a series of operational functions designed to produce a visible whole, which fits the end which it was destined to serve. The end of house building is to live better, the end of road building is to communicate better. There are purposes in becoming, but can becoming be thought to be purposive? Can we understand becoming as it is, when we impute to it a universal and providential plan or design?

Existentially, purposes are directed responses or replies, whereby the individual tries to master or adapt itself to a friendly or hostile situation, which it has not chosen. The direction of the individual is conditioned. Cells and organs may or may not cooperate to further the well-being of the whole organism. The organic finalism is as imperfect as the finalism of individuals in a social whole. But even if we disregard the conditioned and imperfect character of ends, the decisive argument against a universal finalism lies in the uncertainty one purpose has with reference to other purposes. The stronger and clearer a purpose may seem to an active individual, he nevertheless will never know how his partners will react. He may rest assured, though, that the final result of the interaction of many cross-purposes never corresponds to his particular desire. The situation as a whole, the constellation of Becoming, is always different from the purposes whose actualization has brought the whole constellation about. The shapes of becoming, brought about by the cooperation of all individuals, is always different from the purpose of each. But since all becoming is individuated and individuated processes fail to see their own ends realized, there is no evidence anywhere to attribute purposiveness to Becoming. Becoming has purposes, but is itself beyond purpose. My contribution to becoming can not be said to be purposive for becoming as a whole. Universal teleologism is meaningless. The teleological idea is not a model according to which things should evolve, because each phase of evolution realizes its own individual decisions in complete ignorance of any universal purpose of the whole. But if we call the structure or shape of becoming its purposive meaning, which transcends any teleological or antiteleological consideration, then we must say that all purposes are meaningful, in that they help to establish the meaning of evolution, which we already know to be the self-manifestation of being. This perfection of being can never be an aim or an end to be realized, to be planned or to be brought about, because being is at all times perfectly present. It is present in spite of, or through, all purposiveness of individuals who are in functional contact with each other. A prearranged teleological order, which evolution would have to carry out, would deprive evolution of its own responsible decisions, and would degrade former ages to mere means of later ones. In practice, a finalistic interpretation of becoming always amounts to a subjectivistic and selfish perspective, which arranges the importance of things according to the interest or value they have for me in my own time.

The truth of finalism against mechanism is, that finalism acknowledges the individualized character of becoming, hence its character of irrevocable decision, hence the irreversibility of its direction; while the ontological truth of mechanism versus finalism is the emphasis on the blind nature of the environment, which is without idea for the individual. The environment may obstruct and thwart, but it cannot create.

It follows that evolved wholes may be externally described in their structure regardless of the individual aims of its participant members; and secondly, that teleological judgments about evolved or evolving wholes, transgress the limits of such individual judgments. They do not grasp or express the meaning of evolving wholes although they may be accurate expressions indicating the bias of the individual who misjudges.

LEVELS

Phenomenalism, mechanism, finalism, are different methods of interpretation; they are cognitive and human answers to Becoming as experienced. If they are critical, they know that. A critical phenomenalism knows that it talks about the irregular succession of object images, whereas if it is uncritical it talks about Becoming as chaos. But becoming is never chaos, but always the eternal order of being whose unity it presents in everchanging modification and in its irreversible direction. If mechanism is critical it knows that it constructs object-images of Becoming by selecting repeatable patterns. These patterns are, critically understood, ideal and general possibilities of appearing behavior. If mechanism is not critical, and if it projects a method of human control into nature, then it says the world is a machine. If finalism is critical, then it knows that it selects understandable individual processes. If it is uncritical it confuses becoming with an absolute providence.

These three logical or formal levels of understanding are intersecting three material levels of experience, the inorganic, the organic, and the historical. We started out by showing that the experiential classification of these three levels are flowing and blurred, because the outstanding characteristics of one division of life can also be shown to function in the others. Ontologically these levels are self-determinations of universal life and must be made visible as such.

The inorganic world is not a dead and inert matter, but it is in becoming. It is composed of functioning centers or living individuals. They are in universal interaction and consequently change their behavior according to the environing "fields." It might be more fitting to speak of their dancing patterns, wherein they form loose or compact, enduring or fugitive, constellations. Since the life habits of these functional monads seem to be steady and uniform, and since their individual differences are so minute, they may be disregarded for our practical purposes; they may be mechanically treated as if they were exactly alike. But they can not be thought to be dead. Dead would mean something without functional qualities, without resistance, something absolutely isolated. Such a thing would not only be dead but nothing. But what inorganic life lacks is an organizing idea. Its many monads may react similarly and uniformly together, but they do not react as a whole. This is their mass character. That is why they may be divided without offering resistance. They may be compared to unorganized workers in contrast to unionized ones.

The inorganic world is the same universal and individualized life, but not collected into biological wholes, which we call organisms. The transitions from inorganic to organized life would be miraculous if the inorganic world were dead. But inorganic individuals are at any time able to enter an organizing form, as the organized life is constantly dropping its component individuals back into the inorganic life of their own. Every organism, then, is an organized society with a tendency towards a definite form. The organism is able to react as if it were a whole, in order to preserve its particular plan or organization and to defend this its character against dangers from within and from without.

This tendency towards unity and wholeness, that differentiates the organism from the inorganic life, is at the same time a tendency towards constancy of form. The forms are transmitted while their actual carriers disintegrate. This seems to indicate that the organism must be understood as imperfect imitation of being. It is certainly false to derive the organism from a cosmic super-organism; the universe is not only organic, it is inorganic as well. The organic is only in dialectical relation to its opposite, the inorganic. Only in struggle with it can it maintain itself. Being, on the other hand, has its own dialectical opposite in becoming. The universe is not a superorganism, because Being has no environment against which it has to maintain itself. Just as "inorganic" must not be confused with "dead," so the organism must not be thought as an organic cell in a superorganism, which would take the place of Being. The organism is only an imitation of being, in that it tries to bring about a unity and constancy of form, in which being begins to become transparent. The organic form is a conditional and conditioned unity pointing towards the unconditional totality of being. Being is thus both transcendent and immanent in evolution. It is, as Aristotle aptly puts it, the unmoved mover. Plato means the same thing when he says that the organism unsuccessfully tries to be immortal by reproducing its form or idea.

This Platonic idea is the key which discloses the correlation of the organism and the social whole. The organism is a society of individual functions, cooperating more or less perfectly to realize the idea of wholeness and indivisibility in this particular state. This correlation has led to uncritical transgressions, treating states biologically, or antheaps, sociologically.

If we think organisms in Becoming, we see life directed by an organizing idea. The biological form of this modification of becoming is the sexual or non-sexual reproduction of individual organisms. Individuals disappear and disintegrate, while they at the same time transmit their organizing idea to their progeny. The offspring in turn, usually or normally endeavors to reproduce the same organizing idea, but never without individual variation, which may lead to a gradual change of the organizing plan or even to radical mutations. Seen from the point of view of the idea, love is the agreement and ability of organisms to unite and reproduce their kind. The organisms thus serve this idea; they "engender in beauty," as Plato puts it. Seen from the point of view of the organism, love uses the individual organism for ends beyond its own interest in self-preservation. The organism actually does not live on in its progeny. The actual ancestors are never conserved and remembered, because every new variation of life insists on its own individuals and unique newness. What lives on is the idea, symbol of being and unity, continually varied and modified in the dance of life.

Artistic intuition presents this fusion of idea and individual variation in the work of art; in the fine art it is the mutually elucidating synthesis of expressive surfaces, in music it is the moving melody and fugue of individual voices, which celebrate the dialectic of being/becoming in an intensive symbol.

Genetic evolution is only a special kind of becoming. In history the idea rises above the repetitious mechanism of genetic reproduction. Ideas of organization are advanced by individuals and instituted by social groups. We have described this place of man in dialectical reality. Man bursts the limitation of the surrounding environment, selected and defined by his vital-organic mode of existence. He becomes aware of the world, he becomes human in becoming philosopher. He becomes self-conscious, and conscious of nature as that aspect of being which is not conscious of itself. Ontology disloses the possibility of a philosophy of history.

We return finally to the optimistic/pessimistic world views which we found connected with evolution. The pessimist is like a man who looks at the carcass of a horse, in which maggots have a good time, and concludes from the sight that horses are no good at all. Pessimism is connected with materialism. It isolates and abstracts body or matter, and having done so, complains that reality is running low and is constantly disintegrating. But body is the experientially appearing embodiment of universal life and cannot be held in abstraction and isolation.

The optimist, on the other hand, believes that evolution is essentially and necessarily a progress towards higher values. In this contention we must distinguish whether it is a factual statement or an ontological principle. If it is meant as a factual statement, it must clearly formulate the value, which serves as standard to measure "high" or "low." Such values are relative to limited and specific ideas of life. Within such limitations it is quite possible to see that for certain stretches of evolution there is a progress in the sense of working out the idea of a system of law, or science, or a political constitution. But then such factual evolutions are at the same also factual devolutions. They cannot be separated from life. What begins to live begins to die at the same time. What lives forward also lives forward toward its funeral. Every empirical appearance is identical with its disappearance. And since the values selected are values for certain forms of life, the progress of life in one direction may well be the regress in another. A progressive culture of tubercular germs, for example, may well be the regress of a human organism. But, if on the other hand, progress is meant as an ontological principle it is certainly false, because it is impossible to state the value which would serve as a measure for universal life and its evolution and would at the same time include the purposes of all individuations. The organism is always and everywhere imperfect, whether it is a biological organism or a social organization of life, because it is open and conditioned by the inorganic environment and by other organisms in the struggle with which it maintains its idea in self-defense. The universal and omnipresent perfection of Being maintains itself through the everchanging constellation of individualized life. It can neither be a goal to be achieved by organic life, nor a measure of progress from any one point of view because it is eternally realized. The limitations of evolution are at the same time identical with the blessedness of Being. The limits of evolution are the means of a dialectical universe to have and secure at once infinite fullness of life and absolute unity.

The One and the Many

If I believe that someone is able to see what is organized in-wardly (eis) *into one and outwardly* (epi) *into many, him I would follow as in the footsteps of a deity. Whether I name those who are capable of doing this correctly or not, God knows, but I call them provisionally dialecticians.*

—PLATO
(*Phaidros,* 266 BC)

All the nervous tissue of the beehive is the nervous tissue of some single bee: how then does the beehive act in unison, and at that in a very variable, adapted, organized unison? Obviously the secret is in the intercommunication of its members.

—NORBERT WIENER
(*Cybernetics*)

How is the separation of many mutually independent individuals compatible with communication, communion, community? How can one individual select and interpret some gestures which he sees, or sounds which he hears as significant, meaningful directives for his own practice, if on the other hand these gestures and sounds are given to him only in a time sequence of external sense-impressions? How does the individual break the barrier of his individuation, be one and not one? How can many form one organization, which is also not one but many organizations at the same time?

The logical problem consists in the apparent impossibility to think the idea of a total situation, a unified whole of many individual centers or "cells" of life, without sacrificing the independent, distinct character of individuals; and to think the indivisible oneness of one individual together with an indefinite plurality of other individuals all cooperating in a common organism or community. What is the relation of the "one" to other "ones," and of the many "ones" to the unity of all?

THE ONE AND THE MANY

Some empiricists assert that the old Platonic problem of the one and the many is no problem; that it is only a fictitious difficulty of language, while in experience everything is clear and simple. Individuals stipulate their meaning and other individuals understand what is stipulated and so they practically form a technical system of communication. The difficulty is merely verbal; one singular term cannot be itself and at the same time another singular term; what words disunite, practical experience unites, and empirical science describes and explains.

The most successful empirical science, practically or technically speaking, is the explanatory science of the apparent behavior of masses. Can physics explain the communication of the one and the many? If physics is to explain the problem of intercommunication of the one and the many, the solution will necessarily be stated in terms of mathematically constructed machines. But the mechanical aggregate of machine-parts is no *real-living* unity; it is only the *abstract-apparent* unity of a design external to its own parts; these parts are not individuals; they are visible embodiments of mathematical space-time units of measuring; they are alike, and therefore exchangeable; their position and function is prearranged by the mechanical design of the machine. But since in a mechanism neither many individuals nor real oneness exists, the problem has not been solved.

Norbert Wiener's *Cybernetics* is such a perfect statement of the appearing mechanism of communication, that the non-solution of the problem of communication by mathematical-physical methods could not be more obvious. I quote: "If the seventeenth and the early eighteenth centuries are the age of clocks, and the later eighteenth and the nineteenth centuries constitute the age of steam engines, the present age is the age of communication and control. . . . Actually, communication engineering can deal with currents of any size whatever, and the movement of engines powerful enough to swing massive gun turrets; what distinguishes it from power engineering is that its main interest is not economy of energy but the accurate reproduction of a signal. This signal may be the tap of a key, to be reproduced as the tap of the telegraph receiver at the other end; or it may be the sound transmitted and received through the telephone; or it may be the turn of a ship's wheel, received as the angular position of its rudder. . . . Finally the present automaton opens doors by means of photocells, or points guns to the place at which a radar beam picks up an airplane, or computes the solution of differential equations. . . . In such a theory we deal with automaton effectively coupled to the external world, not merely by their energy flow, their metabolism, but also by a flow of impressions, of incoming messages, and of the actions of outgoing messages. The organs by which impressions are received are the equivalents of the human and animal sense-organs. They comprise photostatic cells and other receptors of light, radar systems, receiving their own Hertzian waves; hydrogen-ion-potential recorders, which may be said to taste; thermometers, pressure gauges of various sorts, microphones and so on. . . . The machines of which we are now speaking already exist as thermostats, automatic gyro-compass ship-steering systems, self-propelled missiles—especially such as seek their target—anti-aircraft fire control systems, automatically controlled oil-cracking stills, ultra-rapid computing machines and the like. . . . Thus the modern automaton exists in the same sort of Bergsonian time as the living organism; and hence there is no reason in Bergson's considerations why the essential mode of functioning of the living organism should not be the same as that of the automaton of this type." (Pp. 50-1, 54-6.)

That man may be considered and treated as if he were a machine is an old story. He can be considered in this mathematical-mechanical fashion, when he is given in terms of sensations, or physically. Leibniz compared the brain with an industrial mill—but he added, that entering such a mill and describing its mechanisms would not contribute a thing to understanding this individual in its functioning and thinking. The inter "action" of various electric signals with various metallic gadgets does not constitute communication or message. This may seem so only if we use language ambiguously by meaning "message," once in the real sense of a living function which is important to my life, and once in the sense of the means of communication, by which such a message is transmitted; or by using "information" once in the sense that I have learned something new to me concerning you, and once again in the sense of an "input," "fed" to a machine. If the actual mental communication is confused with the means of such a communication, then communication is annihilated—a telegraphic system is not there to communicate itself, but my message to you. It is such an ambiguity and misuse of language to speak of mechanisms "seeking" their target. Energy-physics describes organs of communication, built by individual centers of life, which prehend one another in their interactions. Qualitatively distinct energy-centers form a continuum, constitute, or are constituted by, a whole situation, a "field"—we recognize in those highly abstract physical formulae of "packages" or "waves" our own original concrete situation of many in one, of one in communication with other individual ones. The scientific description, control, and the technical projections of such organs states externally what constitutes communication of the one and the many as a living actuality underlying all empirical accounts of physical object-thinking.

We now turn from this explanatory-rational to some descriptive sciences concerning organisms; they also do not solve but presuppose the problem. Darwin's biology, for example, explains the variation of species by the "pressure" of the environment and the survival of the "fittest," by which are meant those organisms which could adapt themselves to new environmental conditions. The expressions "fittest" and "survival" contain the whole question, which was to be answered by them. The organisms, apparently, had to interpret the environment. There had to be communication with another, fraught with all the adventurous risk and uncertainty of such guesses, adaptations. The species that did not survive paid for its error in communication, with its extinction. To interpret the environment as friendly, hostile, or indifferent, certain sounds and sights in it had to be selected as meaning something for the direction and possibility of survival of the individual organisms or of the species. There had to be reaction as reply to an action on the part of the surrounding world, the neighboring other. The hypothesis explains nothing but merely describes in general the situation; it presupposes both the independent and sundry organisms and the possibility of a common life and a common understanding of a total situation. And again, the usefulness of the hypothesis for the purpose of pointing out the organic adaptation of polar bears to polar conditions, its empirical correctness, does not alter its ontological blindness. The question remains: how can many differences, qualitatively sundered, act as if they were not sundered but on the contrary conjoined in one total unity of understanding and functional interpenetration?

Another descriptive science, psychology, divides the problem of intercommunication into a series of "stimuli" and "responses." You communicate with me. Translated into the language of physiological "psychology" this may be stated as follows: There is a stimulus, A, emanating soundwaves, B; these are hitting "my" eardrums, C; the vibration of the eardrums causes wavelets of a fluid in the ear, D; they in turn set in motion nerves, E; these in turn are transformed into chemical processes in the braincells, F; and as a final result I know what you mean, G. Now each of these objects in turn is in the same predicament as the object of origin A; they all must be transmitted by the same process as A. The original problem is multiplied indefinitely. But all that this serial and segmental multiplication of visible or audible objects establishes is the restatement of the same problem of the one and the many in each step: how can the many objects, each qualitatively distinct from the other, nevertheless form one continuous unity of communication? The original problem is repeated in every step; the perceivability of the "object" and its interpretation as having a life-value or meaning to me, already takes the solution of the whole problem for granted, presupposes it.

Let us sample psychology, defined this time not physiologically, but as the science of how to understand individual psychical functions. How do I know when I perceive and say "green" that you will perceive and mean the same color as I have in mind? If you are colorblind, we may seem to agree but, without knowing it, refer to entirely different acts of sensation. If you say I know that I mean the same color as you do, because you can show it to me, this is neither ascertaining that I have the correct impression, correct from your point of view, nor does this "showing" answer the question; a pointing gesture is a language no less than a verbal sign; in other words it presupposes what it wants to establish, namely that there is a communicated sameness, a one and same experience, altohugh there are two distinct individuals experiencing. Psychology assumes the possibility of communication and interpretation when it interprets and communicates its own findings to me; it assumes that there can be an identity of life, a oneness of life in all, although this is contradicted by the many individuals in whom life is exclusively organized. You never have experienced life in general; you can only live your own life.

This difficulty has driven some psychologists to the externality of behaviorism, which merely states the correspondence of a sequence of observations by a third observer—a bear comes trotting and somebody's legs begin to move fast—and that, says the behaviorist, is all we know about "fear," which, if true would fill our vocabulary with unnecessary words. Such a standpoint ultimately denies psychology altogether and reduces it to a mechanical physicalism, which is already criticized.

Teleological vitalists, finally, have tried to understand the unity of experiencing life by the principle of finality or purpose. But purpose is no over-soul determining individualities. A determination of individuals by common purposes would eliminate the problem no less than a mechanical causality. I can only say that my purpose feels as if it had become the principle of a common life. Many different individual purposes work out one common, purposive pattern of unity which is different from all purposes of individuals composing it. The ontological question remains untouched by the empirical fact that purposes may agree in peace or disagree in war. Empirical agreement or disagreement of purposes ontologically poses the same unity of a common situation individually shared by all participants.

We conclude: the problem of the one and the many is an all-pervasive, universal and therefore an ontological problem; empirical sciences are all regional, provincial, particular; the one and the many therefore is not a problem of physics, descriptive biology or psychology; the one and the many characterize Being in all its manifestations. The one and the many are presupposed by and appear in all kinds of experience; all empirical interpretations of facts and purposes are more or less correct or incorrect, more or less probable or improbable; the one and the many are present in those interpretations regardless of whether such interpretations are correct or incorrect empirically; empirical object-thinking presupposes ontology as the measure of its fragmentary, inadequate and tentative phenomenalism.

THE ONE

What do we mean when we say that something is? Objects given to sense-perception and subjects perceiving them, scientific propositions, moral imperatives and actions, works of art, errors, dreams, illusions, tragedies, and death, all are; they are something, not nothing. They all agree in being. They are one and the same, in being something and not nothing. Or to put it negatively: what we mean when we say "something is" cannot be answered by pointing to an experience, to something given to my perception and constructed by my object-thinking, because my perceiving and thinking *is* also. Being is prior to any bifurcation or multiplication of experiences. The many presuppose being as their unity. The problem of the one and many is insoluble as long as we ascribe to the many individual entities of experience separate being, if we postulate many beings and then ask how they can communicate or cohere. No sort of experience, no experiential realm is ontological; ontology is prior to all particular experiences or scientific theories; it is their one and common foundation.

We have used the ontological categories of being and unity in correlation, which means that it is impossible to state the one without the other. As ontological categories they are ultimate and universal, there are no concepts more inclusive by which they could be defined or thought. As correlative categories they define or support one another. Being is unity. Unity is. They interpenetrate. To say "something is," is equivalent to saying that it is determined by ontological oneness, by unity. Only when it is one and the same in all of its instances, and when it is identical with itself, can it be referred to, meant as being. Whatever is "belongs to" the universe, presupposes the one world, by virtue of which we can say that it is at all. Being is identical in all that is. There is no gap, discrepancy, disunity in being. Being is wholly and continuously one in all its manifestations. Negatively, something that would contradict this unity of being, something that would disrupt the identity of being, would not be at all, would be nothing. There is no such thing as "Nothing."

But the sophist never dies out. He cuts logic from ontologic. He says what is valid logically may not be true for the nature of being. He may admit that in formal logic the law of identity and noncontradiction operates, but, he holds, this does not mean that being itself must conform to the norms of this "purely human, formal instrument of handling experiences." This distrust directed against ontological thinking has its good right in experience. Skepticism is true when it says that experience may never be adequate. We have seen how this skepticism with reference to appearing experience is ontologically well founded. But to cut thinking from being, the medium of truth from truth itself, is like separating the expression of a poem from the poem itself. To say that being cannot be thought is saying that I know that there is such a being although I do not know it. Sophistic thinking points to a true standard, which is being, and at the same time says that it does not point to such a standard. The term ontology implies the inseparable unity of being and logic. Disrupting this unity merely succeeds in self-contradictions. You never find being in experience, you find it in unity, as identity, and you can know nothing of unity or identity unless you think. Parmenides is right when he says that thought and being are one and the same thing. Thought itself is. And as being it is identical with itself as well as identical with all being. Negatively, if you deny the presence of being in thought, you deny thought itself (as it is always right in experience), but thought digs down to the unity of being that lies beneath the bifurcations of experience in knowing subjects and known objects and this unity is its own certainty of being. Being is known as the one in all.

Another kind of sophistry is the relativistic, pragmatic one. Our philosophical systems of the universe are many and conflicting. They express the poetic mood, the artistic taste, the practical wishes, longings and desires of their human creators. Nowhere is the much vaunted unity of being on display. Reality is much too complex and baffling a concern for any one unified system adequately to express. All this is perfectly true as far as it goes. Philosophical systems are man-made and they do exhibit moods and tastes. Your philosophy is what your character is and your character embodies your philosophy. If you are inclined to gloom, melancholy, and distrust, your world-view may emphasize the sad and distressing features lending comfort to your pessimism; if you are cheerful, trusting, an energetic worker in the vineyard of your Lord, you may find much in your world that speaks of successful adaptation, you will find reality malleable to your will; if you are inclined to orderliness and neatness, you may prefer to stress the laws, types, classes, while on the contrary when you love loose ends and picturesque disorder your whole world may tramp around like an adventuring vagabond. But, as Plato remarks, such pragmatic-subjective universes are wares sold cheaply on the marketplace. Because they are practical and manufactured for needs, they are thereby ontologically irrelevant. They are contrasted with the unity of being as merely representing partial interests. The fact that you are not "at home" for ontology does not mean that you have "dropped out of the universe," or that you do not presuppose it as well as anything else that is something and not nothing. The indubitable dubitability of all pragmatic construction serves to make evident the silent dignity of the one being, which proves and maintains itself through and in the breakdown of all finite, partial, conflicting world views.

We summarize; this summary is based on the basic ontological research done by Plato and Aristotle:

I. The absolute oneness of Being is *evident* to philosophical vision or faith as the ontological ground of that faith.

II. The *ontological necessity* of the absolute oneness of Being is identical with its impossibility not to be or to be other than it is.

III. The *logical necessity* to think the absolute oneness of Being as world-ground is identical with the logical impossibility to think the absolute as Nothing or as being other than it is.

IV. The absolute oneness of Being is identical with its *rationality*. This rationality is the all pervasive universality of its ideal existence (*that* it is), and of its ideal essence (*what* it is). It communicates this rationality to all beings able to share this rationality in *theoria* or logical self-reflection.

V. Philosophical self-reflection logically thus justifies its vision (faith). This logical justification is identical with the self-assertion of reason as that universally open form of man, which can receive and formulate the rationality of the absolute as its (reason's) own "law" *(noesis noeseos)*.

THE MANY

That all being is One whole cannot be logically denied, but the Many exist, which literally means that they "step out" of the unity. How can the one being nevertheless be many? How is experience possible?

Ontological monism has always tended to deny the reality of individuation. For this standpoint individual differences are illusions. The temporality of all experiences and experiencings is illusion. A "past" is as ontologically real now as it ever was; and whatever will be in the future either will be or will not be at all. Our individual perspective from which we call something past or future with reference to us is illusory. But this monistic argument contains its own refutation, as Plato has proved in his "Parmenides," [1] for it assumes the reality of illusion, of false perspectives, of impermissible inflations of the ego. It further contains this contradiction that an individual thinker steps forth and denies in an individual statement that individuals are. He means to speak in behalf of the unity of being, but being itself does not come to pronounce itself one and indivisible. If you deny the ontological reality of individuation you have to take to the mystic path and remain silent. If you evaluate finite experience, the many, as unreal or illusory, you have posited what you deny. How would the absolute ontological unity ever be able to produce the illusion of

---

[1] Cf. Gustav Mueller, *What Plato Thinks*, Ch. 6, "Dialectical Idealism" (Open Court, 1937).

what it is not? If such an illusion exists, then individuals, the many, exist.

Ontological unity is always the unity of something, not of nothing. To unite means to connect, to bring together, to join, at least two different instances, which then stand logically connected. And identity means that something is identical with itself; identity is the logical form of unity of that one something whose identity it is. Unity implies many as its own content, identity implies difference; the one is itself and the other; one postulates the other.

Anything that is, is one *and* many, unity *and* difference, being *and* existing. Experience is ontologically justified, in that individuation of the One being is logically as undeniable as is the agreement of all beings in the One unison. But if empirical individuation is logically undeniable and ontologically necessary, then also error, illusions, practical conceit, and misunderstanding, are undeniable and necessary. Where an individual begins and where it ends is never certain in experience. The experiential many are fuzzy; they have overlapping fringes and unknown backgrounds and recesses, which make their appearance flicker and float. Empirical differentiation as well as empirical "unity" is arbitrary; it is what you take together and call a one. William James is an expert in describing this ontological character of experience: "reality may exist in distributive form, in the shape not of all but of a set of eaches, just as it seems to." (*Pluralistic Universe*, 129.) If you prove the many as necessary, then you also prove the existence of untruth as necessary. Untruth belongs to and characterizes being as experience. Errors are necessarily engulfing us in our individual perspectives.

THE ONTOLOGICAL UNITY OF OPPOSITES

Being, then, is one *and* many. This "and" is a clumsy linguistic expression for the dialectical unity of these opposites. Unity is nothing by itself. If you take unity apart and think it as if it were something by itself, you have isolated it, you think it as if it were an object over against you, as if it were one definite form among others, one of many forms. Unity is wholly and completely unity of the many, which are its differentiations or expressions. The universe is completely and wholly present in each and every one of its different manifestations and is nothing apart or outside or separate from them. *The One is the Many.* Unity remains itself in its own other, just as you remain yourself in your own past and present and future actions, just as you remain one and indivisible in your own many functions and conflicting interests. The many, likewise, are nothing in themselves. If you try to think the many apart from their being many "of" and "in" the one world, of which they are many manifestations, they vanish. For many individual differences unrelated, separated, can neither know nor act nor touch each other in any way. To assume many independent entities would make all communication impossible. The many would not be many of a one, but many as separate eaches; even this is saying too much, however, because separation still presupposes unity. You would end in absolutely and completely separated "ones." If you think many you think many together, you think them linked, aspects of a total situation. You can break down or analyse only what belongs together; you can synthesize only when you have differences; you distinguish or differentiate within a whole; you unite or unify different experiences or you unite nothing. Thinking presents or expresses being and therefore always identifies and distinguishes; both functions are inseparable aspects of one and the same thinking. Ontologically our solution of the problem of the one and the many consists in clarifying their dialectical unity as a unity of opposites in which each side is at the same time its own other. The one being is the many; the many existent individuals all are. Unity is in and through individuation; the individuated many-fold expresses what the one Being is. The unity of Being differentiates itself within itself but remains one and the same in its own self-differentiation.

CRITIQUE OF EXPERIENCE

In experience the one Being appears to and in many existential observers; experience is the external, nonexistential aspect or visible structure the many offer to each other. I experience you, never in your own existentiality, but only as you appear to me in terms in my sensuous, emotive, and practical reaction to you. There is no experience that is not tainted with the experiencer's provincial position in the universe. In our most correct handling of external experiences we experience erroneously. We know that we *exist* in truth because we also know that we *experience* in untruth.

We are able to criticize our nonexistential image of experience. Empirical sciences correct nothing but the accuracy of technical and practical calculations. This kind of correction is like the correction of my eyesight by putting lenses on my nose, or the correction of my hearing by putting microphones into my ears, after which correction I can indulge in the errors of identifying that which I see of the world with its own being-so even more than before, when my short-sightedness or my bad hearing at least made me a little more critical against identifying my view or hearsay of other beings with their own existence. Critique of experience compares experiences and their limited provincialisms with the ontological unity of opposites. The experiential appearance and its mechanism of communication then is made transparent and also understood in its limitation. We cultivate a sense for the unity of being in all experiences. We avoid the mistake of distinguishing too strongly; of laying our hands on phenomena like cosmic robbers.

If our assumption of the absolute ontological unity is true, and we have found our attempts at doubting or destroying the principle to be in vain, then nothing can be opposed to Being. Being has no object against which it could act. Our experiential conflicts and collisions do not tear Being apart, but Being is in them, through them, is equally in all parts. Being is whole and indivisible in all it does, in all of its many, individual self-differentiations or modifications. It always wills what it is; it always is what it wills. What is possible in Being is what it actualizes; what it makes actual is what it is capable of being. From the point of view of the universe actuality and possibility are identical, while from the point of view of our experience what may be or should be never coincides with what experientially is. The pining for absolute and yet unrealizable ideals is an unavoidable moral delusion of a practical experience. We say that the unity of Being is the unity of its very own individuation.

Applied as corrective to our experience, this means that there is an absolute and complete solidarity of Being in all existences; the more we orient ourselves in this solidarity, the more we rise from the unfreedom, the provincialism, the prejudice and superstition, that go together with the experiential outlook; experience always depends on the other and is oriented by what opposes its own way. Freedom is identical with being yourself, is identical with self-realization as universal, rational being. The most fundamental ethical law, that you should treat others as human beings, not only as experiential means but also as ends in themselves, as members of an absolute and ideal community of beings, is precisely an expression of the ontological foundation of all the many in the One. This first correction of experience, then, criticizes the pseudo-absolutization of empirical unities or fixations, seeing in or through them the true or ontological unity.

We have seen that unity is unity entirely in and through its own other, it is unity which is nowhere except in the absolute many of its individuation. There is nothing that is not individually distinct from all other "points," and since at the same time Being is One there are no gaps or discontinuities between all the many. We live in a dense functional continuity of life, all qualitative differences cohering in their one Being. Or, Being is through the constant and fluid action-reaction of its infinite self-modification. Or simply, being is alive; nothing that is, is dead; "dead" would be something without qualitative active-reactive functionality, something out of touch or communication with the rest of being, something that could be exchanged without this making any difference, something, in other words, unthinkable and uncommunicable. Passivity is still some sort of activity and reactivity. When we distinguish between what is dead and what is alive in our perceptions, which are functional reactions to other centers of functionality or activity, we do not classify being, but merely express an experiential prejudice. What we call dead are individuated centers of functionality, whose kind of living energy we do not understand as such and are therefore satisfied to treat them as if their differences could all be evaporated in a mathematical equation of quantities.

If the One is only in the reactivity of the many among themselves, Being is never static and cannot be stabilized. The life of Being is like the life in a work of art, in a symphony, a poem, a dance, in which the figures and movements are all expressive of the one unity of the work, while they seem to appear and vanish on the stage of consciousness. The second correction, then, from the point of view of the ontological many, is to overcome the false distance between the many ones, see through the effort of experience to substitute static "objects" for the fluid dance of living reality.

The formal science stabilizing all experiential contents in a symbolic presentation of space-time relations is mathematics. It is necessary, therefore, to show the difference between the ontological one and the mathematical number one, the ontological many and the mathematical many ones. Logical identity is not identical with mathematical equality, and logical propositions are not mathematical equations. The mathematical "number one" is an abstract, formal symbol for any experiential unity of measurement, such as stretches of space, durations of time, measure-units of force or weight. Such units are never that which we have discussed as logical unity or identity. Mathematically there are many number ones, which can be counted, added, subtracted, multiplied and divided; logically the number one is an identical concept; logically there is only one number one; no matter how many times the mathematician may repeat his one, logically he always manipulates one and the same number one. It is, therefore, possible to think the essence of mathematical equation, logically, but impossible to measure logical truth mathematically. Mathematics does not think but it measures, counts, calculates, and synthesizes. It is a science of space—time-measurements unencumbered by empirical contents. Spatial points in successive moments of time are the *a priori* conditions of all appearances to appear, including the appearance of one observer to another observer. The measuring construction of space and time by mathematics proceeds prior to particular experiences. But as space-time are forms of perceptive contents, mathematics remains a pure and ideal empirical science, the basis for a controlling manipulation of experience. But this very success in fixing experiential aspects in equations of quantitative units of energy is ontologically questionable, if this external manipulation is identified with metaphysics. Mathematical science may make us reality-blind on account of its practical efficiency. It has seduced metaphysicians more than once.

As the logical one is not the mathematical number one, so is the logical many not the mathematical many; the mathematical many are aggregates of the many ones which are all alike, while the logical many are the dialectical other of the one, are its own manyfold content.

We illustrate this relation of the ontological thinking to the mathematical-experiential thinking with the following imaginary conversation between Zeno and the mathematician. Zeno's paradoxes have been most successful in rousing the ire of all literal-minded calculators.

ZENO AND THE MATHEMATICIAN[1]

Achilles had overtaken the Tortoise, and had seated himself comfortably on its back. . . . [2]

Mathematician: You here, Zeno? A pleasant surprise, indeed, as I can now ask you personally what you meant by your paradoxes. Was it jest or was it serious when you said a flying arrow could not move?

---

[1] Nathan Court, "The Motionless Arrow," Science Monitor 63, 249, 1946.

[2] Lewis Carroll, "What the Tortoise Said to Achilles," *Complete Works,* Modern Library, 1225.

ZENO: Newcomers in eternity are always surprised—because they did not acquaint themselves with our ontology when they were still alive. I am just as real now as I was when my existence appeared to the experience of others; and whether my disappearance from the experience of others has taken place a long or a short time ago—a long or a short past with reference to their own times—makes absolutely no difference as to my being. I am.

Mathematician: I would never have thought of that when I was on earth—I was so busy measuring changes, movements and velocities of bodies that I never had time to think—but here I am compelled to admit that you are; I could not have started this discussion with you if you were not. But now, what about your unquenchable paradoxes? I am eager to inform you that we mathematicians have solved them by means of the calculus of convergent series approaching the limit symbolized by zero; and instantaneous velocities are a commonplace in modern physics—we read our speedometers every day, you see. You must enjoy the news that your problem has been solved, even though we ourselves do not understand how we do it: whether there is an actual infinity of numbers in such a series, whether there is an actual simultaneity of events, of numbers in such a series, whether a limit of a system is actually reached or not. Still, we do it. We have made progress. The motionless arrow only seemed a problem to you because mathematical methods were so crude in your time.

ZENO: You advanced mathematicians seem to me no less naive than the simple mathematicians of my time. They said the same thing and also solved the paradoxes *ambulando*. They simply did it. Plato, a friend of mine, says that he has but rarely met a mathematician who could think. And Lewis Carroll, another good friend of mine, says they had better have taken to football than to thinking. I am delighted, of course, that your methods of measuring, adding and subtracting relative velocities in a finite Newtonian system are so nicely perfected now and I celebrate with you such improvements in this art. In Greek we call this *techne*. But my paradoxes, you remember, were written in defense of Parmenides. They were never merely mathematical riddles. If they were only that, they would not be paradoxes.

Mathematician: What is a paradox?

ZENO: Understand, friend, that in asking this question you move outside your calculating habits. And when I say "outside" I do not mean a geometrical position, but a different logical proposition. Now, if you have made your mind up beforehand that only mathematical riddles present serious questions, then you had better abstain from pursuing this further. You are now warned!

Mathematician: I don't know what you are driving at. But for the fun of an argument, go ahead; I am ready to listen.

ZENO: That is something, but I am afraid it is not enough. Nevertheless, may I take your word that you are willing to consider my argument as an hypothesis that "I am," regardless of the time sequence of my appearance?

Mathematician: Yes.

ZENO: Your "hypothesis," then, that I am, must be either true or false.
Mathematician: Do you mean to say that some people have verified your existence in their experience, and have talked about you?

ZENO: That is another hypothesis which must be true or false. How do you verify it?

Mathematician: I myself experienced that other people refer to you as having existed.

ZENO: That is another hypothesis. We need, it seems, quite a "number" of them. And the more you examine them in detail, the more prolific and the more uncertain they become. But take as many and make them as detailed as you please, do all of them prove that I am?

Mathematician: Of course not. All of them only sum up to this that I read, that other people read, that still other people (including yourself) had an experiential impression of a man named Zeno.

ZENO: Yet all the while you tacitly presuppose that you and all the others and I myself *are.* And this ontological presupposition of all the many and fluctuating empirical hypotheses remains one and the same for all of us, regardless whether we lived earlier or later in time or whether we found ourselves located in Elea, Italy, or in Norman, Oklahoma. To verify this one and same Being experientially is impossible, because you and I and everybody must *be,* before we can start having experiences in time or before we can make abstract experiential calculations of temporal data. "Being" *logically* precedes temporal existence and temporal experience, and it is the one and same Being logically "in" all those times, take them as long or cut them as short as you want to. Being is "in" all experiential and existential movements but does not move.

Mathematician: You use undefined terms, and your argument, therefore, makes no sense to me.

ZENO: As long as you do not say it is nonsense, you sit perfectly safe in the dubitability of your earthly memories. Otherwise, if you say either "It is nonsense," or "Only my earthly memories are true," you would end up in saying that "I am" is nonsense—and that would be unconditionally paradoxical, don't you think?

Mathematician: I don't know since you have not defined your paradox.

ZENO: Excuse me, here comes Parmenides who maintains that experience is the seat of all errors. He may enlighten you better than I can who am only his admirer. May I introduce you? Venerable father, here is another one of those mathematicians who complains that we have not told them what the paradox is.

*   *   *   *   *

To understand individuality is to understand how it expresses the unity of Being in its own manner, how the unity of Being is present in this peculiar, unique modification of itself. To misunderstand individuality is to press it into an abstract classification which would leave out its own qualitative character. "Our" scheme of history as "ancient," "medieval," and "modern," is a good illustration of a meaningless experiential superimposition, which does not objectively express what these times were for and in themselves, but only how they are related to the standpoints of an observing egotist.

If we keep both poles of the dialectical unity together, experience appears as a transparent and fluid symbol of Being. If the One is only in its own Many, and if the Many are in constant differentiation and conflict with reference to one another, then Being persists as one precisely through the struggle and perennial conflict of its members. To exist means to exist in differentiation and in communication with the whole qualitative "field," living context, and continuum of all existence. The unity of Being establishes itself constantly through the active-reactive differentiation of all its individuation, just as the unity of a personality establishes itself in the constant reactivity to its environment and through the self-differentiation of conflicting essential interests within itself.

Thus the practical, active, forwardlooking, moral efforts of individuals to establish, to bring about, to impose, and manufacture an experiential unity, are at once necessary and perennially futile. Unity is; it does not have to be established by us. On the other hand, it is equally necessary that existent individuals give testimony to the truth of Being, to symbolize unity in plans and programs of their action. The ontological unity of Being always restores itself through the practical programs of unions now. Practical unity of will is unity in becoming; ontological unity of Being is present unity in philosophical contemplation, the guide for all impartial objectivity. But we may find experience transparent and fluid not only in history, but also in natural sciences, the constancy and invariance of mathematical laws of energy-transformations point towards the pole of ontological unity, while the actual processes of chemical reactivity, of biological associations, adaptations, symbioses, point to the activity and functionality of a constantly struggling historical life.

PHYSICALISM, BIOLOGISM, PERSONALISM

We said that the one Being appears in the experience of many existential observers; this experience becomes transparent if its images are critically corrected. We live in a qualitative continuum of life, in a constant unique self-differentiation of Being which we help to express by our own existence in it. But if we refuse to accept this ontological critique of the image of experience, if we reify appearance, if we ascribe a false metaphysical reality-value to it, experience becomes opaque and the possibility of an understandable communication between the one and the many is broken.

Experience is always the image of appearing objects given to each individual center of reactivity within its own system of reference. I do not say individual human observer, because experience is not limited to human or conscious agents. This would be a human provincialism. There are non-human "prehensions," as Whitehead calls them.

What is given to me (if I take myself as an example of any experiencing agent) is always given in the form of a more or less removed, more or less sharply focussed selection: it is always given in terms of my sense-reactions, and this in turn means that the other is given as strange to myself, as not-I. Experience gives an arbitrary, private world-aspect in the form of alienation. If I take this view seriously, if I confuse this idiosyncrasy with reality, if I say that what I experience is what *is* in itself, I am mad. Insanity in all forms and degrees is the fallacy of confusing experience with existential Being.

If I ascribe ontological reality to my arbitrary experiential selections, then I have erected a barrier which makes communication impossible. The world is then split into overlapping and incompatible projections. I ascribe to the relation between various other individuals the same character of external relations that I have established for myself. In that case I suppose that the relation between a second and a third person is such as I perceive it in my own terms as an outsider and a third observer.

Materialism or physicalism identifies reality with "dead" or physical nature, that is with experience in terms of my sense-reactions falsely transformed into object-qualities, and further thinks these dead objects in external relation to each other, that is, in relations that are not relating. A series of apparent means of communication is confused with communication itself. Materialism is the uncritical use of everything else for the exclusive benefit of the observer regardless of any other individuality. Materialism eliminates both the genuine many, individuation, as well as unity, genuine communication. It cannot understand individuation, neither out of itself nor in unity. If materialism could be consistent, which it cannot be, it would have to eliminate itself, because it cannot find its own standpoint among its own dead world. Used critically, philosophically, materialism expresses the meaninglessness of external experience as such; and since it is impossible to experience anything except as an external "other" from the point of view of one of the many, it follows that you may treat all appearance as if it were given in this form of alienation, provided you remember the fictitious and provisional character of the whole standpoint. The trouble is that we are so accustomed to the absurdity of our experience that we do not notice it. The usual classification of empirical sciences into sciences dealing with physical objects, with organisms, and with personal-social "objects," corresponds to habits of our human perception. But the border lines between these so-called realms of nature are empirically uncertain. Critically understood they are practical divisions of our experience; ontologically they must be rejected; Being cannot be cut into three discontinuous pieces. They are regional descriptions; they are not valid for all of experience. It is impossible to ascribe personal character to animals, plants, chemicals and atoms, because empirically they are never given or experienced that way;

it is equally impossible to reduce the conscious cultural life of man to unconscious biological expressions of races or to comprehend the state and history of man in terms of biological figures of speech, such as Spengler uses when he talks of biological youth, maturity, and old age to comprehend historical cultures. Because these theories are regional, they are thereby invalidated for the comprehension of experience as a coherent whole. In ontological reality this threefold division does not correspond to three realms of nature; it simply expresses degrees of communication, of understanding of the other from the point of view of my own kind of functionality. If my communication is entirely reduced to external contact, I call this communicant dead or physical, in which case I am reduced to a mere noticing or external observation of its appearance to me; if I understand it as functioning out of itself, but as exhibiting a kind of life foreign to my own, I call the communicant organic; while if I understand the other as sharing a life similar to my own I talk of personal experience.

Scientific experience, considered from its formal, logical structure, usually measures appearances or calculates effects. As exact, mathematical science it points toward the one but loses the many; as history it points towards the many, but loses the systematic form. Characteristic of all scientific experience, whether concerned with historical individual concepts, or with descriptive types of classes, or with rational elements and exact quantitative laws, is the dualism, the discrepancy between form and content, between the scientific formula in the book and the living event of life itself. Dogmatic scientism always contradicts itself. It confuses true being with the regional object-image of experience, but nevertheless endeavors to correct this true being to make it more exact. But a completed rational mechanization of the communication relations of the one and its many, would make impossible a true account of being and existence.

Dialectical Theology

Whither shall I go from thy spirit? or whither shall I flee from thy presence? If I ascend up into heaven, thou art there; if I make my bed in hell, behold, thou art there. If I take the wings of the morning, and dwell in the uttermost parts of the sea; even there shall thy hand lead me.

—Psalm 139

THE PHILOSOPHICAL ABSOLUTE AND THE GOD OF RELIGIONS

Throughout we have demonstrated that the idea of reality is not confined to the quantitative calculation of that fragment of the appearing world-process, which is the "nature" of physics; "islands of matter in a sea of emptiness" [1]—islands of physical abstractions in a sea of metaphysical ignorance.

All nations on this little planet earth, in all periods of their self-conscious history, are agreed on relating themselves back to an absolute world-ground which is also the goal of love; the source of existence is responded to in gratitude and awe. *Religio* literally means this "back-tie." Religion is the *consensus gentium*. The many world-religions appeal to the same Absolute in many linguistic symbols. We call a symbol which appeals to the Absolute, a mythical expression. "Tao" or "Central Harmony" in Chinese Taoism or Confucianism, the "Trimurti" of Brahma, Vishnu and Shiva in Hinduism, "Allah" in Islam, "Jehova" in Judaism, "God Our Father" in Christianity, are such mythical appellations. "The realm of God is primarily the invisible church, which comprehends all zones and different religions; secondarily the external church." [2]

---

[1] L. Infeld, *Albert Einstein,* New York, 1950, p. 73.

[2] G. W. F. Hegel, *Sammtlich Werke,* Stuttgart, 1927, vol. III, p. 226.

Man, in saying "I am," expresses his finite existence. The Biblical God is referred to as saying "I am" to express His eternal existence. The finite "I am" reflects the eternal "I am." A being capable of expressing his existence in "I am" is called spirit. The totality of all functions of the human soul are concentrated and involved in this "I am." Religion, hence, "Offers the presentation *(Darstellung)* of the absolute spirit not only for perception *(Anschauung)* and imagination *(Vorstellung)*, but also for thought and knowledge *(Erkenntniss)*. The main function of religion consists in elevating the individual to the thought of God, to produce a unison with him and to give to the individual, account of the certainty of such unison. Religion is the truth as it is found in all human beings." [3]

The philosophical idea of the absolute or unconditional Being to which I am related is identical with the truth of religious faiths. Truth is one and indivisible. This is frequently denied by theologians, who are practical advocates of their particular external church. They are, in such a case, less concerned with the truth of their religion, than with the prestige and power of their particular myths in this world. The labyrinth of the history of the Christian dogmas in the West, bloody inquisitions and mass-persecutions, are the sorry comment on the small and blind "faith" of exclusive churchmen and literal-minded theologians. "Faith" in the sense of assenting to something on hearsay, "saving historical facts," or "saving dogmatic formulas," are artificial restrictions of religion; the touchiness of their addicts is proportionate to the artificiality of their beliefs.

Philosophy of religion is the moment of logical reflection within religion elucidating the universal meaning of faith. To exclude philosophy from religion is to exclude from religion the concern for its truth. The common theological charge against philosophy is that, "philosophy is merely an abstraction from the sensuous world and therefore must terminate in a dead concept." [4] Theologians who argue that way show that their own philosophical education has not passed beyond scientism. It is true that philosophy may start from the sensuous world, because visible nature also belongs to that which is. It is precisely the philosophical critique of scientism which alone expands our concept of reality, so that religion is known to be more than an edifying play with figures

---

[3] Hegel, *ibid.*, p. 225.

[4] Walter Koehler. *Dogmengeschichte*, Zurich, 1943, p. 92.

of speech, and the religious conception of reality becomes logically possible. "The rise above that which is sensuous and finite mediates negatively from our human side religious knowledge, in so far as the sensuous and finite is taken as a starting-point, but as one which is at the same time left behind and known in its negativity. This knowledge of the Absolute is at the same time absolute and immediate in itself; it can have nothing that is merely finite as its own positing ground. . . . To know God is not above reason, reason is reflecting God *(Widerschein)*, and is essentially the knowledge of the Absolute above a scientific intellect and its knowledge of the finite and the relative." [5]

The mythical language of religion colors the Absolute by images from different preferred realms of experience. The Eastern religions prefer the aesthetic perfection of the "lotus flower," in order to worship the eternal perfection of the absolute Being in all manifestations; they rise to this religious contemplation through the discovery of the suffering and insufficiency of all earthly life. The Western, Biblical religions color the Absolute by preferring personal-moral purposiveness; they assure man of the eternal "love" and "mercy" of God in spite of man's moral incompetency.

The Absolute of philosophy is called "God" when it is affirmed in faith and worshipped in religious perspective. Theism emphasizes transcendence: the Absolute is wholly other than, is radically beyond and prior to, any finite and factual temporality. As eternal world-ground the Absolute is "the father," the "creator" of "heaven and earth," "omnipotent power." But the world-process also is. Pantheism or Polytheism worship God in his own "other," in the co-eternal "son," his creation is not real outside or apart from Him, even though it is, as temporal process, not identical with Him. It is God's "goodness" to call into, and to maintain, his creation in existence. It is His "love" to maintain His unity with His own creation. Goodness and love is His Holiness, revealed in and to the man, who responds. In the Christian religion this self-revelation of God as human subject is visible and believed in Christ. Birth, suffering, and grave, is a moment in God's own eternal life. But this temporal suffering and moral incompetence of man is also cancelled and transcended. This is God's wisdom, setting measures, and justice, showing the ultimate unworthiness and insufficiency of all pseudo-absolute fixations of finitudes. Sin, consequently,

---

[5] Hegel, *op. cit.*, p. 97.

is alienation from God, the declaration of independence on the part of man, who is vainly attempting to idolize himself or his own moral-practical designs. But the religious knowledge, that human and divine existence are not absolutely alienated from one another, but that man can grasp in God's "I am" his own ground, is religiously expressed as grace and reconciliation of man with God. This return of man to God is the "holy spirit" of religion.[6]

We now turn to the philosophical formulation of this human participation in the Absolute, having shown its harmony with religious formulations.

The idea of the absolute whole of reality is in itself absolute: It is not derived from something other than what it expresses. The idea of the unconditional Being is "first in dignity and power," as Plato says, although it may appear late in time. Philosophy could not seek reality, if it were not already aware of that which it seeks. We seek what we have half-forgotten, encumbered by experiential cares; philosophy is not wisdom, but "love of wisdom" and "reminiscence."

The Absolute is the unconditional whole and coincidence of all essential opposites; it is the dialectical unity of man and world, process and reality, temporality and eternity, freedom and necessity, affirmation and negation, one and many, being and becoming, transcendent and, in its own otherness, immanent.

It is unique and incomparable. All essential realms of experience, which can be compared and contrasted, can not be compared with the Absolute, which they all presuppose, but which they do not define. The idea of the Absolute thus distinguishes itself from all concepts used in natural or cultural sciences. Every historical concept of individualities is unique too. As such the historical concept is an analogy to the uniqueness of the Absolute. Plato, therefore, compares the *mikrokosmos* of the human soul to the *makrokosmos* of the world-organism, but also points out that both are merely analogies to the Absolute, because they are not unique in the sense of being incomparable.

There is nothing "dead" in the Absolute. The organism also is an analogy of the Absolute. It also is a living whole in which all parts are defined by their function in the whole, and the whole is defined as the totality of its functioning organs. But this too, like the historical individual, is an analogy only, because the universe has no environment, on which all organisms depend.

---

6 *Ibid.*, p. 98.

The universe is concrete. To think it requires a concrete idea as unity of opposites. The universe is the only concrete reality, and philosophy the only corresponding concrete "science." Understanding and transcending ourselves within its eternal being is a thinking of concrete reality inseparable from our fragmentary and transitory existence.

"Nearly all philosophers agree that opposites underlie the many beings and Being itself: for they say that all principles are opposites." [7]

Philosophical participation in the Absolute requires the recognition of abstractions as well as their reintegration in the whole of life. The philosophy of science, practice, art, and so on, considers an abstract but as such real distinction with reference to its contribution to the idea of the whole. The universe is the true measure of all partial and as such abstract truths. Philosophy, further, must recognize irrationality which is irrational with reference to limited systems of rational orders. The most superficial or momentary level of experience is linked to the whole no less than a deeper and more concrete level. Dialectical ontology is the foundation of dialectical anthropology.

THE TRINITY

The Christian dogma of trinity formulates a dialectical conception of God. It distinguishes the Christian religion from any abstract monotheism as well as from pantheism and from polytheisms. Centuries of discussions preceded its final dogmatic fixation in the fourth century by the council of Nicaea (325 A.D.) and on later councils of the church. It was fully accepted and restated by the Reformation.

The trinitarian creed confesses that God is an absolute subject and the creator of subjects "created in his image." God is thus not only the "maker of heaven and earth," the eternal being back of a transitory world-creature, but He is also that absolute Being which reveals Himself as subject. He is a speaking God, *deus loquens,* who gives Himself, who lets Himself be known in human existence. In this self-revelation He distinguishes Himself from Himself, but He remains at the same time Himself; the one and the same eternal being is at the same time appearing in flesh and in human history. God is the "Father" because he is the Father of the Son. The Christian appellation "Our Father in Heaven" refers to the father of His own and only begotten son, refers

---

[7] Aristotle. *Met.,* 1004 b.

to a God whose essence has been from eternity that of a personal subject willing and intending to reveal himself in this, his own capacity. The Christian faith knows God as father and "person" through His son Jesus Christ, the Lord and divider of all times. The times before His historical appearance are the times "before Christ," times of advents, prophecies and premonitions; "after Christ," after hearing God the Word speaking into historical times is the time of faith, acceptance, reconciliation with God through this faith. And so He is "With us to the end of the world" as Holy Ghost, as possibility of recognizing his Grace, as principle of Christian love and of the one and all embracing "kingdom of God on earth," the church.

These three divine modes of being are not three different gods or persons. It is the one and the same God who utters and "others" himself and who eternally returns to his own unbroken unity. The same God who, by accepting the lot of a common human being, by suffering the fate of our blindness and incompetence, reconciles us with our suffering and our cross. In and through faith He imparts to us His eternal life and beatitude, beyond natural competence and under-standing. The Trinity is inseparable from the Christian conception of salvation and reconciliation of man.

What is now called "modernism" consists of two tendencies, which were known in the second century under the name of Ebionite and *Docetic*. They were, and they still are, the two possibilities to deny the Christian conception of God as Trinity.

The first, the Ebionite opinion, holds that Jesus Christ was a wonder-ful, a good, a most inspired individual, who impressed his environment so much, that they exalted him more and more until they finally deified him. Their enthusiasm grew with the distance in time.

The second, the *Docetic* opinion, complements this by saying, that first there were speculative, metaphysical, religious imaginations in the spirit of that time, and they gradually clustered around a symbolic quasi-historical name.

In the first conception the historical individual Jesus became a myth, in the second, myth-making imaginations became Jesus. The first dissolves the *historical* reliability of the New Testament; the other explains the Scriptures as products of religious phantasy. Both ways are the natural human ways of approaching and of handling a human document. But they are both irrelevant to the religious-metaphysical event which is evident to the Christian faith. And from the point of view of this Christian faith it is evident that such an event as that which is believed to have occurred, would cause a lot of disturbance, stories, phantasies and hysterical phenomena in the human scene and in the human reporting of such an event. The appearance of God in our human midst would resemble the stirred motion in an ant heap under a human interference. Men are confronted with an absolute either/or of faith or refusal. And the refusal would inevitably seek cover behind the methods of Docetism and Ebionitism, looking at a highly disturbed scene while at the same time ignoring the cause which goes beyond the possibilities of human prediction as the disturbance in the ant heap would go beyond the comprehension of the categories of the ants. Both methods have led to valid scientific results in historical criticism. But the more valid the results are, the more they confirm the religious view of man as a creature being lost in darkness and confusion, when left to his own devices in matters of faith. The more certain we become, that nothing has happened literally as the Bible reports it, the more certain the human uncertainty of all human reporting becomes, the clearer is the faith and the holy ghost distinguishable from any literalism; they belong to that wholly other dimension which is veiled by the smoke of human reactions. But that smoke is at the same time the sign of the fire. The factual assent to factual reports is never identical with the assent of faith to the Christian Trinity. The Christian faith needs no scientific crutches, but it needs critical scientific intelligence to guard itself against any superstitious literalism and idolatry of alleged scriptural-historical facts.

Augustine, in his book *De Trinitate,* after confessing and explaining the central dogma of Christianity, turns to the study of its analogies and vestiges in man. If man is created in the image of God, he must be created in the image of the Trinity. Augustine finds this vestige or image of the trinity in human existence, which is prior to any of its functions. Man is the subject of all he knows, wills, feels, loves and produces. All those functions are inseparably one with myself, with my basic existence, but this basic existence is at the same time more than they are, it transcends them as the ground transcends its own consequences. When, for example, I conceive a work of art, produce it in the finite and visible form of a particular medium of expression, I am both the author of that work, and insofar it is my production, and can not be separated from my self-activity. On the other hand, it gains an objective and expressive appearance for you, and if it does that, its producing idea may be reproduced in you and thus returns to the realm from which it sprang, the realm of an ideal conception.

The human being is a trinity of eternal existence, which is and will always be that which it is; of finite life and expression, working itself out in pain and effort in time; and a longing for eternal being and beatitude, participated and anticipated in faith.

Augustine finds the vestige of the trinity in the created world, which unites being, the same in all, with particular, individual modifications of that being, which express the universal being in infinite modifications, and which are all cancelled, withdrawn, and preserved in the moved image of eternity, which is God's creation.

Eight hundred years later, Thomas Aquinas interprets the trinity with the categories of "procession" and "internal relation." (*Summa Theologica Q. 27-43.*) "As there is an outward procession corresponding to the attending to external matter, so there must be an inward procession corresponding to the act remaining within the agent." The divine Word, proceeding from the speaker, yet remains within him. God also "may be compared to created things as the artisan is to the works of his art." "In God the act of understanding (his Word) and his Being are the same." This is so in distinction from our understanding, where our conception of a thing is only partly identical with the thing itself, as "there is no identity of nature" between my conception of a thing and that thing itself. But God not only expresses in his living word his understanding of Himself, but also His will and love, "whereby the object loved is in the one who loves." This, again, is only partially true for us, whereas in God this openness and being-there for others is revealed in the limitless openness and being-there for others in the Savior. This love of God for man does not cease with its actual appearance in time, but remains the realm of freedom, in which we are invited to be moved by love to join in the community of the holy spirit.

Again, three hundred years later John Calvin in the thirteenth chapter of his *Institutes of the Christian Religion,* reaffirms the Trinity as the essential and central dogma of the Christian religion. He is, however, afraid of philosophical formulations of it; we should "not curiously penetrate into the sublime mystery, to wander through a multitude of vain speculations." Instead, he goes through the Bible to prove the scriptural source of the dogma. "When the Scripture speaks of the Word of God, it certainly was very absurd to imagine it to be only a transient and momentary sound, emitted into the air, and coming forth from God himself; of which nature were the oracles, given to the fathers, and all the prophecies. It is rather to be understood of the eternal wisdom residing in God, whence the oracles, and all the prophecies proceeded. . . . Therefore, as all the Divine revelations are justly entitled the Word of God, so we ought chiefly to esteem that substantial Word, the source of all revelations, who is liable to no variation, who remains with God perpetually one and the same, and who is God himself." Without apprehending the one God in his eternal threefold function, "we have only a bare and empty name of God."

The Reformation thus restricted religious thinking to Biblical thinking and divorced philosophy from it. This disrupted the harmony between philosophy and religion; it accented their difference. The result was the emergence of a philosophy of religion, which in turn understood the religious thinking as a particular sort of apprehending the absolute being in pictorial or imaginative symbols. Biblical thinking is indeed a non-philosophical, symbolic thinking in stories and images. It is the apprehension of the Absolute in the form of quasi-sensuous representations. Thus we come to the last turn of the trinitarian idea, which we illustrate in the philosophy of Hegel.

The absolute Being, the one and all-embracing concrete universe, elucidates and manifests itself also in the Christian Trinity. If it is apprehended in its truth through the Christian symbol, it is apprehended religiously, in the representational form of religious-mythical thinking. But it can also be apprehended as the same truth in philosophy. This philosophical comprehension includes the Christian representation as one of its own dimensions. The one and same truth, which is the whole, contains many avenues to itself in itself.

Hegel sees the same truth in the Hindu trinity, the Trimurti, the eternal identity of creation and destruction; it is one and the same eternal and living universe, which brings forth and creates world-systems, cancels them again and preserves itself in this process as the one and the same absolute being.

He also sees it in the Platonic-Aristotelian dialectic, in which Being is eternally that which it is in itself, but also and at the same time that which it is not, its finite self-manifestations of its activity, which it brings forth and takes back to itself. Being, as Plato says, is and contains its own negation, its non-being as essential to itself within itself.

The absolute truth can be worshipped. In worshipping perspective and in representational images it is named Father, Son, Holy Ghost. "This eternal idea is expressed in the Christian religion as that which is called the Holy Trinity." [8] "God the Father is the universal being as it is in itself; it is not solitary, but breaks open in the creation of nature, which is the same being but as external to itself and as being apart from itself (*Sichselbstäusserliche, Aussersichseiende*); and creates itself as his own 'I am' and views himself in his son; to see himself in another as one with oneself is love, through which he returns to his own unity; this concrete unity, mediated by self-distinction and self-unification is the concrete life of the holy spirit which has its existence in the true Christian community of believers." [9]

The absolute is manifest in truth, love, and spirit. Man is, in spite of his animal finitude, privileged and dignified to participate in this immense dialectical life of the Absolute. Apart from the trinitarian absolute he is bound to fall in fixations and abstractions of his own limited experiences.

THE ONTOLOGICAL ARGUMENT, ABSOLUTE IDEALISM AND THE "FOOL"

We said the Absolute is world-ground of creation. The philosophical problem is, whether or how such a statement can be justified. Is it only a human, imaginative fiction or "idea" in my head? To say that the subjective-human idea of the Absolute is the Absolute itself is the standpoint of so-called "absolute idealism" or gnosticism. I am not sure whether anyone has held that view. If anyone does then that which Hegel calls the otherness of the world-process or the "seriousness of negativity" has gone. The idea-of-the-Absolute is absolute itself, yes; but it is not the Absolute.

This confusion of the idea of the Absolute with the Absolute is traditionally known as the "ontological argument." It is usually stated like this: The idea of an absolute and perfect being implies the existence of that being, because it would neither be perfect nor absolute if it lacked existence. The existence of the absolute being is thus logically assured. The logical thought, my idea, implies existence.

This argument is ascribed to Anselm of Canterbury. Historians of philosophy are almost unanimous in this assertion. Already Anselm's contemporary, the monk Gaunilo quotes the argument in that form and quite rightly replies, that he could think a perfect island, whose per-

---

[8] Hegel. *Werke*, Stuttgart, XVI, 227.

[9] *Ibid.*, X, 27. In the original this is all one sentence.

fection would imply its existence, since a non-existent island would indeed be far from perfect, but that such good logic does not guarantee the actual existence of such an island. Kant repeated the same refutation with the vulgar example; he could think one hundred perfect dollars in his pocket, but he could not go and buy anything with them.

Now this is all very well and good—but it does not touch Anselm's ontological argument. The historians of philosophy should have quoted his text, instead of taking Guanilo's or St. Thomas Aquinas' word for it. Anselm actually says the exact opposite of what his critics "quote" him as saying. Here are his own words:

> And so, Lord, do thou, who dost give understanding to faith, give me, so far as thou knowest it to be profitable, to understand that thou art as we believe; and that thou art that which we believe. And, indeed, we believe that thou art a being than which nothing greater can be conceived. Or is there no such nature, since the fool hath said in his heart, there is no God? (Psalms xiv, I) But, at any rate, this very fool, when he hears of this being of which I speak—a being than which nothing greater can be conceived—understands what he hears, and what he understands is in his understanding; although he does not understand it to exist.
>
> For, it is one thing for an object to be in the understanding, and another to understand that the object exists. When a painter first conceives of what he will afterwards perform, he has it in his understanding, but he does not yet understand it to be, because he has not yet performed it. But after he has made the painting, he both has it in his understanding, and he understands that it exists, because he has made it.
>
> Hence, even the fool is convinced that something exists in the understanding, at least, than which nothing greater can be conceived. For, when he hears of this, he understands it. And whatever is understood, exists in the understanding. And assuredly that, than which nothing greater can be conceived, cannot exist in the understanding alone. For, suppose it exists in the understanding alone: then it can be conceived to exist in reality; which is greater.
>
> Therefore, if that, than which nothing greater can be conceived, exist in the understanding alone, the very being, than which nothing greater can be conceived, is one, than which a greater can be conceived. But obviously this is impossible. Hence, there is no doubt that there exists a being, than which nothing greater can be conceived, and it exists both in the understanding and in reality.

God cannot be conceived not to exist. God is that, than which nothing greater can be conceived. That which can be conceived not to exist is not God.

And it assuredly exists so truly, that it cannot be conceived not to exist. For, it is possible to conceive of a being which cannot be conceived not to exist; and this is greater than one which can be conceived not to exist. Hence, if that, than which nothing greater can be conceived, can be conceived not to exist, it is not that, than which nothing greater can be conceived. But this is an irreconcilable contradiction. There is, then, so truly a being than which nothing greater can be conceived to exist, that it cannot even be conceived not to exist; and this being thou art, O Lord, our God.

So truly, therefore, dost thou exist, O Lord, my God, that thou canst not be conceived not to exist; and rightly. For, if a mind would conceive of a being better than thee, the creature would rise above the Creator: and this is most absurd. And, indeed, whatever else there is, except thee alone, can be conceived not to exist. To thee alone, therefore, it belongs to exist more truly than all other beings, and hence in a higher degree than all others. For, whatever else exists does not exist so truly, and hence in a less degree it belongs to it to exist. Why, then, has the fool said in his heart, there is no God (Psalms xiv, I), since it is so evident, to a rational mind, that thou dost exist in the highest degree of all? Why, except that he be dull and a fool?[10]

II & III, pp. 7-9.

What Anselm says, then, is this that the Absolute exists, because the idea of the Absolute is *not* the Absolute itself. The Absolute reveals itself through the negativity, through the breakdown of any human effort to form an adequate conception. The only adequate conception is a *negative* conception, which declares that it is *not* that which it pretended to think, namely a "being greater than which *nothing* can be conceived." The human idea of the Absolute is transcending itself by *negating itself* as an absolute idea. The Absolute is that being which *cannot* be conceived to be identical with any human subjective notion in anybody's head. Its briefest notation is the paradox: A *is* not-A.

This logic of the dialectical paradox is the logic of the Absolute. It is the shadow of the Absolute. The absolute Being is that which *is not* identical with any one of its many and opposite creations in

---

[10] St. Anselm, *Proslogium,* tr. by Sidney Norton Deane, Open Court, 1926, Chs.

which it appears as this ground. It is that which it *is not*. But dialectically it is also and likewise the negation of this negation, it *is not* outside and apart from the many transitive reflections and notions which the creature forms of it. As Being in its absolute and fully concrete sense it exists precisely in those transitive processes, in whose breakdown and transitivity its absoluteness is revealed. It is not what becames visible as its empirical or ideal manifestation, and it is not allowing them to stay in themselves as if they were absolute themselves. It negates this negation of itself and takes it back to itself.

The ontological argument says that the all-embracing, self-sufficient Absolute cannot be thought in any experience, but that no experience can exist without it. For this *dialectical* reason, the idea of the absolute is the only idea, whose thinking involves reality. If the Absolute Being "greater than which nothing can be conceived" were only an "idea in my head," it would not be the idea which we pretended to think and to understand, since an "idea in my head" is not that "Being greater than which nothing can be conceived." The idea of the Absolute *is not* the Absolute, it radically denies its perversion, which is the misunderstanding known as "Absolute Idealism," which conjures the Absolute out of its own idea of the Absolute.

To put it differently: everything (whether worlds, or ideals, or negations) is something and not nothing. Their Being is different from their being this, that, and the other thing. However, their Being cannot be thought behind or separate from their being this or that. Every concrete determination, the "thisness" or "whatness" of any object or any idea is not Being. But since Being is not outside or apart from its manifestations, these manifestations must be thought as negations of Being, insofar as they are something and not nothing in addition to their Being. Or what they are "in addition," *is* also, it does not drop out of Being, although Being is not only "that." Or, Being "contains" its own negation, its other, its death and limitation within itself. It is One-And-Other. Hence the formulation above, that my subjective understanding of Being involves its reality through the *negation* of my subjective, particular idea. If the Absolute is thought, it is more than mere thought. Since it is not given here or there or anywhere in particular, but since it is not thinkable apart from my particular realization of it, the Absolute is formulated as one with dialectical thinking. As unity of whatever is, it is also a unity of its own negations and of opposites within itself. The Absolute is a dialectical Being. Particular experiences, taken in and by themselves are not Absolute

Being, but apart from it they are nothing. Being cannot be thought to be a summation of nothings. The sum of negations is not Being.

Anselm's "fool" is as undialectical as the gnostic "absolute idealist." He is agnostic. He separates the idea of the Absolute from the Absolute. But the Absolute Being cannot be separated from the proposition which says what it is and what it is not. Making the Absolute independent of the idea-of-the-absolute would reduce the idea to nothing. Being, to which there is no legitimate access through thinking it, would be "a thing in itself," of which nothing could be predicated, not even that it is not experience. To separate is also to relate. The ontological argument thinks the Absolute negatively through the predicates that are excluded from it. It is in relation to that which it is not. It is not a perception, opinion, practical vehicle of communication; it is not any isolated system of experience; but again, it is not separate and apart from all these experiences. Being is the unity in and through what it is not; Being is itself and its own other; Being is the unity of Being and Non-Being.

The Absolute cannot be predicated of itself except in a negative dialectic. It is the link between a one and an other, which are united and differentiated. Their unity is Being, their distinction is Non-Being. Both belong together. Without distinction there is no unity; without unity there is no distinction, since distinction is also a unifying relation.

As unity of opposites, as synthesis of one and other, the Absolute can never become a dogmatic fixation, because the dialectical movement from position to position, the unfinality of all standpoints and fixations is the dialectical life of the Absolute. There can be no position which does not meet a challenge, and no question which does not in some sense demand a solution. The dialectic of one and other is present in all stages of experience.

The particular, one-sided negation of Being, such as evil, ugliness, and error, *is* as the other-than-God. Calling it illusion and unreality makes it not less real, but on the contrary magnifies its negative reality. If Non-Being were not, everything would be equally real and equally true and good. The unity and universal harmony of Being must be thought in and through all those realities, which in themselves are suffering from their very real insufficiency.

Non-Being, the disruptive other-than-Being, is ontologically dependent on the affirmation. Every negation presupposes in the connecting "is" the priority of a unity, which is broken up and which nevertheless maintains itself in its own disruption.

Being and Non-Being are always the one and inseparable Absolute. If we say that it is whole and part, one and many, eternal and temporal, same and different, absolute and relative, knowing and being known, and so on, we always characterize it by something other than it, but we also always take this otherness back, because whatever we say also is. The Absolute as unity of all opposites, of being and non-being, is a dialectical process, a dialectical becoming. And it shows or manifests itself to be this dialectical process in each of its steps, situations, achievements.

It is as impossible to separate God from the world as to identify the world with God. If we try to separate the unadulterated one Being, we can do that only by saying what it is not; hence we characterize it negatively by the predications which we exclude; we draw it back into the living process of dialectic. If we try to separate the other, Non-Being, we must say that it is, which negates its negativity and fixes it back again in the dialectical process. Undialectical "absolute idealism" is just as impossible as empiricistic agnosticism.

The ontological argument confronts you with the most radical Either/Or: Either you *think* absolute reality, and then you absolutely think *reality,* or you do not think reality at all—which does not prevent you from thinking stars, organisms, historical documents, or social problems.

Anselm's "fool" is in very numerous company nowadays. Among them we find all kinds of relativism, subjectivism, naturalism, positivism, nominalism, and the like. Their common counter-argument is, that we cannot think Being, but only experiences. They identify thinking with the thinking of some given factual stuff; for them there is only a logic of scientific or empirical procedures, but no logic of philosophy. They deny Being, because they do not find it among their things or particular essences. They deny the ontological argument either by saying that it is a mere tautology, an empty generality, or on the contrary that Being must be some given stuff and that the ontological argument does not help us in "real" knowledge, by which they mean empirical knowledge.

But this opposition simply reaffirms the ontological argument from its negative side. Entrenched in the finite, subjective, and particular experience, those thinkers are unable to see anything except in isolation and abstraction. But that Being can not be thought behind, beyond, separate, or in abstraction from, experience, is precisely the thesis of the ontological argument.

Another form of the same opposition is the fictionalism of an "as if" or will-to-believe philosophy. Absolute Being is not to be thought, but you may believe that there is such a thing, if that edifies you. This "belief" itself, however, is something real. Unbeliefs are also real, as are all these experiences. They presuppose, therefore, the problem of Being, but Being does not presuppose their belief in order to be in and through them.

This leads us from the scientific-empirical to the moral-practical objection. The moralist is infuriated by the ontological dictum that "what is rational is also real." He knows that his experience is not as it ought to be. He thinks the real being as an end to be brought about, as a purpose to be fulfilled. He, therefore, misunderstands the ontological dialectical rationality as rationalism. He overlooks the fact that the rational ontological argument contains the other, the negative and disruptive moment in Being. Moral experience with its tensions and problems is one of the many contradictory realms of experience which exist. Ontology cannot be replaced by "living a good life," or practicing morality, because moral practice, the bringing about what ought to be, takes place in concrete situations, in responsible decisions here and now. Neither can ethics, the dialectic of moral standpoints, replace ontology, because ethics is the theoretical perspective of moral experience. Being is not to be brought about, but exists in this practical tension. Its dialectical nature is merely exemplified in the ethical dialectic of the good.

The agnostic (scientific-empirical, subjectivistic, and moralistic) negation of ontology, is the necessary counter-point against the dogmatic undialectical affirmation of it. Dogmatic-empiricistic ontology recognizes the problem of Being, but takes "the results of science" and constructs them into pseudo-absolutes. For example, as naturalistic-realistic metaphysics, it constructs a world-view, in which Being is seen as a necessary evolution "from the nebula to the superman"; or, as a pseudo-religious, theosophical, or even astrological system, it constructs Being in terms of a providential "higher" knowledge. Such dogmatic ontologies overlook the critical, negative provision of the ontological argument, according to which all experiences are contingent, unnecessary. Nowhere in experience is there something which has inevitable or absolute Being, which might not just as well not be. A dogmatic ontology stops the open and problematic process of scientific research and covers the uncertainty of the practical world by a seeming and illusory, constructed "certainty." *Agnostic protest and dogmatic speculation demand each other.* This they have in common— they misunderstand Being in terms of experiential beings, the one positively, the other negatively.

ANALOGIA ENTIS

Thomas Aquinas criticized the pseudo-ontological argument, but replaced it with his "analogy" argument which is not a bit less dialectical than Anselm.

> Ex hoc autem quomodo in rebus *possit* similitudo ad Deum inveniri vel *non possit,* considerari potest.
> *Summa contra Gentiles,* Cap. **XXIX**.

The doctrine of *analogia entis* or *analogia proportionalitatis* is completely and tersely stated by Thomas Aquinas in chapters 29-32 of his *Summa contra Gentiles;* it is already the central problem of his first systematic work, *De Ente et Essentia.* It is the governing peak of his metaphysical landscape, or, to use another metaphor, the very heart of his system. In his own words this "proof" of the absolute Being is a rational method, by means of which we transcend our empirical knowledge of sensuous things, a safe bridge from the world to God. Sensuous things by virtue of their "being," resemble the absolute Being, and it is the task of reason to state this resemblance (VIII).

Thomas seeks this rational method, because the beliefs of different religions and what they accept or reject as revelation, are hopelessly at odds (II, 7, 8). Against this variety of religious experience reason is able to ascertain its own absolute ground (III, 4). Although sense-knowledge is its starting point in time, reason is nevertheless capable to infer the Absolute, using the empirical starting-point as evidence which implies its "first cause" (III, 5).

Our intention is to show that the *analogia entis* is no such logical-scientific method of transcending, but that it is a dialectical unity of opposites, a subtle balance of a "Yes" and a "No." The "yes" is the *via affirmationis,* according to which all beings participate in the Absolute; and the "no" is the *via negationis* according to which the Absolute is radically different from all other beings. The identity is just as ultimate as the non-identity. The way of affirmation may be compared to the art of the painter, who makes us see a whole by putting his colors on canvas; the way of negation proceeds like the sculpture who makes us see the whole by chiseling away imperfections; and the way of analogy is analogous to the poet who conjures up a vision of a whole of life by words which are quite unlike the vision itself.

Plato discovered dialectic as the logic of philosophy in distinction from the non-dialectical logical methods of sciences. In Aristotle's *Metaphysics,* dialectic is latent[11]—Hegel rightly observes that, had Aristotle followed his own formal logic he could not have written it. The situation is similar in Thomas Aquinas. He practices dialectic without knowing it. He assumed the formal Aristotelian logic to be the only logic, yet his own dialectic thrives in breaking through the barriers of formal logic. Had he been acquainted with the dialectical dialogues of the later Plato he could have found dialectic as the logic of his own philosophy in them. That he develops and practices dialectic against his own intention is no small tribute to Thomas' philosophical genius.

But then, other parts of his system would have collapsed. I mean especially his dualism, according to which "God" and "Matter" have absolutely nothing in common, are radically *diversa* (XVII, 6). In a dialectical *universum* there can be nothing that is not related in spite of and through difference.

THE AFFIRMATIVE WAY

Aristotle's metaphysics intends to think "being *qua* being." In contrast to partial and one-sided metaphysics, such as materialism or spiritualism, empiricism or rationalism, which seek the ultimate nature of reality in arbitrary reductions to one "sort of thing" or even one sort of method (subjectivism), the Aristotelian-Thomastic metaphysics is fully aware of an ontological complexity, which defies any such reductionism. What do we mean to say, when we attribute Being to so many radically different beings? Or, how can the unity of Being be thought, when all we meet are differences which seem to have nothing in common; when this unity of Being is nowhere on display?

We have an indefinite and undetermined pure potentiality or "first matter"; an infinite and determined multitude of individual forms of nature and of life; "above" those potential and factual realities, the

---

11 See my "Platonic Aristotle," *Proceedings of the Philosophical Congress,* Mendoza, Argentina, 1949.

thinking mind finds itself and, in correlation to its thinking ideal possibilities, logical forms of order, which may be thought in their essential ideality, suchness or whatness, regardless of whether they occur factually or not.[12] The logical category of quantity orders those forms in ascending degrees of extension or generality. The worldly beings are composites of ideal essence and factual existence; of genus, species, and individual differences: of substances and their attributes. Thought distinguishes and also holds together in thought that part of reality which is known and that which is not known. Laws (for example of causality) and relations of qualities and locations in space and time, bind those composite complexities in partial identities (XVIII).

Reason reaches "beyond" those worldly composites because all distinguishable categories or kinds of composite beings, are not Being as such. Being as such, as a whole, as a One, is the transcendental idea of reason (*transcendentalia*). As ground and goal of reason it is also the ground and goal of all truth. As ground and goal of love it is the ground and goal of all values (virtues) and of our beatitude. Values of life, including also the aesthetic value of the beautiful, are new ideal beings or entities, which accrue to man as he opens his rational vision to the Absolute.

We have reached the "affirmative way" of dialectical ontology. The Absolute is fully present, and one and the same in all of its own self-differentiations, although each taken by itself or abstractly, is not the Absolute. The Absolute is both itself and its own Other (*aliud, aliudquid*). This dialectical truth is in harmony with the Christian revelation where the absolute and eternal Being appears at the same time as this mortal individual.

When we affirm that Being is One, or that the One IS, we have affirmed both identity and difference, Oneness and Not-Oneness. "Everything that in any way is, is from God." (*Summa Theol.*, I.q 7, 8). The Absolute is unique and infinite, because nothing (factual or ideal, potential or actual) can be added to it or subtracted from it.

Being is identical with truth, so that the position of all things in Being is also their position in truth. This is the principle of all partial truths and to reach it is the endeavor of all research. And it is also true that we are not in possession of truth.

---

[12] This has recently been elaborated again by Husserl's Phenomenology.

Opportet igitur ultimum finem universi esse bonum intellectus. Hoc autem est veritas. Opportet igitur veritatem esse ultimum finem totius universi: et circa eius considerationem principaliter sapientiam insistere . . . sic enim est dispositio rerum in veritate sicut in esse (*Ibid.*, I, 6).

To cultivate wisdom, then, is our participation in the dialectical life of the whole, our similarity to, or analogy with, the Absolute.

THE NEGATIVE WAY

We now take the "negative way." The dialectical nature of Being is indirectly demonstrated through the insufficiency of formal logic. This *via negationis* terminates in two negations which cancel one another. The first negation is that nothing can be predicated "univocally" of the absolute Being on the one hand, and of the relative composites within it on the other hand (Cap. 32). The second negation denies that these opposites must be thought "equivocally" (Cap. 33), as if they had nothing in common. The argument hinges on these two terms *univoc* and *aequivoc*.

A predication is *univoc,* if the predicate has the same (identical) meaning for all subjects determined by it; or if all subjects belong to the same type of existence, the whole general essence is expressed by their general class-concept. Thus "organism" is predicated univocally of lions and men.

A predication is *aequivoc* if the predicate does not have the same meaning for different subjects; or if they do not belong to the same type of existence. Thus "healthy" is predicated equivocally of a medicine and of a man.

Categories can not be predicated univocally. What is, for example, factually real is not real in the same sense as that which is logically possible, and this in turn can not be said to be apodictically necessary. This holds also for the transcendentals. We have already seen that the true position of anything in the Absolute is not identical with the knowledge we may possess of it.

Our transcendental concept "being" is a most general class which seems to be valid for all things, when we say that they are something and not nothing; or when we say that everything is what it is. But in order to form this concept we have to disregard all significant differences in Being. We retain an empty general abstraction which is nothing in particular. But "nothing in particular" is not that which all beings are, or have in common. The attempted unification of "being" turns out to be its very opposite which is sheer equivocation. And we likewise merely fool ourselves if we think that formal logical unity is identical with the concrete unity of the Absolute. The transcendental concept becomes a mere *ens rationis*, a pale abstraction in our minds, if we try to predicate it univocally of all beings.

Formal logic, therefore, can not handle dialectical ontology. General and essential forms predicated of individuals may disregard their factual existence. The general nature, the whatness of a thing, is indifferent to its factual existence. Existence is not logical (*individuum ineffabile*) but is added to the logical possibility which says what it essentially is, what kind of a thing it is.

The species are coordinated among themselves and subordinated to their genus: but this logical order is not identical with the factual occurrence of those individuals which are logically determined by this order. Individual differences accrue to forms empirically.

The absolute Being, on the contrary, does not lie "outside" or "above" its own self-modifications. It contains all of its differences within itself *"per intrinsecam modificationem."* It manifests itself in all its realms, potential and actual, empirically real and logically ideal, truth and untruth alike. Only if it could stand like a genus outside or above itself and its individual manifestations, could it be predicated univocally.

We cannot identify the absolute Being with any one of its self-differentiations. But neither can we separate all the realms of Being from itself. This would be equivocation, which would leave us with absolutely unconnected fragments or a *"multi-vers," "diversa,"* which contradicts the idea of reason which demands systematic or "architectonic" unity and concrete totality of all realms.

THE ANALOGIA IS DIALECTICAL

Affirmation and negation meet in the dialectical *analogia entis* (Cap. 34):

> Sic igitur ex dictis relinquitur quod ea quae de Deo et rebus aliis dicuntur, pradicantur neque univoce neque aequivoce, sed analogice: hoc est, secundum ordinem vel respectum ad aliquid unum ... sicut *ens* de substantia et accidente dicitur ... non quod substantia et accidens ad aliquid tertium referantur.

The "order" or "respect" within which "God" and "all other things" are thought to be, and to be one, is like (*sicut*) the order within which a substance and its accidents are said to be, and to be one: this unity and being lies neither outside of this their analogical or dialectical relation, nor can it be attributed to one of the opposites exclusively.

In the complex world of human experience we meet an infinite manifold of individuals, and of types, levels, and kinds of beings, which all *are*—but none of them is absolutely or necessarily. But on the contrary they all are and have their being in the eternal and necessary truth of the absolute Being. The absolute Being is infinite not in the sense of an infinite manifold but in the sense that nothing can drop out of it and nothing can be added to it. The Absolute, therefore, is both One and its own Other, both infinite Oneness and finite manyness, both itself and not itself, both in harmony and discord with itself. This is the dialectical relation of the Absolute as Being-in-itself (*ens a se*) to itself as creation or appearance (*ens ab alio*).

This dialectic is ultimate, because the opposites are ultimate—they can not be overarched or subsumed under a "third," a general being "which would contain both God and World as its aspects"; the mind (*intellectus*) in Thomas participates at once in the absolute Being as well as in a genuine finite situation within which alone its formal logic is valid.

We find the same situation in Plato or in Kant. Kant's noumenal Reality or "World-itself" stands in a dialectical relation to itself as phenomenal, "world-as-appearance," which appears to scientifically knowing subjects, whose scientific knowledge is limited by formal logic and perceptual materials. Kant's man also participates at once in the phenomenal and noumenal opposites.

> "Every single experience is only part of the whole sphere of its domain, but the absolute totality of all possible experience is itself not experience."
>
> (Kant, Prolegomena)

If man could not participate in the Absolute, then his terms "Necessary and eternal Being" would be empty and meaningless: he could know or say absolutely nothing about it. If, on the other hand, man were sunk in finitude, if finite realms of experience and appearance were all he could know, then he would be like an animal unaware of his finitude and mortality. That he can take his finite existence seriously, that he can know himself and other experienced beings as not Being in the eternal, infinite, and absolute sense—this, his failure and privation of Being which he *is*, is also the reason for his self-transcendence.

The *analogia entis* is also referred to as *analogia proportionalitatis*. We saw in the quoted passage that the dialectical relation of God to "all other things" is *like* the relation of the substance to its accidents.

The absolute Being is one whose existence, *that* he is, is identical with his essence, *what* he is—namely, manifest in creation. The absolute Being is its own ground, *ens a se*. All other beings are groundless, apart from their absolute ground. They participate in the absolute Being and are absolutely dependent on it, they are *ens ab alio*.

Finite substances, particularly man, are beings which are active out of themselves; as conscious subject, man is for himself that which he is, he is *ens per se*. But as composite being he consists of matter/form, potentiality/actuality, existence/essence, which constantly fall apart. In the cognitive situation this falling apart is evident, in that formal or essential knowledge requires perceptual, factual, existential filling to become actual; on the other hand, mere existence requires the attainment of essential forms and values to become human actuality. In other words, man requires an object or an other, a you, belaboring which he becomes and finds himself. He depends on an other, an object, a material, a neighbor, a partner in order to realize that he is active out of himself. His *ens per se* is at the same time *ens in alio*. The dialectical proportion or analogy between the Absolute and men, then, is this that the Absolute is to its own Other, what man is to his own self-embodiment; *ens a se* is to *ens ab alio* what *ens per se* is to *ens in alio*.

That this analogy of proportion is a dialectical unity of opposites becomes clear when we compare it with a one-dimensional, non-dialectical proportion. In the abstract and ideal dimension of mathematical quantity, X is to Y what N is to M (6:4 what 3:2). In such a formal proportion the proportionate members are undetermined. They belong, on the other hand, all to the same series. In the dialectical proportion, on the other hand, the opposites are determined and the two sides of the proportion are both identical and different, similar and dissimilar. They agree in being unity and they also agree in being opposites.

An immanent pseudo-dialectic thinks along the line of the mathematical pattern. Empirical differences and conflicts, for example, conflicts of economic interests, which in one century seem to be incompatible are resolved by a later time. ("Dialectical" materialism.) What is compared here belongs to the same dimension, is the same sort of thing (Economic). It moves entirely *"in alio."*

The conflicting interests are in some respect similar, in that they are both economic, in another respect different, in that they disagree about the organization or distribution of economic power.

The ontological analogy is genuinely dialectical, because the members compared do not belong to a "third" general system, in respect to which they would be partly identical and partly different. Their opposition is their unity, their unity is at once also their disunity. The argument is not, as Thomas believes, rational in the sense of a logical inference.

The ontological analogy contains three dialectics rolled into one argument:

1. A is non-A—the eternal Being is itself in its own temporal process and becoming; the Absolute remains itself in the relative; the infinite is at once this finite individual; the One is the Unity of its own infinite manifold; it remains identical, it is what it is, in its own difference and otherness.

2. Man is self-activity and self-alienation. His relation to himself is an unavoidable and problematic relation of existence and essence. Finite beings in general and man in particular can not choose not to be problematic. Their potentiality and their actuality, that they are and what they are, are constantly falling apart. Finite existence is a dialectical struggle, but as such it is *absolutely;* we can not choose not to be it.

3. The absolute Being and man are analogous or similar in that both are dialectical; the dialectical structure of Being is reflected in the dialectical structure of finite existence. This proportion is itself a dialectical unity of opposites, a comparison of incomparables, an identity of contradictions.

There are three possibilities to replace dialectical ontology with a non-dialectical metaphysics. We can either fix the contradiction and make of the Absolute a "wholly other" in which case we have *dualism;* or we can absolutize experience, which is *empiricism;* or we can experientialize the Absolute, which is "the speculative fallacy" of *sitting in God's council.*

Referring once again to the Kant quotation: the unity and totality of all experiences radically transcends all experience and is no experience—but this absolute and concrete unity of all possible experience which is "world-itself," is also nothing outside and apart from that which appears. The phenomenal world is not the appearance of nothing. Ultimate reality both is and is not, identical with its own self-manifestations.

This dialectic excludes one-sided metaphysical standpoints, which think in abstract either/or—either the absolute Being is "wholly other," totally unrelated to the worlds of experience, in which case nothing can be said or thought about it, not even that it is and is "other"; or, the Absolute is identical with (and not also contradictory to) the worlds of experience, in which case experience is falsely and ontologically constructed, as if we could know it as a necessary Being; or, as if hypothetical and tentative empirical knowledge would gradually disclose the Absolute. Again in Thomistic terms: Ontological knowledge is neither *"aequivoc"* nor *"univoc,"* but it is analogical, or, as we prefer to say, dialectical.

THOMAS IN THE HISTORY OF DIALECTIC

We return to our introductory observation that the historical Thomas Aquinas is more dialectical than he knows. I hope I have now justified this contention. In following his own argument carefully, its dialectical structure has become apparent. If "God Is" and if "man is," then the meaning of this "is" can only be stated as a together of mutual affirmations and negations. Both are mutually exclusive and inclusive; God transcending himself becomes immanent, man transcending himself ceases to be merely finite and immanent (in the world). But if it is thus true to say that Thomas is more dialectical than he knows it is also true to say that he is less dialectical than he knows; and this for three reasons:

The first is logical. He believes that his *analogia entis* is a logical inference leading logically from the creature to the Absolute. He does not recognize that the ontological dialectic of Being and beings is presupposed and the argument is therefore merely the dialectical-rational exposition of this presupposed ontological dialectic. And he does not see that it is the breakdown, the "foundering" (to use Jaspers' term), of formal logic which is the evidence for dialectical truth.

The second reason is, that he mixed the *analogia entis* with an argument from causality, the nerve of which has been cut by Kant's critical philosophy. Causal relations make sense as logical links of "if/then" applied to temporal successions of "when/then." Thomas applies causality, however, to a religious-metaphysical idea of creation, as if this idea could be "proved" by causality. Thus, instead of making the idea of creation logical, he falsifies and weakens both logic and the religious-metaphysical idea. Metaphysics becomes pseudo-rational and logical reason becomes pseudo-metaphysical.

The third and main reason for his underestimating the power of dialectic is his religion. God thrones in "heaven," he dwells in an absolute "Beyond." He makes himself available in revelations, quasi-historical stories. If man were not graced by these quasi-historical revelations he would be lost in sin, darkness, and nothing. Responding to them in faith, he rises from his death and is united with his risen savior.

Thomas wants to keep this religious realm of experience outside of dialectic. He does not dare to assert, what Hegel will assert later, that the truth of this religion is the ontological dialectic, which is religiously represented in the form of mythical imagination; this imagination is the medium of feeling, of worship, and the symbol around which worshipping communities can be assembled.

Yet, this trinitarian movement of a God who "others" and utters himself, and takes us through this process of incarnation back to his immutable eternity—is the religious image, the well from which the Platonic-Aristotelian dialectic was nourished and strengthened. Thomas is a dialectician because he is a Christian who wants to understand what he believes—Hegel is a Christian because he sees ontological dialectic also in its religious symbolic manifestation.

Thomas thinks dialectically not only in the *analogia entis*. He practices dialectic when he thinks the irrationality of the concrete individual, whose existence is shown to be more than the logical possibilities or ideal essences, in which it can be determined and classified. Dialectic thinks logically the non-logical opposite of itself.

The systematic outline of philosophy in the introduction of the *Summa contra Gentiles,* is dialectical. Dialectic not only thinks the irrational, pre-scientific realm of immediate experience, logically, *qua* non-logical; in contrast to the scientific-rational realm of object-thinking; it also thinks logically and systematically the non-logical essential realms of value-experience, such as problematic existence, practical-moral, and aesthetic life, as determining each other by their irreducible oppositions; and all of them are dialectically united with reference to the supra-rational whole of reality, which is their concrete unity. To isolate this transcendent whole as if it were a "thing-in-itself" would be an undialectical fixation of an empty abstraction, mere "equivocation."

Thomas Aquinas is one of the great dialecticians between Plato-Aristotle and Kant-Hegel, and thus an important link in *"philosophia perennis."*

KANT AND THE ONTOLOGICAL ARGUMENT

Kant is supposed to have refuted the ontological argument and to have laid it to rest once for all—which did not prevent Hegel to restore its truth in his last lectures on the so-called proofs of God's existence, which he gave immediately before his sudden death.

Kant's philosophical authority is such, that we cannot afford to by-pass in silence his critique of the ontological argument. Fortunately, a scrutiny of this greatest critic has brought this result, that his refutation is not at all the refutation of the ontological argument, but merely a refutation of the spurious, the pseudo-ontological argument in its Gaunilean or Thomistic version. And *that* refutation stands. Kant says against this pseudo-ontological argument the same thing, which Gaunilo already had said, namely that the idea of a perfect being, including the existence of that perfection, does not therefore assure us of its actual existence, just as the "idea" of the hundred dollars does not buy us any goods. The real ontological argument, on the contrary, is not only not refuted, but Kant's whole critical philosophy itself rests precisely in its dialectic between an impossible "absolute idealism" and an equally impossible agnostic empiricism.

To demonstrate this thesis and to understand the systematic function of Kant's "critique of the ontological argument," it is necessary to remind ourselves briefly of the general outline of his critical philosophy.

The main thesis of the first part of the *Critique of Pure Reason* and of the *Prolegomena,* is this: that any known reality (reality as object of knowledge) is a "synthesis *a priori*" of a perceivable given material, appearing in the universal *a priori* or pure forms of intuition (space and time), and of logical *a priori* and pure functions of reason, formulated as categories. The principle of this synthesis says, that conditions which make propositions possible and true, are the same identical conditions, which make objects of knowledge real.

"Die Bedingungen der Möglichkeit der Erfahrung überhaupt sind zugleich Bedingungen der Möglichkeit der Gegenstände der Erfahrung und haben darum objektive Gültigkeit in einem synthetischen Urteile *a priori*." This implies that a *critical idealism* can describe scientific experience from the side of the logical functions, which formulate the rules according to which true judgments can be formed, since no "things themselves" walk into our minds to announce what they are; but it also implies that a *critical realism* can describe the same logical functions as laws constituting the formal pattern of objects and their behavior. Both standpoints are merely moments within the whole synthesis of experience; and they both are critical, if they remember that they present merely the events of experience when they are known. The events themselves, however, happen and meet observers as they are perceptually given. The total synthesis of known reality thus is a synthesis of opposites, which can neither be separated nor identified. *Kant's "experience" is a dialectical unity of those opposites of logical form and material content.*

But against this experiential reality in the form of being-known stands the existential reality of man in the form of being-doing. This human existence, enacting itself, producing itself as its own product, is governed by "the idea of practical reason." This practical reason Kant calls the faculty of the unconditional *(Vermögen des Unbedingten)*. It is rooted in the idea of an unconditional unity, which appears in the "categorical imperative": Unify your life! Bring about a harmony of your many interests! And treat others as organs of the same unconditional task, as ends in themselves and not merely as means to your own private pleasures, profits, and ends! The idea of reason functions in knowledge as a regulative view of an infinite process. It enables man to call any achieved and formulated knowledge in question and to demand proof and verification. But reason itself can not be called in question, because it is that by virtue of which anything given is questionable. Life, under the guidance of practical reason ought to be harmonious, unified, agreeing with itself. This is an "ought" because experience fails to offer it as a fact to observation. Practical reason is never a given fact, but as the idea of a "divine man in man" it serves as a standard, in comparison with which we shall judge ourselves. If we try to picture it, we have nothing but the "mere fiction" *(blosse Erdichtung)* of Utopian novels. The idea of practical reason remains a principle of ethical self-knowledge, and enables man to constantly renew his good will and to constantly practice his sense of practical fairness. It prevents his claim to possession of goodness, or to dispose over others for their own good.

We note: practical reason no less than scientific reason is a synthesis *a priori* of an unconditional formal unity, and of given tendencies and living interests. *It is an existential unity of those opposites of ethical form and living content.*

If we call that which is known as factually given "world," and that which is characterized by the ethical demand of what ought to be "soul," then world and soul form a new pair of contrary opposites. How are these to be thought together as manifestations of the one and same universe? Kant wavers here between two possibilities. In the last part of the *Critique of Pure Reason (Methodenlehre)*, he says that they cannot and shall not be thought together. True knowledge is restricted to its scientific use, and true action is restricted to the simple fulfillment of moral obligations in action. Philosophy comes in only as a police court comes in, when there is trouble. Trouble arises on the one hand, when science transgresses its restrictions, and becomes scientism. Instead of resigning itself to the empirical-logical construction of objects, it renders pseudo-metaphysical verdicts on metaphysical questions which are out of its reach. And trouble arises on the other hand, when sophists dispute and blur the dignity of practical reason. Philosophy as critique watches the property lines between world and soul and does not brook transgressors. Philosophy in this sense is merely analytical. It reflects upon the two syntheses, analyzing their constitution. Metaphysically, this aspect of Kant's philosophy expresses the existential human situation as one barred from access to the Absolute. It expresses the respect for the Absolute by not identifying it with any finite synthesis. *But this, we note, is precisely one premise in the ontological argument itself!*

In the chapter, entitled "The Ideal of Reason," however, Kant thinks through a second possibility. The Absolute, he says there, is "The sole genuine ideal of reason" ("das einzige eigentliche Ideal der Vernunft"), because it comprehends the ideas of "world" and "soul" in its own totality. Reason rises "inevitably" from different sets of conditions to the idea of an unconditional whole of all such sets, and thinks this totality as a sufficient ground of all realities. And it is for this very same reason that Kant rejects the Wolffian type of ontology, which confuses the object-world of the scientific intellect with the Absolute. For the rationalism of Wolff it was the same absolute thing-in-itself, which was known empirically in confused perceptions and rationally in clear concepts. For Kant this whole object-world is phenomenon only, appearance of absolute reality, but not identical with it.

The ideal of reason is rather disclosed to an "intellectual intuition" *(intellektuelle Anschauung)*, in which we think reality as we must think it, if we let all lines of theoretical as well as of practical knowledge converge in the unity of an absolute universe.

As Being of all beings *(ens entium)*, the Absolute has nothing that would stand over against it. Nothing is given to it. Whatever there is, in any sense—is posited in and by the Absolute itself. The ideal of reason thinks a totality of all possible predicates as coherent and determined by reality itself. Each moment in it would express in its own modest modification the nature of reality as such. Reality as such is thus a self-determining whole which is identical with freedom. And since nothing can drop out of it, nothing can be separated, extracted, or abstracted, from it, the Absolute is strictly individual.

What, then, happens to the finite, relative, non-absolute realities? They can only be thought as negations or negative self-determinations of the Absolute. This negation, Kant explicitly states, is, of course, not merely a logical but an ontological negation: there can be no realities, which could maintain themselves as absolute, and this impossibility is the Absolute's own negation of their ontological independence *(Fürsichsein)*. There are, nevertheless, such finite and relative realities, and they do not let go of their own relative identity, they want to be as they are—finite and relative. Hence there are self-limitations of the Absolute, posited by it, and existing in it. Kant uses a geometrical analogy to express this ontological negativity in and of the Absolute; he says these self-limitations are like the geometrical figures limiting the one and infinite space. Applied to our finite thinking of the Absolute this ontological negation states that our finite idea of the Absolute is never the Absolute itself, but that this, its own non-absoluteness, is precisely the position of the Absolute in and through its fallibility, mortality, and subjectivity. In other words, the ideal of reason is the Unity of absolute opposites. *And this is the second premise of the ontological argument!*

Kant goes on to say that the Absolute must not be quantified. Its individual modifications and self-limitations do not "divide" it in quantitative units. But they likewise are not logical "consequences" from it, as if the Absolute were their logical antecedent. The Absolute is neither a pantheistic aggregate nor a panlogistic rational-logical "sum."

The Absolute, finally, must also be thought as the ground and perfection of all practice *(ens summum)*. As supreme unity of value and reality the Absolute stands in a dialectical relation to the human synthesis of practical idea and vital interests. The unity and harmony of life, which in practice is an "ought" and not a "fact," is completed and perfected in the Absolute. Reality is not to be made perfect in the future, but it is eternally perfect. All tensions and oppositions of all experience are posited and justified in the eternal and perfect order of the Absolute. Our practical life lives eternally in a tension between "ought" and "is," and that practical dialectic itself is eternally willed and created as our destination. The Absolute justifies the non-absolute life in all its uncertainties and in all its problematic tensions. In relating it back to the Absolute, the finite life knows itself grounded and anchored in all its own groundless and floating transitoriness.

And then comes Kant's amazing transition to the critique of the so-called ontological argument. The ideal of reason, he says, is faultless *(fehlerfrei)*, but "whether such an absolute Being *(Wesen)* exists, we do not know ("wir sind in bezug auf die Existenz eines solchen Wesens in völliger Unwissenheit").

"Reason assumes this idea only as a ground, without requiring that it be objectively given and to constitute itself as a thing" (Vernunft legt diese Idee nur zum Grunde, ohne zu verlangen, dass sie objektiv gegeben sei und selbst ein Ding ausmache"). But where does the ontological argument require that the Absolute be a "given object" or "a thing!"? Yes, in Gaunilo's and Thomas Aquinas' "quotation" on the "ontological argument"—but not in the ontological argument as Anselm formulates it! The ontological argument is in complete harmony with Kant, that the Absolute is not—of course it is not—a "given object" or "a thing"! And Kant's philosophy of object-thinking has made it amply clear, that "given objects" and "things" are not—of course they are not—absolute reality itself. Kant most successfully then refutes the idea which tries to think the Absolute as a separate "absolute being" *(besonderes Urwesen)* apart from, and in contrast to experience. Ontology pervades all realms of experience. He goes on running through wide open doors in saying that the idea of Absolute would include its existence, if it were "given," just as a triangle must include three angles as soon as a triangle is given. But because the Absolute is not "given" in the idea of the Absolute, the idea therefore remains a mere possible idea, which does not "give" its reality. But what Kant here calls a mere possible idea is exactly that which Anselm calls an "idea in my head." Anselm's ontological argument and Kant's critique of Gaunilo's pseudo-ontological argument are again in perfect agreement! Kant's "ideal of reason" and Anselm's ontological argument are identical. But Kant fails to draw the necessary dialectical conclusion from his own premises, which are the premises of his whole philosophy; historically he left it to Hegel to draw it. Instead he falls back on his philosophy of science and measures ontological metaphysics by standards of physics, as if the Absolute were a scientific "given object." And this critique, we repeat, is valid—but it misses the point.

And this strange missing of the point has baneful consequences. In the *Critique of Practical Reason* those weak substitutes for the ontological argument are offered as "practical postulates." Kant says to think the Absolute is a "speculative crime" *(spekulativer Frevel)*, but to believe it practically is all right. Man may "choose" in its favor, may "give his vote" for it, may make this practical "decision." What sense has this popular plebiscite, if there is nothing to be voted on? Instead of "thinking what we believe," (the *"credo ut intelligam"* of Anselm), Kant proposes to believe and not think what we believe. He overlooks that his thinking of practical reason is also thinking and not acting. To evaluate his practical reason is philosophy, and not doing practical deeds. What does it mean to say, that "God is a practical postulate"? If it means God is not, but He has to be fabricated in the future, then the term "God" is a most superfluous term, which should be replaced by an ethical program for action now. If it means on the other hand, and this is Kant's intention, that all practical actions should be related to the idea of reason, then his so-called practical postulate is identical with the "speculative crime" of the ontological argument and his own ideal of reason. But if dialectical ontology is to be replaced by a philosophy of practice, then we have the self-contradiction, that we pretend to act when we merely think what practical action is.

The philosophy of practical reason becomes a substitute of the ontological argument for Kant, because he thinks, in his moral law, a "Being greater than which nothing can be conceived"—by him! He falls back on his moralism, as he fell back on his philosophy of science. But in both cases he retains limitation of the scientific as well as of the practical-moral sphere. And by these limitations he demonstrates that which the ontological argument pronounces. If he has nothing but scientific experience, then we could not know the limitation of that experience. If we were nothing but practical we could not become aware of a limitation of practice. In becoming aware of both we make manifest the limited nature of all finite syntheses. And this is point of the ontological argument. The "ideal of reason" comprehends those limited unities of opposites within itself; they are the self-limitations and self-negations of the Absolute. If we use a finite standpoint to ward off the Absolute, then we affirm our negativity, our contradictoriness, as an essential moment of the life of the Absolute, without which it would not be what it is. We cannot hold on to our imperfections as if they were final, ultimate, absolute, and we cannot think the Absolute if we deprive it of our imperfections which it both affirms and which it negates. The Absolute is the paradox:—that it is not that which it is, and that in its Non-Being, it nevertheless maintains and eternally restores itself.

Index*

---

* I thank my secretary, Miss Dovie Leister, for this Index.

INDEX

Inorganic, 170, 178
Insanity, 40, 51, 200
Intellectual intuition, 230
Intension, 148
Inter-action, 172
Inter-communication, 182
Introscendence, 71, 81
Intuition, 21, 22, 135, 143
Ironical, 102
Irony, 44; and dialectic, 114
Irrational, 70, 105, 111, 134, 145, 152, 133
Irreligion, 106, 114
Islam, 58, 104, 202

James, William, 134, 135, 191
Jaspers, Karl, 39, 226
Judaism, 39, 58, 202
Judgment, 72, 146, 147

Kant, 16, 18, 21 22, 65, 78, 88, 97, 120, 134, 147, 156, 212; 223-234
Knowledge, 36, 67
Koehler, Walter, 203
Koran, 58

Language, ceremonial, 114; mythical, 204; philosophical, 114; physical, 111; poetic, 110; sign, 112; symptom, 111
Law, 34, 43, 45, 51, 53, 95, 104, 156, 160, 167, 201; of thought, 67
Legal, 33, 54
Leibniz, 78, 88, 105, 163, 172, 184
Lenin, 51
Levels, 111, 115, 120; of abstraction, 174; of meaning, 110
Liberalism, 87
Life, see psycho-physical
Limit, 17, 28, 32, 40, 123, 137, 233
Literal, 32, 203, 208
Locke, 78, 154
Logic, 53, 56, 84, 123, 125, 163, 188, 216; of philosophy, 73, 81, 82, 216, 219
Logical, 43, 44, 51, 69, 93, 95, 104, 105, 182, 231; forms, 135, 229; idea, 124; levels, 160; necessity, 190; quality, 70, 147; quantity, 69; self-reflection, 190
Love, 32, 33, 91, 137, 148, 179, 202, 204, 211
Lucretius, 46

Machiavelli, 87
Machines, 46, 56, 88, 102, 178
Man, 39, 57, 73, 75, 81, 90, 96, 104, 123, 124, 138, 180, 184
Mann, Thomas, 119
Many, 136, 182, 183, 187, 190, 191, 198, 216
Marx (ism), 47, 48, 52, 53, 80, 87, 92
Mass, 51, 178, 94, 156
Mass movements, 46
Materialism, 180, 200, 219
Mathematical, 18, 35, 57, 117, 122, 133, 194; laws, 165, 199; logic, 88; quantity, 224; sciences, 16
Mathematics, 156, 194, 195 201
Measure, 19, 26, 134, 174, 194, 195, 196, 233
Mechanical, 17, 20, 183
Mechanism, 19, 174, 180, 175
Melville, 119
Memory, 24, 25, 26, 30, 40, 117, 118
Metaphysics, 14, 42, 77, 115, 123, 195, 219
Modalities, 107, 151
Monads, 178
Monism, 137, 162, 190
Moral, 26, 41, 55, 102, 113, 158, 160, 187; law, 56, 233
Moralism, 107, 233
Morgan, Lloyd, 167
Mortality, 14, 28, 29, 37, 71
Motion, 17, 18, 20
Muses, 116, 117, 118
Music, 110, 111, 180, 194
Mutations, 164, 179
Mystic, 136, 190
Myth, 35, 60, 61, 139, 202, 207, 210, 227

Naturalism, 32, 45, 46, 47, 122, 130, 216
Naturalistic speculations, 31; naturalistic negations, 47
Nature, 42, 44, 45, 92, 93, 122, 138
Necessity, 83
Negation, 36, 71, 128, 134, 151, 155, 161
Negative way, 221
Negativity, 231, 233
Neuroses, 118
Newton, 16, 18, 96
Nihilism, 72, 77
Nominalistic, 154, 216
Non-being, 32, 170

INDEX

Thales, 154
Theism, 204
Theodicy, 86
Theologians, 203
Theological speculation, 31
Theoretical, 112, 135, 190
Theory of ideas, 56
Thinking, 192, 195, 216
Thomas Acquinas, 209, 218, 219, 226, 232
Time, 13-37; biological, 33; clock, 15, 19, 23, 26, 45; eternal, 22, 27, 29; existential, 23-27, 15, 31, 32, 33, 41, 44, 64, 75; experiential, 15-18, 19, 20, 24, 26; finite or infinite?, 13-15; mathematical, physical, psychological, 18-21, 22; ontological, 21-23; operational, 20; scientific, 15, 16; importance of, 32-35; myth of, 35-37; temporal dialectic, 25, 29-32
Time-rhythm, 27
Totalitarianism, 40, 60, 70, 104
Totality, 22, 23, 24, 230
Toynbee, Arnold, 91
Tradition, 25, 26, 36, 173
Traditionalism, 62
Tragedy, 103, 107, 119
Transcendence, 81, 136
Trinity, 206, 207
Truth, 28, 29, 50, 52, 56, 57, 123, 126, 130, 142, 143, 146, 159, 192, 211, 220
Truth table 140, 141

Ugliness, 215
Uncertainty, 22, 27, 73, 102, 124, 146
Unconditional, 229; totality, 179; whole, 230
Unique, 43, 205
Unity, 173, 182, 187, 191, 215
Unity of opposites, 134, 215
Universal, 91, 134, 135
Universality, 69, 124
Universality of Becoming, 167
Universe, 124, 206
Untruth, 145, 191, 192

Valid, 135
Value, 31, 33, 40, 42, 43, 62, 75, 101, 133, 158, 186; cultural, 29
Value tensions, 64
Values of existential time, 26
Vice, 160
Virtue, 160
Vitalists, 186

Werther, 119
Whitehead, 199
Whole, 216
Wiener, Norbert, 182, 183
Will, 40, 41, 99, 102, 199
Will-to-believe, 217
Wisdom, 68, 79, 221
Wolff, 230
World-ground, 170, 202
World-itself, 74, 114, 136, 230

Zeno's paradoxes, 195

5/
4.00